Foundation Fireworks CS4

Grant Hinkson, Craig Erskine, Matt Heerema, Chuck Mallott,
Matthew Keefe, Hugh Griffith

friendsof

DESIGNER TO DESIGNER™

an Apress® company

Foundation Fireworks CS4

Credits

Lead Editor	**Associate Production Director**
Clay Andres	Kari Brooks-Copony
Development Editor	**Production Editor**
Douglas Pundick	Laura Cheu
Technical Reviewers	**Compositor**
Matthew Keefe, Sarthak Singhal	Lynn L'Heureux
Editorial Board	**Proofreader**
Clay Andres, Steve Anglin, Mark Beckner,	Lisa Hamilton
Ewan Buckingham, Tony Campbell,	
Gary Cornell, Jonathan Gennick, Jonathan Hassell,	**Indexer**
Michelle Lowman, Matthew Moodie,	Carol Burbo
Duncan Parkes, Jeffrey Pepper, Frank Pohlmann,	
Douglas Pundick, Ben Renow-Clarke, Dominic Shakeshaft,	**Cover Image Designer**
Matt Wade, Tom Welsh	Corné van Dooren
Project Manager	**Interior and Cover Designer**
Richard Dal Porto	Kurt Krames
Copy Editor	**Manufacturing Director**
Ami Knox	Tom Debolski

CONTENTS AT A GLANCE

CONTENTS

PART THREE **FIREWORKS IN ACTION** **225**

Chapter 12 **Web Site Case Study #1: Blog** **227**

Chapter 13 **Web Site Case Study #2: CSS Sprites** **245**

Chapter 14 **Web Site Case Study #3: E-Commerce** **255**

FOREWORD

Even though Fireworks has been around for more than a decade, I've lost none of the original passion and excitement that I felt on its original release from Macromedia. In fact, Fireworks was the first application developed from the ground up at Macromedia, and it was born of the same energy and burst of creativity that greeted the web boom of the 1990s. Designing a user interface to fit within the limitations of 640 by 480 pixel screens was difficult, but there was seemingly no end of great ideas.

Now it's called Adobe Fireworks, and it's very much an integral part of Adobe Creative Suite 4, especially the Web Suites. With its superior optimization, interaction, and slicing model, Fireworks allows designers and developers to create rich user experiences. Output formats include Adobe AIR, PDF, standards-compliant HTML/CSS, and various image formats for maximum flexibility. New cooperative workflows emerged when core Adobe libraries were integrated in CS3, and now CS4 has added even more, including the Adobe Type Engine, native Photoshop import/Save As functionality, and native Illustrator CS4 document support. Fireworks CS4 is truly an integral component of the Adobe ecosystem.

However, it's the passion of Fireworks users that really fuels my fire to succeed. When I speak to user groups and teach Fireworks to professionals, I strive always to learn as much from the users as they learn from me. I know Fireworks saves them time and money. We've built that into the product. But it is their creative use of Fireworks that constantly surprises, pleases, and keeps me focused on making Fireworks even better and more useful.

You see, I too worked in the trenches using Fireworks to build web sites and create compelling user experiences—so many, in fact, that I've lost count. But I've never looked back. If it weren't for devoted Adobe community experts such as Grant Hinkson, Matt Heerema, Matthew Keefe, Craig Erskine, Chuck Mallot, and Hugh Griffith, I wouldn't be at Adobe passionately working day and night with the Fireworks team to create an amazing product that enables you to rapidly design and prototype for the Web.

Happy reading!

Alan Musselman
Application Architect, Adobe Fireworks
Adobe Systems

ABOUT THE AUTHORS

Grant Hinkson is director of the Experience Design Group at Infragistics, a software company specializing in application user experience and user interface tools. He is passionate about design, usability, and technology and is rewarded by working with a team of people who share similar passions. Grant is a Microsoft Expression MVP, a contributing author to both Silverlight 1.0 and Silverlight 2 Programmer's Reference (published by WROX), and a contributing author on Adobe Developer Center. He has spoken at Adobe MAX, Microsoft ReMix, and Devscovery and is active in the Fireworks, WPF, and Silverlight communities. When not coding or designing, Grant enjoys playing both the piano and organ.

Craig Erskine is a full-service web developer working out of Wisconsin and has specialized in designing and building standards-based web sites since 1996. He's been a longtime advocate of using Fireworks for web site prototyping and maintains a modest Fireworks tutorial collection on his portfolio site, `http://qrayg.com`. When he's not feverishly designing or coding, Craig is usually spending time with his wife and daughter, nerding out with some video games, or swinging the sticks on the golf course. You can find out more about Craig at his blog, `http://craigerskine.com`.

Matt Heerema is a front-end designer and developer who has been making web pages since 1999 and has been using Fireworks from the very beginning. He currently works as principal designer for Weblogs, Inc. at AOL/Mediaglow and on occasion consults on web interface, usability, and accessibility issues through his business, Direct Steps. Matt works out of his home in Iowa where he lives with his wife, two daughters, and a cat. In his spare time, he enjoys music, reading, outdoor sports, and the fellowship of his church. You can find out way more than you want to know about him at `www.mattheerema.com`.

Chuck Mallott is a web craftsman passionate about improving the experience for users of Internet technology. He has been using Fireworks to make web pages shine since 2000. He currently works for Rosetta Stone as senior interaction designer. When he's not pushing pixels, Chuck spends time with his family and enjoys reading books, listening to music, and following his favorite sports teams. In his spare time, he runs a freelance design consultancy and blogs about web-related topics at `www.oaktreecreative.com`. He works from his home in suburban Dallas, where he lives with his wife and three children.

Matthew Keefe (Carver, Massachusetts) is a new-media designer, developer, author, and trainer with a strong background in application development for the web and offline platforms. Originally a full-time graphic artist, he found that much of the programming associated with his design work was being outsourced. Matt quickly learned programming for the Web and uncovered a valuable but little-known skill set in this industry, that skill set being the ability to build a site and also powerfully design it.

Matt has worked with such companies and studios as Inverted Creative, Delphi, PhotoshopCAFE, Kineticz Interactive, Organi Studios, Bent 360, and OrcaMedia.

Recently, Matt authored the *Flash and PHP Bible* and was the lead author on the *Java and Flex Integration Bible*. He has also contributed to various Flex/Flash magazines and runs http://scriptplayground.com as a resource for other programmers.

You can find more information about Matt on his personal site: http://mkeefe.com.

Hugh Griffith has been focused on design for most of his career, and while some might consider that a flaw, he would disagree. He could have attempted to be an all-in-one wonder, but he chose instead to be the best at one discipline. Skilled in two facets of that discipline—interaction and visual design—he has designed blogs, retail e-commerce sites, large-scale web applications, and everything in between. An ex-pat Canadian, he is currently living the American dream in the foothills north of Boise, Idaho.

ABOUT THE TECHNICAL REVIEWER

Sarthak Singhal works for Adobe Systems on the Fireworks engineering team. He has seen multiple Fireworks version releases and enjoys working on this technology every day. Apart from engineering responsibilities, he writes articles for Adobe Developer Center and submits extensions on Adobe Exchange. He communicates with Fireworks customers in multiple ways, blogging being the primary one. You can find his postings at http://blogs.adobe.com/sarthak. He is considered the voice of customers internally. When he is not involved with Fireworks, Sarthak spends time admiring nature, travelling, and capturing moments with his camera. Some of his shots can be found at www.sarthaksinghal.com.

ABOUT THE COVER IMAGE DESIGNER

Corné van Dooren designed the front cover image for this book. After taking a brief from friends of ED to create a new design for the *Foundation* series, he worked at combining technological and organic forms, with the results now appearing on this and other books' covers.

Corné spent his childhood drawing on everything at hand and then began exploring the infinite world of multimedia—and his journey of discovery hasn't stopped since. His mantra has always been "The only limit to multimedia is the imagination," a saying that keeps him moving forward constantly.

Corné works for many international clients, writes features for multimedia magazines, reviews and tests software, authors multimedia studies, and works on many other friends of ED books. You can see more of his work at and contact him through his web site, www.cornevandooren.com.

If you like Corné's work, be sure to check out his chapter in *New Masters of Photoshop: Volume 2* (friends of ED, 2004).

LAYOUT CONVENTIONS

To keep this book as clear and easy to follow as possible, the following text conventions are used throughout.

- Important words or concepts are normally highlighted on the first appearance in *italics*.

- Code is presented in `fixed-width` font.

- New or changed code is normally presented in **`bold fixed-width font`**.

- Pseudo-code and variable input are written in *`italic fixed-width font`*.

- Menu commands are written in the form Menu ➤ Submenu ➤ Submenu.

- Where I want to draw your attention to something, I've highlighted it like this:

  Ahem, don't say we didn't warn you.

- Sometimes code won't fit on a single line in a book. Where this happens, I use an arrow like this: ➡

  ```
  This is a very, very long section of code that should be written all ➡
  on the same line without a break.
  ```

Part 1

LEARNING FIREWORKS

The chapters in this book are divided into three parts: "Part 1: Learning Fireworks," "Part 2: Using Fireworks," and "Part 3: Fireworks in Action." In this first part, we start by introducing you to the Fireworks application—where it lives within the Creative Suite, what makes it unique, and why you would use it. You'll be introduced to the bitmap and vector tools and learn how to export your artwork to the Web.

Each chapter consists of a number of walkthroughs, so if you don't already have Fireworks CS4 installed, be sure to do so before you start making your way through the book. To take full advantage of the tips and techniques offered in this book, you'll want to follow along with your copy of Fireworks running in front of you.

Chapter 1

WELCOME TO FIREWORKS

Welcome to *Foundation Fireworks CS4*! This book is designed to meet the needs of both novice and expert, with plenty of fundamentals and advanced topics as well. If you're new to Fireworks, welcome aboard! It's going to be a fun ride. If you're a seasoned user, you're sure to find plenty of new tricks and introductions to new features. Adobe Fireworks CS4 builds on the solid foundation of many previous releases and delivers a flexible, powerful design tool for web and user interface design.

Many people are often confused about the role Fireworks plays in the Creative Suite, questioning, "Why use Fireworks? Isn't Photoshop (or Illustrator) the right tool?" The truth is, most of the things you can achieve with Fireworks *can* be achieved with Photoshop, Illustrator, or both. However, the number of steps you have to perform or tricks you have to know often complicate what is generally a simple task in Fireworks. And—and this is a big "and"—it is often difficult to refine your actions in these other tools. Fireworks is the tweaker's design tool—everything is infinitely editable, changeable, tweakable, and ultimately removable. I have introduced an entire team of user interface designers to Fireworks, each of whom had never used the tool, and they now swear by it, saying things like "It's the only tool for the job."

When asked, "Why Fireworks?", most of us who have been using Fireworks for years always answer with something similar to this: "Fireworks is this hybrid bitmap and vector-based design tool that lets me edit with vector-level precision, and then zoom

3

in at a pixel level and see exactly how my vector artwork is going to be rendered. I can constantly tweak and change my artwork until I'm happy." This is the key feature of Fireworks for us—we are in control of the pixel-level rendering of vector-based objects. For those who are control freaks and perfectionists, Fireworks is the tool that satisfies their need for control.

Beyond the pixel-level precision, Fireworks CS4 embraces a number of metaphors that make it *the* choice for web and application design. Key among these is the **page** concept. You can organize your artwork into conceptual pages that map to different physical web site pages or application "pages." Instead of maintaining separate files (or separate layers) for each page in your site, each page can be housed in a single document. Additionally, each page can have multiple states, further tying your artwork and mockups to the mental map of your final output. (Note: If you've been using Fireworks for a while, states are the same as frames in previous versions of Fireworks, only the name has changed.)

Once you have all of your pages in place, you can quickly publish the pages to PDF, or generate a simple HTML-based walkthrough. Both of these features are excellent tools for gathering feedback from your teammates or clients. Being able to step through clickable pages can quickly give you insight into whether or not certain elements make sense for your design. And, since these walkthroughs are 90% automated, you don't feel like you've wasted hours and hours creating throwaway HTML layouts.

Before jumping right into the tool itself (that's what the rest of this book is for), let's take a look at some of the many ways Fireworks is used in the design and software industries today.

Fireworks as a web design tool

Fireworks was initially created as a web-focused design tool and was released as a complement to Dreamweaver following Dreamweaver's release a few months earlier. Over subsequent releases, features were added to both Fireworks and Dreamweaver to enable round-tripping between the two tools. Layouts and supporting artwork could be created in Fireworks and exported to a Dreamweaver site. Metadata files generated by Fireworks were consumed by Dreamweaver to provide a link between the two tools. With a Fireworks-exported image selected on the design surface in Dreamweaver, an Edit in Fireworks button would appear on the Property inspector. When clicked, the original source PNG file was opened in Fireworks for editing. These features are still alive today, only evolved many times over.

In addition to Dreamweaver round-tripping, Fireworks includes image-slicing tools that live natively in the main design environment. This was a unique concept introduced by Fireworks that led to further adoption by web designers everywhere. Figure 1-1 shows slices drawn directly on the design surface.

Each slice is drawn using the Slice tool, which behaves like the Rectangle tool. Slices are stored in a special layer named Web Layer alongside all of your custom defined layers, and individual slices may be toggled on and off based on your export needs. When you're ready to export, you can choose either table-based or the new CSS-based export introduced in Fireworks CS4. Fireworks' CSS export even preserves your text as HTML text!

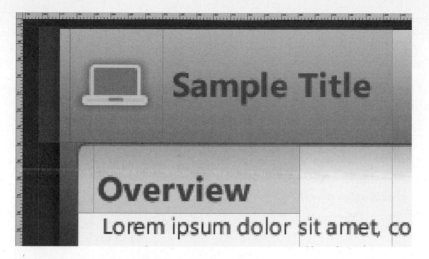

Figure 1-1. Slices on the design surface

Further strengthening its position in the world of web design, Fireworks includes a built-in preview mode that provides a live preview of your export settings. In Figure 1-2 the computer icon slice is selected.

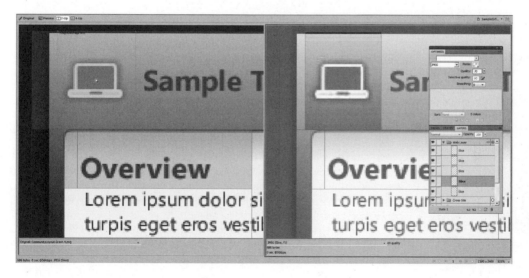

Figure 1-2. Image exporting with live previews

Custom export options can be specified for each individual slice, allowing you to use PNG compression on one slice and JPEG compression on another. We have specified JPEG compression with a Quality setting of 70 for the selected slice and will continue to adjust the quality setting until we are happy with both the resulting image and file size shown in the lower-left corner.

To recap, these are some of the common features that make Fireworks a great tool for web design:

- Built-in slicing tools
- Live preview tabs
- Slice naming
- Dreamweaver round-tripping
- HTML export (table-based)
- HTML export (CSS-based)

Fireworks as a design and illustration tool

Fireworks was primarily designed with screen output in mind. Pages are sized in pixel dimensions with resolutions that are generally similar to target monitor resolutions (1280×1024, 1024×768, and so on). When zoomed in on the design surface, you see pixel-based anti-aliasing, much like you would see in Photoshop. This often comes as a surprise to new users, considering most of the tools used to draw on the design surface are vector based. Coming to Fireworks from Illustrator, you expect to see sharp vector rendering regardless of how much you zoom in on the canvas.

With these screen-focused eccentricities, you may not expect Fireworks to be an excellent tool for design and illustration, but core features of the tool have led Fireworks to be widely accepted as an excellent tool for cutting-edge artwork. Fireworks' Live Filters are largely to thank for this. Filters (such as Blur, Drop Shadow, and Hue/Saturation) can be applied to any object on the canvas, even vector-based objects. Once applied, these filters can be edited infinitely, giving you the freedom to refine the settings until you've reached the desired effect.

Figure 1-3. Camera icon on design surface at 100%

When designing illustrations for the Web (a key destination no doubt), designing at the native output resolution is perfect. You can design your illustration with vector-level precision and know exactly what the final output will look like when exported as a PNG or JPEG. If you're designing for print but have come to rely on Fireworks' design capabilities, you can always resample your illustration in Fireworks to the target resolution and export as a 32-bit PNG file that can be imported into your print-based layout in Illustrator, In Design, Photoshop, or another tool of your choice.

Figure 1-3 shows a camera icon at 100%, while Figure 1-4 shows the same icon zoomed to 400%. All of the path nodes have been selected with the Subselection tool to reveal its underlying composition.

Figure 1-4. Camera icon zoomed to 400%

Zooming in reveals the rasterization that will occur when the illustration is exported to its final bitmap output. Being able to see this rasterization on the design surface while precisely editing the underlying vector artwork is a core strength of Fireworks as a design tool. For one final example, Figure 1-5 shows the top-left corner of a button on the design surface.

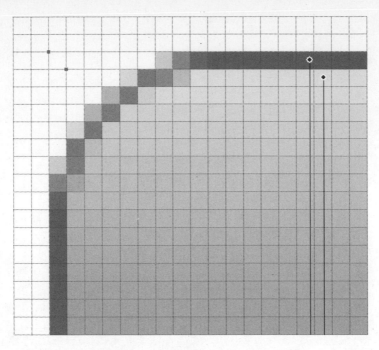

Figure 1-5. Pixel-level editing of vector-based objects

Two rectangles make up this button background, one nested 1 pixel within the other. The Grid feature of Fireworks has been turned on with its dimensions set to 1 pixel on both the x and y axis. At this zoom factor of approximately 2500%, you can clearly see and adjust the pixel-level output of the objects on the design surface. Being able to see the pixel grid and snap the artwork to the grid enables sharp, clean rendering, a technique essential for creating high-quality, screen-based illustrations and interface elements.

To recap, these are some of the common features that make Fireworks a great tool for design and illustration:

- Vector-based objects
- Live Filters
- Rasterized display when zoomed
- Pixel-based grid
- Pixel-based snapping

Fireworks as a prototyping tool

After much research and many face-to-face user meetings, it became clear to the Fireworks team that Fireworks has been embraced by application and user interface designers. They witnessed time and time again designers dropping screenshots of scrollbars and check boxes and radio buttons onto their forms, and then painstakingly masking out text and replacing it with their own. They witnessed scrollbars being diced into multiple pieces and stretched laboriously to represent the actual width or height needed by the layout. In short, they saw the pain that users were experiencing to create application mockups that resembled their final output when running as a true application.

To ease this pain, the Common Library (Window ➤ Common Library) was created. Figure 1-6 shows the Common Library panel with the Flex Components category expanded.

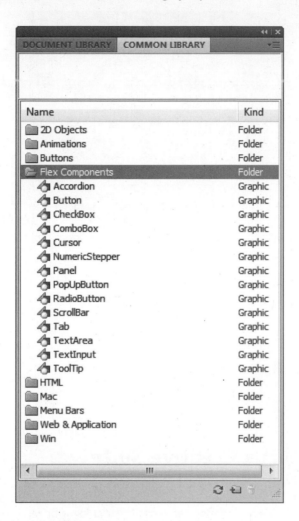

Figure 1-6. Common Library panel

A large number of controls have been implemented as Fireworks symbols that you can drag from this Common Library directly to your page. In addition to Flex-styled controls, there are both Mac- and Windows-styled controls, as well as a number of non-OS-specific controls and icons to speed the creation of your layouts. Figure 1-7 shows the Flex, Mac, and Windows versions of the RadioButton symbol. The Symbol Properties panel is used to set common properties on the selected control, such as Text and State (Normal or Selected, for example).

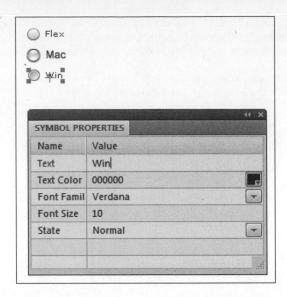

Figure 1-7. Setting RadioButton symbol properties

These are some of the common features that make Fireworks a great tool for prototyping:

- Pages
- States
- Common Library
- Create AIR Package command
- Export Flex Skin command
- Export FXG command
- PDF export
- HTML export

Fireworks and the Creative Suite

While Fireworks can stand on its own as a design tool, it doesn't have to. And, because of its strengths and history in web design, Fireworks is often used as an integration tool prior to slicing and exporting images for use on the Web, bringing together assets (such as logos or retouched images) created in other tools. It's important that you be able to import artwork created in these other tools and export to their native formats as well. The Fireworks team (along with the rest of the Adobe engineering team) has gone to great lengths to develop an effective workflow between Fireworks and the other Creative Suite tools, such as Photoshop, Illustrator, and Flash.

The fastest way to move artwork from one program to the other is by simply copying and pasting artwork. For example, you can select an object on the Photoshop stage, copy that object, and then paste that object directly to the Fireworks stage. Likewise, you can copy artwork on the Fireworks stage and paste it into other Creative Suite applications. While the copy/paste approach is fast, it does not always give you the level of control that is needed when moving from one application to the next. In the following sections, you'll see how Fireworks gives you extra control over importing and exporting artwork to Photoshop, Illustrator, and Flash.

Photoshop support

Fireworks can both open and save Photoshop PSD files. Figure 1-8 shows the Photoshop File Open Options dialog, launched when you open a PSD file (a similar dialog is displayed if you choose File ➤ Import and select a PSD).

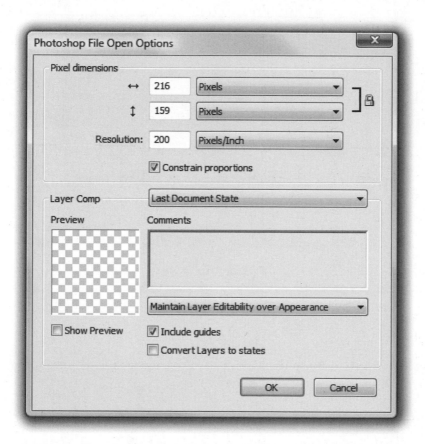

Figure 1-8. Photoshop File Open Options dialog

When opening a PSD, Fireworks lets you choose how the underlying artwork is imported. By default Maintain Layer Editability over Appearance is selected from the last combo box. When this option is selected, Fireworks tries to convert Photoshop elements into native Fireworks objects. If you just want to drop a Photoshop element into your existing layout and have no need to edit the artwork, select Flatten Photoshop Layers to Single Image to ensure the imported artwork looks exactly as it did in Photoshop.

Fireworks also lets you save your file as a Photoshop PSD and offers export options similar to the import options just seen. Figure 1-9 shows the Photoshop Export Options dialog.

Figure 1-9. Saving as a Photoshop PSD

This dialog is displayed by clicking the Options button of the Save As dialog after selecting Photoshop PSD from the Save copy as combo box. Just like importing, the settings you choose here should be dictated by how the final exported PSD will be used.

Illustrator support

Like Photoshop files, Illustrator files can be opened directly via File ➤ Open or can be imported into an existing Fireworks document by selecting File ➤ Import from the main menu. Once you've selected an Illustrator file, the Vector File Options dialog is displayed, as shown in Figure 1-10.

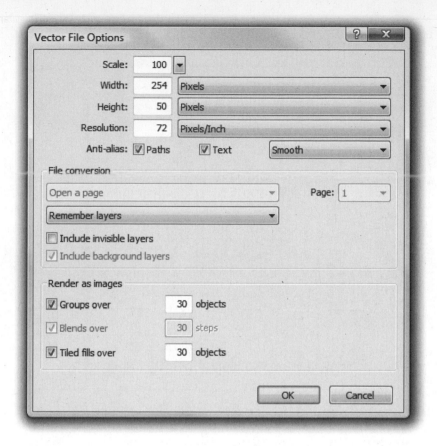

Figure 1-10. Vector File Options dialog

This dialog lets you customize the way Illustrator artwork is imported into Fireworks, letting you specify the scale and resolution and whether or not you want large groups rasterized (in the Render as images section). Save Fireworks documents as Illustrator files by selecting File ➤ Save As from the main menu and selecting Illustrator 8 from the Save copy as menu. When saving Fireworks files as Illustrator files, Fireworks will generally rasterize any objects that use filters or unsupported fill types.

Flash support

Flash is a common destination for artwork created in Fireworks. And (surprise, surprise) Fireworks includes a custom Adobe Flash SWF Export Options dialog that lets you customize the way Fireworks artwork is treated when exported. Select Adobe Flash SWF from the Save copy as menu of the Save As dialog, and then click the Options button to see the dialog shown in Figure 1-11.

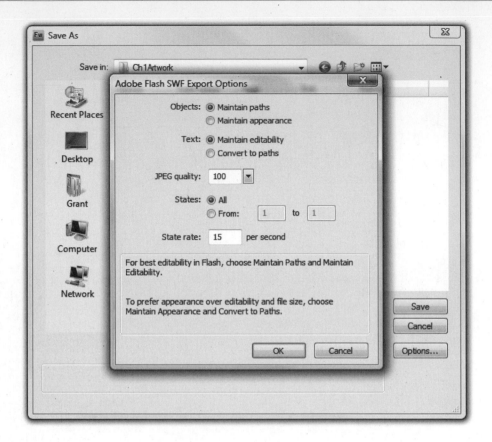

Figure 1-11. Adobe Flash SWF Export Options dialog

When exporting to SWF, like exporting to Illustrator or Photoshop, you have options to preserve edit-ability or appearance. The resulting SWF can later be imported to the Flash design surface by selecting File ➤ Import from within Flash. Further, as mentioned in the "Fireworks and the Creative Suite" section earlier, you can copy objects on the Fireworks stage and paste them directly to the Flash stage. Flash automatically launches a custom import dialog as shown in Figure 1-12.

Figure 1-12. Import Fireworks Document dialog in Flash

Once again, you're presented with options that let you find the right balance between editability and appearance preservation. Unlike interoperability with Photoshop and Illustrator, Fireworks does not have a way to natively open artwork created with Flash. You can get around this by exporting Flash artwork to an Illustrator file, and then importing the Illustrator file into Fireworks.

Summary

You should now have an idea of who uses Fireworks, why they use Fireworks, and how they use Fireworks with other tools of the Creative Suite. In the chapters that follow, you'll be introduced to the Fireworks toolset from the ground up. You'll see how to create highly popular (and polished) effects, learn about Fireworks extensibility, and even be shown how to extend Fireworks yourself. You'll see why Fireworks is used by leading web designers, illustrators, graphic artists, and user interface and user experience professionals, and be prepared to join their ranks. By the end of this book, you'll be well on your way to becoming a Fireworks pro yourself. So, push up your sleeves—it's time to get started!

Chapter 2

FIREWORKS AND CS4 INTEGRATION

Fireworks CS4 boasts of much better integration with other CS4 applications. This chapter begins with highlighting the need and advantages of integration. After that it delves into integration of Fireworks specifically with Photoshop, Illustrator, and Flash. The various settings and options involved with files being passed across these applications are discussed in each application-specific section. This chapter serves as a start for users to explore those functionalities in depth. To understand the text in this chapter, we advise you to install the CS4 applications discussed in this chapter apart from Fireworks, namely Photoshop, Illustrator, and Flash. The 30-day-trial editions for all these applications are available at www.adobe.com.

What is integration?

Integration is the process of connecting multiple applications or tools to create a final product. In designing, integration is the act of using multiple applications to create a picture or piece of art.

If you have ever designed a 3D scene and then imported it into Photoshop, you have integrated two tools to create a finished piece. In fact, many tools exist that work well with each other. Adobe has built the Creative Suite around this concept to make the designers' and developers' lives a lot easier.

How integration helps

The goal with integrating multiple applications is to speed up the design process and make changing an existing project faster as well. You will find that integration also makes working in a team environment smoother and more seamless. A team designer proficient with Photoshop might not migrate to Fireworks or vice versa. In such a situation, designers can use the application of their choice and still get their designs worked upon by other team members.

The reason integration abilities benefit teams is because the designer can focus on his or her skill set and not have to worry about preparing the design for the developer. The developer can take the files from the designer and simply import them without any modification.

Another less-known advantage of integration is the ability to keep your designs in sync, because you never have to export the individual elements of a project. This in turn means fewer chances for errors in the design and development process.

Now that you know what integration is and how it can help you, let's take a look at how integration works within the Creative Suite.

Integration within the Creative Suite

You will find most of the applications within the Creative Suite offer some level of integration. Some examples of integration would be the ability to load PSDs directly into Dreamweaver or the ability to create a Fireworks PNG (the default Fireworks file format) and load that directly into a Flash application. Copying text objects from Illustrator or Photoshop and pasting them into Fireworks with all the attributes editable is another integration example among Adobe CS4 applications. A symbol created in Fireworks intelligently converts into an editable component when copied and pasted into Flash.

This chapter will cover the integration of Fireworks with Photoshop, Flash, and Illustrator. We will look at the similarities and differences as you start sharing files across the applications.

Once the fundamentals have been examined, we will wrap up the chapter with an exercise of building a basic Flash interface using Fireworks as the basis of an application.

> *For this chapter, you will need to have Flash, Photoshop, and Illustrator installed on your system. Thirty-day trials can be downloaded from www.adobe.com if you do not already own these software programs but would still like to follow along.*

In this section you learned what integration is and how it can help. Now we will start looking at integration features available in Fireworks CS4.

You will quickly realize how well the CS4 applications work with each other.

Integration with Photoshop

The first application we will work with to cover Fireworks integration features is Photoshop CS4. Fireworks has the ability to work with the PNG format by default, but it can easily load a PSD file (native Photoshop format). You can access a PSD file in Fireworks in two ways: either open it or import it into any page of the Fireworks PNG file.

Importing a Photoshop file

To import a PSD in Fireworks, select File ➤ Import and navigate to a PSD on your machine. Once you have found a PSD you want to import, click Open, and the Photoshop File Import Options dialog box will appear.

This dialog, as shown in Figure 2-1, allows you to choose which contents should be imported. It has a variety of abilities, such as previewing the PSD and allowing you to choose specific layer composites to import.

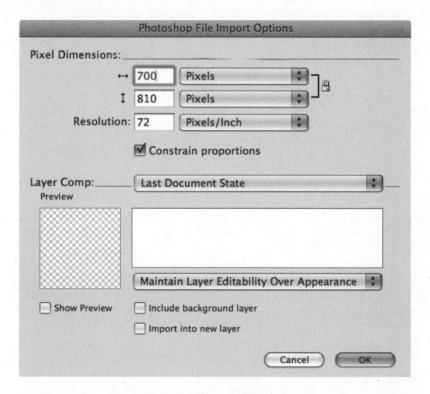

Figure 2-1. Photoshop File Import Options dialog in Fireworks CS4

The three check box options at the bottom of the Photoshop File Import Options dialog are unchecked by default, but the settings will persist when modified. Also, the drop-down selection options persist on further PSD imports.

> *When importing multiple PSDs, we recommend you enable the option* Import into new layer *to ensure the document is easy to work with in the future. This option is found at the bottom of the* Photoshop File Import Options *dialog.*

Pixel Dimensions

The Pixel Dimensions section of this dialog is pretty straightforward. The size of the imported objects can be set here. Most of the time you will want to leave the resolution at the default setting of 72, but you do have the opportunity to change that setting in this section as well. The last option in the Pixel Dimensions section, Constrain proportions, is used to keep the same ratio when you modify the height or width.

Layer Comp

Photoshop allows you to create states in your document called **layer comps**. These are most often used to demonstrate many options to a client or colleague without your needing to generate multiple files. The Layer Comp option can also be used in other apps, such as Fireworks.

Using the drop-down, you can choose a specific layer comp to import. If you're unsure which layer comp you want to load, you can check the Show Preview option. This will display a thumbnail of the specific layer comp.

The last drop-down box allows you to select from the following four import options. These settings define how elements in the PSD file are brought into Fireworks. The option you should choose depends on the use cases of the document objects being imported into Fireworks (e.g., you want the objects to be editable or retain custom settings) after importing.

- **Maintain Layer Editability Over Appearance**: This option will ensure you are able to edit the objects within the imported document and even sacrifice some appearance specifics to make sure editing is still possible.
- **Maintain Photoshop Layer Appearance**: When you prefer to preserve the display of the imported graphics, this is the option you would use. This will favor the original Photoshop graphic quality over editability.
- **Custom Settings From Preferences**: Rather than choosing settings each time, you have the option to set up a default one in the Preferences dialog box under the Photoshop Import/Open category. This option tells the importer that you would prefer to use previously defined settings, rather than the settings from this import dialog box. This allows users finer control on how the objects should appear when they are imported in Fireworks.
- **Flatten Photoshop Layers to Single Image**: Occasionally you will have a document that doesn't look good when imported, or maybe you have no intention of editing the document. When this is the case, this option will ensure the appearance is pretty much identical to the one found in Photoshop, because the imported file will become a flattened graphic. This setting will convert the PSD file contents into a single bitmap object, losing the capability to make any edits.

The last two options available when importing a PSD are Include background layer and Import into new layer. Both options are pretty straightforward. Sometimes, when creating a graphic in Photoshop, the background is required for layers to properly be blended. If this is the case, you would ensure the background layer is included when importing the PSD.

The Import into new layer option is important if you have a complex document and don't want elements of that design to get misplaced. This option would ensure that all the objects of imported graphics would be placed on a new layer in the Fireworks document.

Once you have made all the changes to the settings for this import, click OK to import the PSD. Your mouse cursor will change to an "L" on its side. This special cursor is used to define the bounds where the document will be placed. Click and drag to define the width and height. By doing this you are defining the crop point. This means the final object will only display within the regions you define.

The object will be resized based on the size you define. Once you have defined the required size, release the mouse button, and the object will be placed.

> *If you just click once when the "L" sign is visible, the actual dimensions of the objects within the PSD file will be applied to the imported objects.*

Opening a Photoshop file

To open a PSD in Fireworks, select File ➤ Open and navigate to a PSD on your machine. Once you have found a PSD you want to import, click Open, and the Photoshop File Open Options dialog box will appear.

You also can open a PSD without an existing document available. When you open a PSD versus importing one into an existing Fireworks document, you will be presented with a set of options similar to those in the Photoshop File Import Options dialog, aside from the check box options at the bottom, as shown in Figure 2-2.

These options are replaced with two new ones. The first, Include Guides, allows you to include the guides that were created in Photoshop. The other option, Convert layer to frames, will convert the layers found in the PSD to states in Fireworks. This option is commonly used when you are creating an animation, such as animated buttons for a web project.

While importing/opening a PSD file with the drop-down option Custom Settings From Preferences selected, the settings from the Photoshop Import/Open section of the Preferences dialog are applied, as mentioned previously. In the preferences settings is the check box option Prefer native filters over Photoshop Live Effects. This option, which has been added in Fireworks CS4, is helpful for designers wanting either a Fireworks or a Photoshop appearance for filters. When the check box is checked, all the effects applied to an object are mapped to Fireworks effects. When the check box is unchecked, the effects on the objects are mapped to Photoshop effects. This may change the appearance on some occasions.

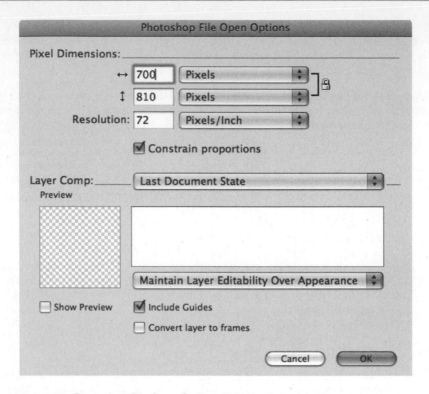

Figure 2-2. Photoshop File Open Options dialog in Fireworks CS4

The advantage of using Fireworks filters is that all the filters are individually listed, thus allowing their movement in the hierarchical order in which they are applied. The multiple Photoshop live effects when applied are shown as a single effect in the Property inspector, restricting the individual effects' hierarchical movement.

> *If the PSD file to be imported/opened has a color profile attached to it, Fireworks will ignore it. This may result in color shifts for certain files.*

Photoshop Live Effects

You probably already know you can create graphics with filters in Photoshop. However, did you know that the filters can be re-created in Fireworks? When you import a PSD with filters that Fireworks can work with, it adds a Photoshop Live Effects entry in the Filters section within the Property inspector, as shown in Figure 2-3.

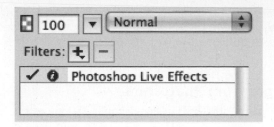

Figure 2-3. Photoshop Live Effects entry in the Property inspector

If you click one of the objects that has a filter applied and then look in the Property inspector, you will see the Photoshop Live Effects item. With the object still selected, if you double-click the filter, a dialog box will appear, as shown in Figure 2-4.

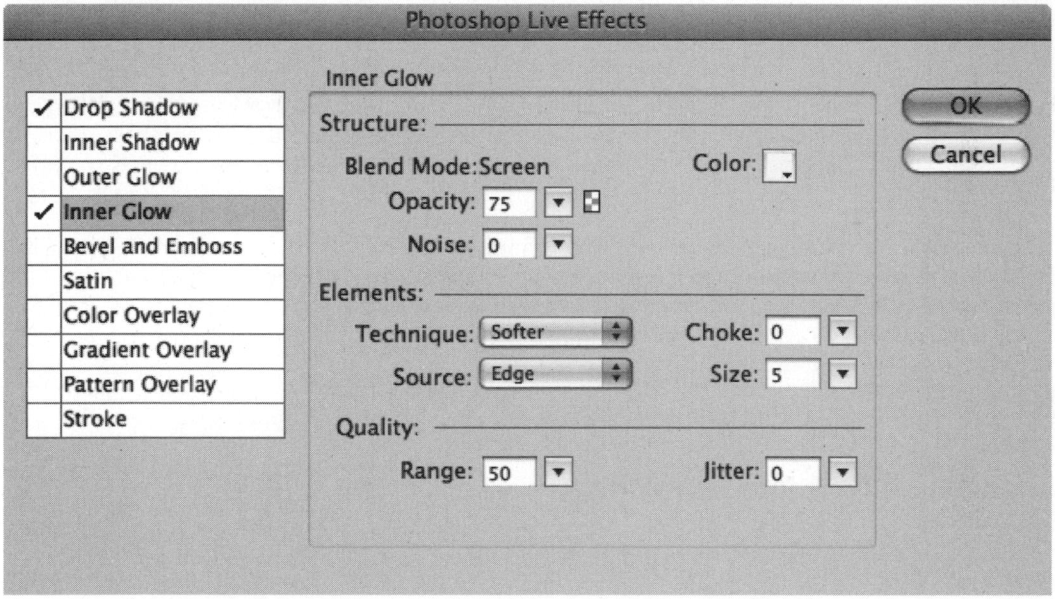

Figure 2-4. Photoshop Live Effects dialog box

Most designers familiar with Photoshop will notice that this dialog box is very similar to the one found in Photoshop. In fact, it is a lot more user friendly for these designers due to the similarities.

Filters imported from the PSD will display a check box in front of their name, as shown in Figure 2-4. Clicking a filter entry will reveal the settings for that filter. The starting values of filters found in the imported PSD are also carried over, which makes it easier to edit and manage.

After you are satisfied with the changes you have made in the Photoshop Live Effects dialog box, you can click OK to close it, returning to the Fireworks document. You can double-click the filter entry at any time to make more adjustments, which makes the integration abilities between Fireworks and Photoshop very useful.

Working with shapes from Photoshop

Now that you know how to import a PSD in Photoshop, let's look at one of the cross-application advantages of the Creative Suite. When you create a PSD with a shape layer and import that PSD into Fireworks, the shape is still editable when the preference is set to Maintain Editability Over Appearance while opening/importing the PSD file.

Start by creating a new PSD in Photoshop. Choose the Rectangle tool and draw a rectangle on the stage, leaving all the default settings as they are. Now save this PSD somewhere on your computer and import it into Fireworks.

When you open the PSD in Fireworks, you will see your shape on its own layer. However, the interesting ability you will discover is when you select the shape, you can still modify its attributes like fill or stroke color, or any effects applied to it.

Fireworks has the ability to edit more than just rectangles. In fact, you can pretty much modify any of the shapes that Photoshop can create. To demonstrate this, we have created a custom shape, Blob, in Photoshop, which is included with the downloads for this book available from www.friendsofed.com, and added some basic filters.

Now when this PSD is opened in Fireworks, you can see the paths of the Blob shape are still editable, but you can also see the Photoshop Live Effects that were added in Photoshop. To show the easy editing features, we have added a soft inner glow to the Blob shape in Fireworks and lowered the intensity of the outer glow.

As you can see, the editing options between Fireworks and Photoshop offer great integration that ultimately allow you to seamlessly modify graphics and keep a consistent appearance.

Importing a PNG into Photoshop

It is important to understand a PNG file cannot be opened in Photoshop with the layer data intact. This means the file will be opened as a flattened document. If you save this PNG in Photoshop, the Fireworks layers would be discarded.

Photoshop is aware of this limitation and warns you of this any time you open a PNG in Photoshop that contains Fireworks information, as shown in Figure 2-5.

You can, however, save the Fireworks document as a PSD in Fireworks and then open that in Photoshop. You could even save the PSD, open it in Photoshop, make changes, and reimport it back into Fireworks. Unfortunately, doing so can result in color profile mismatching and is generally a dangerous idea because the applications do differ.

Figure 2-5. Photoshop warning dialog that appears while opening a Fireworks PNG file

It is best practice to import a PSD into Photoshop only when changes are required, rather than constantly passing the file back and forth, or round-tripping.

Another integration that is possible between Fireworks and Photoshop is the copying and pasting of text objects between the applications. When you are in the text editing mode of Photoshop and a text object is copied, it will become a native Fireworks editable text object with complete fidelity when pasted into Fireworks. Text objects can also be copied from Fireworks to Photoshop. Copy a text object in Fireworks, select the Horizontal Type tool in Photoshop, and then paste to get editable text in Photoshop.

Saving as PSD

Fireworks CS4 allows users to save a file as a PSD also. It can be customized by users using options similar to those available while importing/opening a PSD in Fireworks, as shown in Figure 2-6. Depending on the settings chosen by users, various options can be specified for the objects when saved as a PSD.

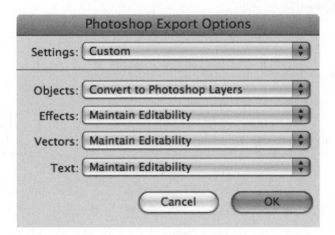

Figure 2-6. Photoshop Export Options dialog

You should now have a pretty solid understanding of the abilities of integration between Fireworks and Photoshop.

Now let's take a look at how integration can be used when working with Illustrator files.

Integration with Illustrator

In the previous section, we covered the integration abilities of Photoshop. In this section, we will look at integration between Fireworks and Illustrator, another popular product shipped with the Creative Suite 4. When working with an Illustrator file (AI format), you can import the file into an existing Fireworks document or create a new Fireworks document with an AI file as the base.

Opening an Illustrator file

To open an Illustrator file, you can either double-click the application background (if the app frame is displayed) or select File ➤ Open and navigate to the AI file. When you click Open, the Vector File Options dialog box, shown in Figure 2-7, is displayed, and this is where you can modify the settings used when opening the AI file into a Fireworks document.

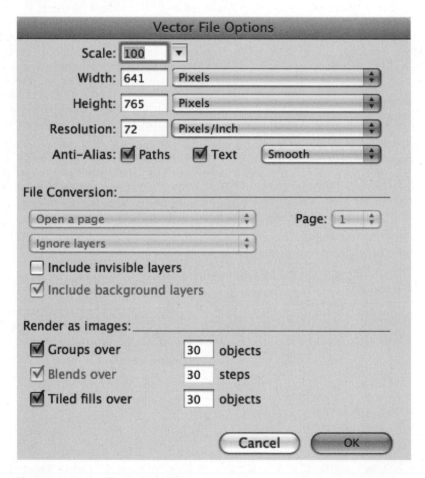

Figure 2-7. Vector File Options dialog

Scale

An Illustrator file is in vector format, which means the graphics can be scaled without degrading the original image quality, unlike a raster graphic from Photoshop.

Width and Height

The Width and Height options are self-explanatory. You can define the width and height of the graphics using the drop-down boxes to the right of the options to set the unit of measurement to be used.

Resolution

You would normally want to keep the Resolution setting at the default, 72, when working with web graphics, but you do have the opportunity to change it here.

Anti-Alias

When importing the AI file, you can tell Fireworks to anti-alias, or soften, the lines of paths and text. The drop-down to the right of the Paths and Text check boxes allows you to set the anti-alias mode, similar to the text settings found in Photoshop.

File Conversion

If your document contains more than one page, you have the option to choose which page to open. If there is only one page to open, this option will be disabled. The use of multiple artboards has been introduced in Illustrator CS4, and Fireworks CS4 has the intelligence to understand them also. The Page field drop-down menu allows users to choose which artboard to be imported. When a multiple artboard file is being opened, this option is grayed out, as all the artboards appear as pages in Fireworks.

Fireworks has the ability to create layers based on those defined in the AI file. You have the option to override this by ignoring layers and converting the layers to states, which is especially useful when working on web graphics, such as buttons and other multistate objects.

The Include invisible layers option will make sure the invisible layers within the AI file are included when importing the document. This can be useful when you have a fairly large document that has the majority of the layers hidden, but you want to still include them in the Fireworks document.

Similar to the PSD import feature, the Illustrator import feature also lets you import the background.

Render as images

When importing a large Illustrator file, you may find the quality is not always maintained in Fireworks due to the complexity of that file.

The Render as images option converts certain objects to graphics based on the values set in the input boxes. This ensures the overall quality of a complex document will be preserved.

Once you have modified all of the options, click OK, and the AI file will be imported into Fireworks. The time this takes depends on the complexity of the AI file.

As you begin to open more varied AI files, you will learn that Fireworks can only re-create so much of the design of these files. This is due to the complexity of the starting file. The only way to avoid this is by simplifying the objects in the AI file and/or modifying the settings during the import process. The best way to determine the simplicity needed is to first import the AI file with no changes, and then simplify until the graphic shows the desired result.

Importing an Illustrator (AI) file

The process of importing an AI file is identical to the process of opening one. Unlike the PSD Import and Open commands, the import process uses the exact same Vector File Options dialog box, with all of the same options and settings, as the open process.

The copying and pasting of text between Illustrator and Fireworks is much improved due to the same text engine being used by the applications.

Integration with Flash

The integration process between Flash and Fireworks is a little different. Fireworks does not have the ability to open a Flash file (FLA format), but Flash can open and import a Fireworks file. This book is obviously about Fireworks, but this section is going to explain the process of importing a PNG file into Flash.

With a Flash file open, select File ➤ Import ➤ Import to Stage and choose the PNG that you want to import. When you click Open, the Import Fireworks Document dialog box, shown in Figure 2-8, is displayed. This dialog box is where you define the settings to be used when the file is being imported.

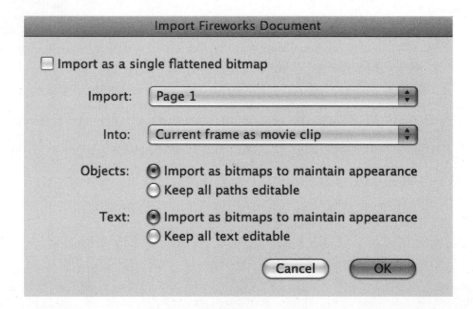

Figure 2-8. Import Fireworks Document dialog

Import as a single flattened bitmap

When the Import as a single flattened bitmap option is checked, the PNG is flattened into a simple bitmap, which means the files will no longer be editable. This option is useful when you don't want to create a new PNG from the Fireworks document, but only need a single graphic.

If you choose this option, all the other settings will be disabled because they no longer will have any effect. If you uncheck this option, those disabled settings will become enabled once again.

Import

The Import option lets you define which page will be imported if the document contains more than one page in the Fireworks document.

Into

The Into option determines whether the imported graphic will be placed within a movie clip or on a new layer in the Flash document.

Objects

When you import a PNG into Flash, you have the option to keep the imported file editable. The Objects option is where you can modify this setting, depending on whether the imported file is complex or not. When the file is complex, we recommend you choose Import as bitmaps to maintain appearance to ensure the document's overall appearance is preserved.

Text

Imported text has an option, Text, which is similar to Objects, to convert the text to a graphic. This is important if Flash doesn't have the ability to render the font used in Fireworks or if you know that the text will not need to be edited. For instance, when importing a logo, it is important to keep the original design. This would most likely not need to be edited, so the Import as bitmaps to maintain appearance option would make more sense here.

Once you have modified all of the settings for your PNG to be imported, the last step is to click OK, and the file will be imported into Flash. For more information on importing or other aspects of Flash, we recommend Adobe's web site or a book that covers Flash at a more in-depth level, such as *The Essential Guide to Flash CS4 with ActionScript* by Paul Milbourne et al. (friends of ED, 2009).

Summary

In this chapter, you learned how Fireworks can integrate with other applications in the Creative Suite. You first learned how to integrate Photoshop and Fireworks, as well as how to import a PSD into Fireworks and modify the filters in a system similar to the one found in Photoshop.

You then learned how to import and work with Illustrator files, which allowed you to better understand vector properties in Fireworks, such as scaling and appearance.

The last part of the chapter covered integration with Fireworks and Flash, explaining the process of importing a PNG into Flash and how to modify settings during the importing process.

Chapter 3

WORKING WITH BITMAPS

One of Fireworks' greatest strengths as a design tool is the way it combines bitmap and vector tools in a single environment. You can mask bitmaps with vector paths, convert bitmap selections to paths, apply live filter effects to bitmaps, and much more. While most of your time in Fireworks will likely be spent using the vector tools, the bitmap tools will still play a key role in your daily workflow.

If you're designing web layouts with Fireworks, it's highly likely that you'll be including photos or some type of bitmap-based artwork in your layouts. You'll probably need to adjust the color, mask the background, or even convert the image to vector art. All of these things can be done inside Fireworks without having to jump to a dedicated bitmap-editing tool (like Photoshop). Even when we're not working on layouts and just want to quickly crop or resize an image, Fireworks is the tool we open first. Fireworks makes it much faster for us to get the results we want than other tools.

In this chapter, you'll learn how and when to use the bitmap tools and see how the pairing of bitmap and vector tools can empower you to create compelling layouts. By the end of the chapter, you should have a solid grasp of Fireworks' bitmap-editing capabilities.

Bitmap layers

Fireworks draws a distinction between vector-based objects on the design surface and bitmap objects on the design surface. For example, if you import a JPEG image into your document (using File ➤ Import from the main menu), you'll see the text "Bitmap" listed next to the layer preview in the Layers panel. Figure 3-1 shows the Layers panel for a document with an image on the design surface.

Figure 3-1. A bitmap object in the Layers panel

All of the bitmap tools are designed to target bitmap layers such as this. You can also create empty bitmap layers by clicking the icon next to the trash can icon in the Layers panel. When you create an empty bitmap layer, you can use the bitmap drawing tools to draw into the bitmap layer, and you can use the Paint Bucket tool to fill the bitmap layer.

Bitmap tools

The bitmap tools, housed in the Tools panel (Window ➤ Tools), are highlighted in Figure 3-2.

Icons in the Tools panel with a down arrow indicate a group of related tools is available to choose from. Press and hold the icon to see the submenu of tools. In Figure 3-2, the lasso tools menu is shown, revealing the two types of lasso tools available: the Lasso tool and the Polygon Lasso tool.

When working with any of the bitmap tools, additional configuration options are available on the Property inspector (Window ➤ Properties). Click through each of the tools, and watch the Property inspector respond accordingly. Figure 3-3 shows the Property inspector when the Rubber Stamp tool is active.

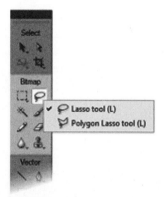

Figure 3-2. The Fireworks bitmap tools in the Tools panel

Figure 3-3. Property inspector when the Rubber Stamp tool is active

We'll go into these properties in the sections that follow, but know that any time you're asked to adjust tool settings, this is where you'll be making those adjustments.

Selection tools

Much of your interaction with bitmaps in any program involves creating selections. You select pixels to delete, copy, color, apply effects to, and more. Fireworks offers three types of selection tools: the marquee tools (for making rectangular or elliptical selections), the lasso tools (for making free-form or polygonal selections), and the Magic Wand tool (for like-color selections). Working together, these tools can cover the full range of your selection needs. Figure 3-4 shows an image with a lasso tool–based selection.

Figure 3-4. A lasso tool–based selection

The dotted lines indicate the edges of the selection. When a bitmap layer has a selection applied, only pixels within the selected area can be operated on. For example, if you select one of the bitmap drawing tools, such as the Brush or Pencil, you will only be able to draw within the bounds of the selection. Likewise, if you press Delete on your keyboard, the contents within the selection will be deleted, while the rest of the bitmap will remain untouched. In the sections that follow, we'll look at each of the selection tools in depth.

Common selection techniques

When working with any of the selection tools, both the Alt and Shift keys can be used to augment the behavior of the active tool.

Shift key

Press the Shift key while using either of the marquee tools to add to the current selection. As you hold down the Shift key, you should see a plus icon added to the current cursor.

Alt key

Press the Alt key while using any of the marquee tools to subtract from the current selection. As you hold down the Alt key, you should see a minus icon added to the current cursor.

Arrow tool and arrow keys

Use the Arrow tool or your keyboard's arrow keys to move an active selection.

Live marquee option

Once you've selected one of the marquee tools (Marquee or Oval Marquee), simply draw the marquee on the design surface as if you were using the Rectangle or Ellipse tool. Select a bitmap layer prior to drawing the selection to ensure the selection targets that layer. You can also select the target bitmap layer after drawing the marquee. Simply draw the marquee first, and then select the target bitmap from the Layers panel. This tool has a Live marquee check box option in the Property inspector when selected. The Live marquee option allows you to dynamically change any of the selection properties after you have drawn the selection. For example, if you initially draw a rectangular selection with a hard edge, you can later change the edge to be feathered. There's no need to start over and re-create the selection. Simply check the Live marquee option in the Property inspector, and make all of the changes you like. Fireworks will dynamically update the selection and show you the results instantly.

Marquee tool

Marquee tools come in two flavors: the standard rectangular Marquee tool or the Oval Marquee tool. Quickly select one of these tools by pressing M on your keyboard. Repeatedly pressing the M key cycles between the two tools.

> *For any of the tool groups, repeatedly pressing the group's shortcut key cycles through the available tools in the group.*

With either of the marquee tools selected, the Property inspector will include the options shown in Figure 3-5.

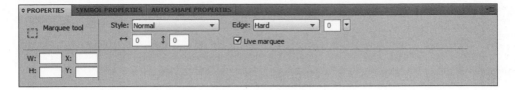

Figure 3-5. Property inspector settings for the Marquee tool

The following list details each of the marquee tool settings:

- Style
  - Normal: Lets you freely draw rectangle and oval selections in any dimensions
  - Fixed Ratio: Locks the aspect ratio of the selection in a user-specified ratio
  - Fixed Size: Locks the size of the selection in user-specified dimensions
- Edge
  - Hard: Makes the edge of the selection hard or have no aliased edges
  - Anti-aliased: Makes the edge of the selection smoothed by a 1 px (pixel) feather effect
  - Feather: Makes the edge of the selection feather by a user-specified amount
- Live marquee
  - Allows the properties of the selection to be changed after the selection has been created

> *Double-clicking any bitmap object with the* Pointer *or* Subselection *tool will automatically select the rectangular* Marquee *tool.*
>
> *Hold down the Shift key while drawing your initial selection to create a perfect square or circle selection. You can still use Shift to add to the selection after your initial selection has been drawn.*

Lasso tool

The Lasso tool is used to create free-form selections. You draw selections on the target bitmap just as you would trace an outline of an object on paper. The Polygon Lasso tool (available from the submenu) is used to create more precise selections. Instead of being a completely free-form tool, the Polygon Lasso tool, as its name suggests, is used to create polygon-based selections. This is the tool to start with if you want to cut out the outline of a building in a photo.

The Lasso tool settings are similar to those of the Marquee tool, only the Style options have been omitted. In Figure 3-6, you can see that the Edge and Live marquee settings remain.

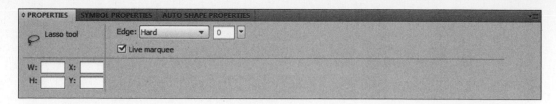

Figure 3-6. Lasso tool settings

> Hold down the Shift key while dragging or clicking to snap the currently drawn area to perfect 45-degree increments.

Magic Wand tool

The Magic Wand tool is great for quickly creating complex selections that would take a lot of manual work with the lasso tools. To use the Magic Wand tool, click anywhere on a bitmap layer to create a selection. This tool selects all colors similar to the color initially clicked. In Figure 3-7, you can see that a Tolerance property has been added for this selection tool.

Figure 3-7. Magic Wand tool settings

The Tolerance value is used to set the threshold for **likeness**, which means color similarity. With very low Tolerance values, only colors that are very close to the original color will be selected. As you increase the tolerance, the size of the selection will grow. The Magic Wand tool really shows off the power of the Live marquee feature. Try it yourself by selecting an area of your target bitmap with the Magic Wand tool. With Live marquee checked, increase and decrease the Tolerance value and observe how the size of the selection changes.

Figure 3-8 shows the difference between low and high Tolerance settings on the same coffee cup image we showed previously in the chapter.

Figure 3-8. Magic Wand tool Tolerance settings

In order to create the final selection shown previously in Figure 3-4, we started with the Magic Wand tool, adjusting the tolerance so that the selection did not bleed into the clear glass area (this was a pretty low Tolerance setting). We then used the Shift-click technique to add to the selection, clicking in different areas of the image to select different colors as the base. Once the selection was pretty close, we chose Select ➤ Select Inverse from the main menu. Inverting our selection resulted in the coffee cup itself being selected instead of the whitespace around it. We further refined our selection using the Lasso tool and the Shift and Alt modifier keys to precisely add to and remove from our selection.

Converting selections to paths and vice versa

An often overlooked feature in Fireworks is the ability to convert selections to paths. This is a great technique if you're working with a low-res logo or illustration. You can use the Magic Wand tool and other selection tools to create a selection, and then convert that selection into a path that can be further refined, scaled, and manipulated. To convert a selection to a path, simply create a selection, and choose Select ➤ Convert Marquee to Path from the main menu.

Figure 3-9 shows a new path that has been created from the final coffee cup selection.

Figure 3-9. Path created from a selection

We set the opacity of the path to 70% so that you can see the original image behind it. This path definitely needs to be cleaned up a bit, but it's a create start, and it was much faster than creating the path by hand (OK, maybe not for this coffee mug, but for more complex outlines it's a time-saver!).

Similarly, you can convert paths to selections. If you're really skilled with the path-editing tools, it may be faster for you to create a really precise shape to act as your selection. Once you have your path the way you want it, select Modify ➤ Convert Path to Marquee from the main menu. Your original path will be lost completely if you do this, however, so you may want to create a copy of your original path for later editing or tweaking.

Drawing tools

In addition to the selection tools, Fireworks includes a number of tools that let you paint, erase, and alter your target bitmap. We'll step through each tool and review its capabilities and settings.

Pencil tool

The Pencil tool is used to draw fine lines at 1 px in diameter. It's great for drawing very small, precise bitmap objects like bullets or arrows, or cleaning up resized icons for better clarity at low resolution. To use the Pencil tool, press the B key until the Pencil tool icon is highlighted in the Tools panel. Now click and drag on any bitmap layer or object.

Figure 3-10 shows the Pencil tool's Property inspector settings.

Figure 3-10. Pencil tool settings

The following list details each of the Pencil tool settings:

- Color: Specifies a color for the Pencil tool.
- Anti-aliased: Toggles between a hard or smooth line.
- Auto erase: Uses the fill color instead of the stroke color.
- Preserve transparency: Prevents the Pencil tool from drawing in transparent areas of the bitmap. You can only draw on existing pixels.
- Opacity: Allows you to adjust the opacity of the drawn pixels from 0 (transparent) to 100% (opaque).
- Blend mode: Allows you to use any one of the 46 built-in blend modes. These blend modes contain all of the built-in Photoshop blend modes and consist of effects like Darken, Lighten, Overlay, Difference, Hue, Reflect, Additive, Invert, and Erase.

> *Create straight lines or polygons by holding down the Shift key while drawing with the Pencil tool. Click once to set the start point, and then continue to click in other areas of the bitmap to create straight lines between the points.*
>
> *Quickly select colors from the canvas by holding down the Alt key while the Pencil tool is active. You will temporarily switch to Eyedropper mode. Click to select a new color, and then release the Alt key to return to Pencil mode.*

Brush tool

The Brush tool uses Fireworks' built-in brushes to allow you to paint with tips other than a single fine line. These brushes range from a solid hard line to randomly sized and oriented patterns that change in opacity depending on how fast or slow you move your mouse. To use the Brush tool, press the B key until the Brush tool icon is highlighted in the Tools panel. Figure 3-11 shows some of the many brush tips that can be used.

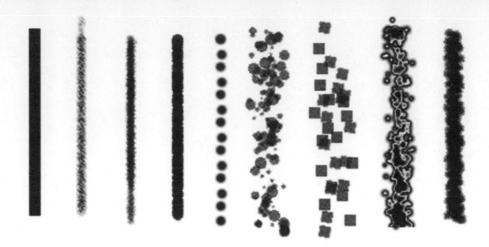

Figure 3-11. Sample brush tips

Unlike the Pencil tool, the Brush tool includes a number of options that you can configure using the Property inspector, as shown in Figure 3-12.

Figure 3-12. Brush tool settings

The following list details these settings:

- Color: Allows you to specify a color for the brush.

- Tip size: Increases or decreases the diameter of the brush tip from 1 to 100 px.

- Stroke category: Lets you select one of the 54 available brushes. In Figure 3-12, Soft Rounded is selected.

- Edge softness: Adjusts the softness of the brush tip's edge from 0 (hard) to 100 (soft).

- Texture: Selects a texture to apply to the drawn pixels. You can choose from one of 52 built-in textures. These textures range from grids to dots to lines, to organic textures like burlap and smoke. You can even load an external image for use as a custom texture.

- Amount of texture: Changes the amount of texture applied from 0 to 100% opacity.

> *Most of the brush tips are speed sensitive, meaning their properties vary depending on how fast you move your mouse while drawing.*
>
> *Hold the Shift key while drawing to constrain the brush in straight lines at 45 degree increments.*
>
> *Hold the Shift key and click different portions of the canvas to draw straight lines between the points.*

Eraser tool

The Eraser tool, as its name implies, is used to erase pixels from a bitmap layer. Like the Brush tool, the Eraser tool lets you adjust its tip size, edge softness, shape, and opacity. Using the settings shown in Figure 3-13, you can precisely and subtly remove unwanted areas of your bitmap.

Figure 3-13. Eraser tool settings

Image adjustment/effects tools

The next set of tools is used to apply subtle effects or adjustments to your bitmap layers. The first two, Blur and Sharpen, work hand in hand, letting you soften or sharpen areas of your image. The next two, Dodge and Burn, let you lighten or darken areas of your image. The third tool, Smudge, lets you push pixels of your image almost as if you were finger painting.

Blur and Sharpen tools

The Blur tool is often used to soften or blur the focus of areas in your image. You can cover up imperfections in a skin by lightly blurring them as well. Alternatively, you can sharpen the edges of objects in your images using the Sharpen tool. This can be useful if you have a photo that is slightly out of focus that you want to add some clarity to. It may not bring your best friend's face into focus, but it can make your flower shot look a little more professional. Both of these tools share the same settings in the Property inspector, as shown in Figure 3-14. These settings should look familiar by now, as you've seen them in the Property inspector for previous tools.

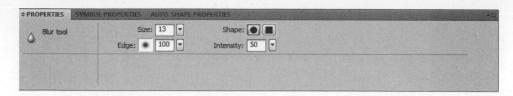

Figure 3-14. Blur and Sharpen tool settings

In Figure 3-15, the first letters of the words "SHARPEN" and "BLUR" have been modified using the Sharpen and Blur tools, respectively.

SHARPEN BLUR

Figure 3-15. Effects of the Sharpen and Blur tools on text edges

Notice the edges of the "S" in "SHARPEN." It should look more pixilated to you. Likewise, the edges of the "B" in "BLUE" are softer than those of the other characters. Together, these tools can help you refine a not-so-perfect bitmap, whether the contents of that bitmap are vector art or text, or a slightly out-of-focus photo.

Dodge and Burn tools

The Dodge and Burn tools can be used to lighten and darken areas of your image, respectively. Together, these tools can enhance photographs, bringing out areas in shadows and darkening areas that have been washed out. Figure 3-16 shows the settings for the Property inspector for these two tools.

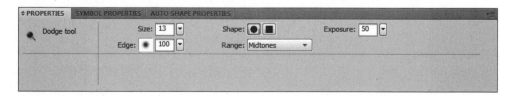

Figure 3-16. Dodge and Burn tool settings

In addition to the familiar Size, Edge, and Shape settings, both Dodge and Burn tools include Range and Exposure settings. Use the Range setting to select a color range to target with the current tool:

- Shadows: Targets dark areas of the image
- Highlights: Targets light areas of the image
- Midtones: Targets the middle range per channel of the image

The Exposure value is similar to the Amount value in previous tools. Adjust this setting to affect how strongly the dodge or burn effect is applied.

The photo shown in Figure 3-17 was taken at sunset. Getting the exposure right for both the light-house in the foreground and the sky in the background always proves a difficult task.

Figure 3-17. Bringing out the details of an image using Dodge, Burn, and selection tools

We've masked the body of the lighthouse and started to lighten the tower using the Dodge tool. You can see the effects of the tool at the bottom of the tower where we haven't completed painting. With a little patience, the Dodge and Burn tools, along with some precise masking, can really enhance the quality of your photos.

Smudge tool

Use the Smudge tool to subtly blend colors or create more dramatic melted or finger painted looks. Like the previous tools, you can adjust the Size, Edge, Shape, and Pressure settings of the Smudge tool, as shown in Figure 3-18.

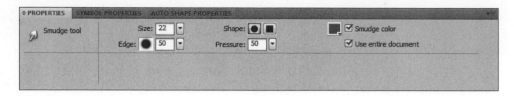

Figure 3-18. Smudge tool settings

In addition to these common settings, you can enable the Smudge color option. When enabled, the smudge will start with the color you specify. The result is like working with a combination of the Brush tool and the Smudge tool. You can also enable Use entire document. When this option is checked, colors from all layers in the document will be used in the smudge, but they will continue to be drawn on the active bitmap layer.

Additional retouching tools

The final set of bitmap tools are used for retouching areas of your image by either cloning pixels, replacing colors, or removing red-eye from your photos.

Rubber Stamp tool

The Rubber Stamp tool is great for fixing blemishes on photographs or even creating seamless textures. To use the Rubber Stamp tool, press the S key until the Rubber Stamp tool is highlighted in the Tools panel. Now, hold down the Alt key and click any existing bitmap layer or object to set your target clone area. Once you've selected your target area, continue holding Alt and position your cursor where you want to start cloning pixels. When you have your cursor positioned, release the Alt key and begin drawing. Figure 3-19 shows the Rubber Stamp tool settings.

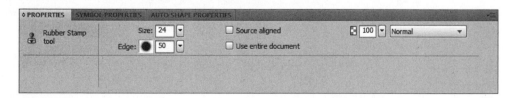

Figure 3-19. Rubber Stamp tool settings

In addition to Size and Edge settings, which adjust the size and softness of the brush, you can enable the Source aligned property. When enabled, the source location remains fixed as you perform multiple paint operations. When deselected, the source area moves relatively with the cursor. This is one of those features that is really difficult to describe, so to fully understand the effects of this property, you really need to experiment with it yourself. Figure 3-20 demonstrates how the Rubber Stamp tool can be used to remove unwanted areas of an image.

Figure 3-20. Using the Rubber Stamp tool to remove areas of an image

We were quickly able to paint out the rivets of this sign without masking the image at all.

Replace Color tool

The Replace Color tool is almost like a hybrid between the Magic Wand tool and the Brush tool. You can select a target color, specify Tolerance and Strength values, and then paint over the target color with a selected color. Using the Replace Color tool, you can paint individual flowers, change a shirt color, or create any number of effects. Figure 3-21 shows the Property inspector settings for the Replace Color tool.

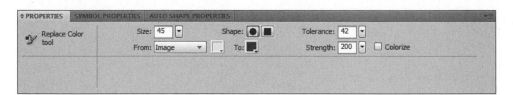

Figure 3-21. Replace Color tool settings

You can specify a replacement color either by specifying a color swatch or by clicking the target color you want to replace. Choose Swatch from the From combo box to select a specific replacement color, and then select a color from the first color box. When you start painting, only pixels similar to the color you set in the color box will be altered. If you select Image from the From combo box, the first color you click when you start painting will become the target color. This is a faster method, but it may not be as precise as selecting a single target color. Adjust the Tolerance setting like you would for the Magic Wand tool. The higher the value is, the greater the range of colors that will be replaced.

In Figure 3-22, we used the Replace Color tool to change the paint color of the background wall.

Figure 3-22. Changing the wall color with the Replace Color tool

In this example, we just used the Replace Color tool, and you can see that the results are quite good. For a true production-quality modification, we would probably mask some of the more difficult areas to ensure that our new color doesn't bleed into any unwanted areas.

Red Eye Removal tool

The Red Eye Removal tool is perhaps the easiest of the bitmap tools to work with. You simply draw a rectangle around the red-eye in your photo, and Fireworks takes care of the rest. The Property inspector settings for this tool, shown in Figure 3-23, offers Tolerance and Strength adjustments that can be used to tweak the tool quickly.

Figure 3-23. Red Eye Removal tool settings

Figure 3-24 shows the effectiveness of the Red Eye Removal tool. On the left is a photo exhibiting typical red-eye symptoms. On the right is the same photo after processing. Two simple rectangles are all it takes to restore balance to your world!

Figure 3-24. Red Eye Removal tool results

Summary

The bitmap tools included in Fireworks cover all of your daily editing needs as an interface and web designer. It's only when you need to edit hi-res images, edit in CMYK, or perform sophisticated processing and retouching of images that you need to turn to a tool like Photoshop. Using the Path to Marquee and Marquee to Path commands is a great way to create precise selections or quickly create vector artwork from bitmap artwork. Take the time to master the bitmap tools discussed in this chapter, and your design workflow will be that much more streamlined!

Chapter 4

WORKING WITH VECTORS

In this chapter, you will discover the world of vector graphics. You'll discover how vectors are different from bitmap objects, or raster objects, learn how to use various tools to draw vector objects within Fireworks, and explore scenarios for using vectors to achieve unique graphical effects.

One of the chief attractions of Fireworks is its prowess as a rapid prototyping application. Fireworks provides easy-to-use drawing tools to create vector-based graphics along with bitmap graphics. The ability to create vector-based graphics and modify them on the fly right there within the prototyping tool gives Fireworks a distinct advantage over its competitors.

Raster graphics are representations of images based on pixels. Because of this, raster images lose clarity and become pixelated when resized, especially when enlarged. Vector graphics are different from raster graphics in that a vector object is a mathematical description of an object. Vectors are created using geometric objects such as points, curves, and lines based on mathematical computations to define their shape and dimension. One distinct characteristic of vector images is they can be scaled indefinitely without degrading, which makes them particularly useful for the low-resolution demands of the Web.

Using the Vector tools

The Vector tools (see Figure 4-1) can be found in the main Tools palette. To save space in the main palette, related tools are stacked, as indicated by the small down arrow next to certain tool icons. To select a tool other than the one displayed, click and hold to display the tool options. Let's take some time to look at the vector drawing tools Fireworks provides and explore how these help us create common graphics in everyday situations.

Figure 4-1. The Vector tools section of the Tools palette in Fireworks CS4

Line tool

The Line tool is a very basic tool, and it does exactly what you think it does—it draws a line. The Line tool will create a line in its truest sense—a straight line with a beginning point and an ending point (see Figure 4-2). To draw a line, select the Line tool from the Tools palette. Then, just click and drag from the beginning point to where you want the endpoint of the line to be.

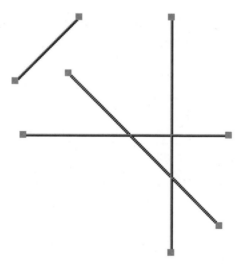

Figure 4-2. A simple line drawn with the Line tool

Holding down the Shift key while dragging will force the line to be perfectly straight. With the Shift key pressed, moving the mouse around will snap the line segment to 45 degrees.

Because this line is drawn with vectors, it is fully editable. If you decide later that the line needs to be longer, shorter, or moved to a different location, just use the Subselection tool to select an endpoint and move it either with the mouse or the arrow keys to the desired coordinates.

Pen tool

In other drawing programs, the Pen tool may be referred to as a Bézier tool. For us, the Pen tool is the workhorse tool of the bunch—you can draw virtually any shape with it. Drawing polygons with straight lines is easy, but you can also draw more organic shapes with curved edges. The Pen tool takes a lot of practice to be comfortable drawing with it, but once you've got the hang of it, it is indispensible.

There are a couple different ways to handle the Pen tool, and each has its own useful purpose. To draw straight-edged shapes (a square, for instance), you click once to begin drawing a line, click again at a different location to initiate the next point in the shape, and repeat until you get back to the original point (see Figure 4-3). Fireworks has a couple of built-in helpers. First, it enables you to draw a perfectly straight line by holding down the Shift key as you move your cursor. Second, it provides a few visual cues to help you understand what will happen on your next click, such as whether your click will close a path or add or subtract points.

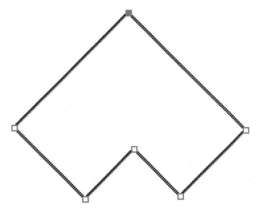

Figure 4-3. A simple straight-edged vector object drawn with the Pen tool

When you are using the Pen tool to draw a shape and are about to close it, the cursor changes to a pen with a small circle, indicating your next click will complete that shape. Let's say you have already drawn a perfectly nice square, but you'd like to add a point. With your square highlighted and your Pen tool selected, as you hover over any one of the segments of the square, the cursor changes to a pen with a plus sign next to it, indicating that your next click will add a point. Conversely, hovering over an existing point, your cursor changes to a pen with a minus sign next to it, which means clicking there will remove that point from the shape.

You can also draw curves and organic shapes with the Pen tool. This requires a slightly different technique. Instead of clicking and moving the cursor to the next point, you click and drag the cursor, which creates a curve using Bézier handles. These handles control the shape of the curve and can be moved in tandem or alone for different effects (see Figure 4-4).

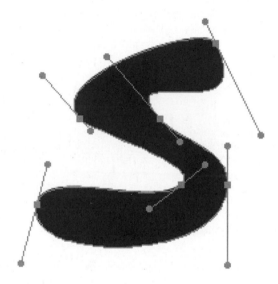

Figure 4-4. A curved contour vector object drawn with the Pen tool

Vector Path tool

 Similar to the Line tool, the Vector Path tool (which you bring up by clicking the arrow beside the Pen tool) allows you to draw a line, but unlike the Line tool, it allows for more than just straight lines. Straight lines, curved lines, even scribbled freeform lines can be drawn that will be converted to a vector-based path (see Figure 4-5). The Vector Path tool also allows you to "close the loop," creating a shape that can have a solid color fill. You can then edit any of the points along the path to change the line.

Figure 4-5. A random line drawn with the Vector Path tool

Rectangle tool

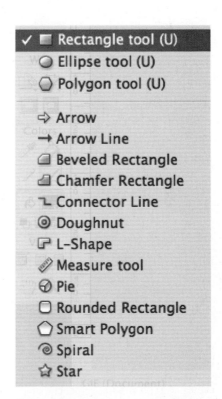

As mentioned previously, the small inverted triangle next to any icon in the Tools palette indicates that other related tools are available but not shown. To reveal these other options, just click and hold on the icon, hover over the desired tool, and release the mouse key to select that tool. The most common tools available in addition to the default Rectangle tool are the Ellipse and Polygon tools. Selecting any one of these will allow you to create the shape by clicking and dragging to the desired dimensions. Holding down the Shift key while dragging will force the tool to create an exact square or circle, depending on the tool selected. Other autoshape tools include the Star, Arrow, Chamfer Rectangle, and so on (see Figure 4-6).

Notice in Figure 4-5 the diamonds (which will appear yellow on your screen) associated with the star shape. Many of the autoshapes contain these yellow diamonds, which are configuration points. Each configuration point changes the shape in some way. For example, by adjusting the roundness configuration point, a star like the one in Figure 4-7 can be changed to look like the stylized star in Figure 4-8.

Figure 4-6. Drop-down revealing alternative autoshape tools

Figure 4-7. An ellipse, polygon, and star drawn with the autoshape tools

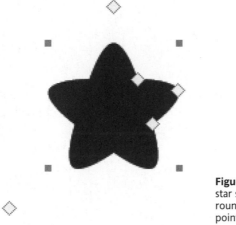

Figure 4-8. A simple
star shape with the
roundness configuration
point adjusted

Text tool

The Text tool allows the creation of text boxes and gives the user a great deal of flexibility and options when dealing with text in a Fireworks document (see Figure 4-9). The Property inspector shows all the different options for changing the properties of the selected text.

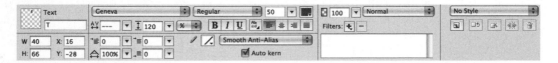

Figure 4-9. The Text Properties panel

Everything from font selection and size to line height and justification is controlled in the Text Properties panel.

Fireworks allows text to be converted to paths for further editing of letter forms (see Figure 4-10). To convert text to paths, just select the text and choose Text ➤ Convert to Paths. Converting text to paths is a good idea in certain situations. Perhaps you're creating a graphic with text set in a particular typeface. You'd like to send the file to a colleague so he or she can make further changes, but you know your colleague doesn't have that font installed on his or her system. Converting text to paths disassociates the text from a specific font, making the letterform's vector paths instead of characters in a text box. Now your colleague can manipulate the text, and you can be assured that the font you chose for the graphic is intact. Or perhaps you are creating a graphic with text, but you need to modify the look of the typeface. Since converting text to paths changes the characters to individual vector objects, you have complete control over the size, shape, and contour of each character.

Figure 4-10. Text that has been converted to vector paths

> *When text is converted to paths, all the individual text characters are grouped into a single group, and elements in the path objects cannot be converted back to text objects apart from an undo.*

Freeform and Reshape Area tools

The Freeform and Reshape Area tools, which are grouped, are very similar. Both tools allow a path to be changed with the push of the cursor (see Figure 4-11). Select a vector shape, click the path of the shape, and drag to "push" the element into a different shape, creating new points and tangents along the path as needed. In the Property inspector, the size and pressure can be adjusted for varying effect.

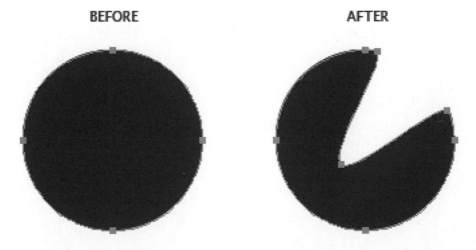

Figure 4-11. An ellipse after a swipe of the Freeform tool

Knife tool

 The Knife tool allows for the bisection (see Figure 4-12) of one or more paths of a vector object, resulting in two separate and independent elements on the canvas.

BEFORE   AFTER

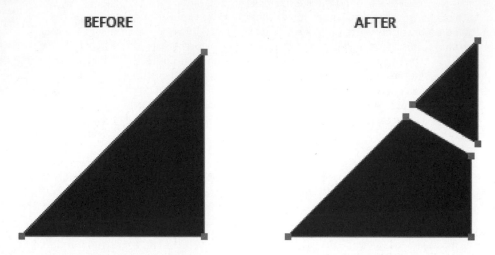

Figure 4-12. A triangle bisected with the Knife tool (shapes separated so you can see them)

Using the Paths panel

A vector shape is an outline that comprises different lines. The shape contains nodes, which define the flexibility in editing the shape for its roundness. Each of these nodes can be modified independently using the Subselection tool. These individual nodes are used to modify the contour of the shape created.

Some of the tools described previously are used to modify points, which in turn changes the shape of the object. Fireworks provides several different ways of modifying points and paths. These different means of modifying the complete vector path or individual points of the path can be found in two menu items located at Modify ➤ Combine Paths and Modify ➤ Alter Paths.

Apart from the menu locations, Fireworks CS4 makes accessing path modification options much easier by combining them all in a special new Paths panel (see Figure 4-13). They've also added several new options that are accessible only from the Paths panel. The Paths panel is located in the Workspace panel, which appears on the right side of the canvas; alternatively, it can also be found by selecting Window ➤ Others ➤ Path.

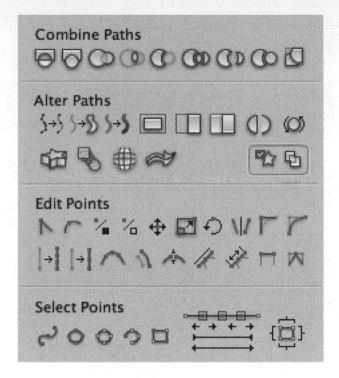

Figure 4-13. The Paths panel

Within Fireworks all the vector objects can finally be converted to the lowest level as a path. You can see this for yourself by ungrouping vector shapes until the Layers panel reflects the name of the object as a path. Lines are paths by default when created using the Pen tool.

The Paths panel is organized into four different categories based on the type of effect you are trying to achieve:

- Combine Paths: This section contains functionality such as union, intersection, punch, and combine that will work on the shapes as a whole.
- Alter Paths: The commands within this area will modify the shapes for functionalities such as extrude and blend.
- Edit Points: The individual nodes in a vector shape can be manipulated through these functions. Some of the functions present are smooth, straight, and sharp.
- Select Points: This will allow for selection of nodes in the vector shape that can then be worked upon using functionalities present in the Edit Points section.

To demonstrate how paths and points can be combined, altered, and edited, let's use two basic shapes for our common example for each technique.

Combining paths

While working with vectors, sometimes its necessary—and sometimes downright beneficial—to combine the paths of two separate objects. For our examples, let's use two different shapes—an ellipse and a square (see Figure 4-14), each on a separate layer—and overlap them to demonstrate the effects of combining paths on two vector objects. We'll use the same two shapes throughout for consistency.

Apart from the Paths panel, the options we'll be exploring are also available under the menu item Modify ➤ Combine Paths. However, using the panel provides ease of click execution compared to submenu navigation and then function execution.

The following commands appear from left to right in the Combine Paths section.

Figure 4-14. Two simple shapes, slightly overlapping

> *Note also that hovering over a particular tool in the Paths panel will bring up a tooltip with that tool's name.*

■ The Join Paths command allows you make one vector shape out of two, which is different from grouping the two objects. Joining their paths also "knocks out" the area where the two objects overlap, as shown in Figure 4-15. Split Paths will do the opposite of Join Paths. This command can also be used by selecting Modify ➤ Combine Paths ➤ Join.

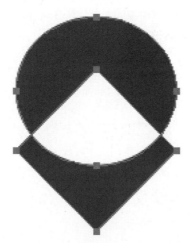

Figure 4-15. The Join Paths command in action

- Selecting Union Paths actually makes one object with a new path that is made from the merging of the two objects (see Figure 4-16). While Join Paths will knock out the overlapping areas, Union Paths will not; instead it removes any extra points, merging the two objects together as one. This command can also be used by selecting Modify ➤ Combine Paths ➤ Union.

Figure 4-16. The result of using the Union Paths command on our example shapes

- Intersect Paths allows you to make a single shape from the paths where the two other shapes overlap, as shown in Figure 4-17. Selecting this tool removes the parts of the objects that are not within the overlapping area. This command can also be used by selecting Modify ➤ Combine Paths ➤ Intersect.

Figure 4-17. Applying the Intersect Paths command to our circle and ellipse gives us this shape.

- Punch Paths also works with the overlapping area shared between the two objects, functioning much like an everyday cookie cutter. In this case, Punch Paths uses the object that is in front or on top per the hierarchical order to cut into the shape below, thus redrawing the path using the shape of the object in front and removing that object (see Figure 4-18). The Punch Paths tool relies on layer order, so keep in mind which objects are in which layers. This command can also be used by selecting Modify ➤ Combine Paths ➤ Punch.

Figure 4-18. The Punch Paths command at work

- Divide Paths will create new shapes from two or more overlapping objects (see Figure 4-19). The key here is the overlap. Any overlapping area gets divided into its own separate shape, in addition to the areas outside the overlap.

Figure 4-19. Our example shapes after applying the Divide Paths command (with shapes separated for easy viewing)

- Exclude Paths is the inverse of Divide Paths. When two objects are overlapping and the Exclude Paths action is used, it will remove the overlapped area, resulting in two separate objects, which were the areas outside the overlap (see Figure 4-20).

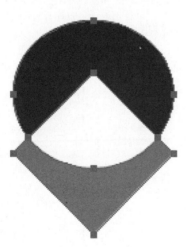

Figure 4-20. The Exclude Paths command gives us shapes outside an overlapping area.

- Trim Paths will create two new and separate objects from the overlapping shapes. This is similar to Punch Paths in that it relies on layer order, but it does not remove any part of the objects (see Figure 4-21).

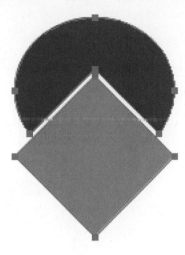

Figure 4-21. The results of applying the Trim Paths command to our example shapes (with shapes separated for easy viewing)

- Crop Paths is similar to Intersect Paths in that Fireworks will keep only the shared area between two overlapping objects (see Figure 4-22). This command can also be used by selecting Modify ➤ Combine Paths ➤ Crop.

Figure 4-22. The Crop Paths command's results are similar to those for Intersect Paths.

Altering paths

Within the Paths panel under the Alter Paths section are several options for modifying and adjusting the path points of a specific object. Most of these tools perform automatic adjustments and make editing paths with precision much easier than manually modifying an object's path. Let's explore some of the options in this section of the Paths panel. Some of the same functionalities can be accessed from Modify ➤ Alter Path.

Generally, the more points along a path, the more complex the object is or can be.

The following commands appear from left to right in the Alter Paths section:

- The Simplify Paths command reduces the number of points in a given path, which smooths the contour of an object's path (see Figure 4-23). Remember the Vector Path tool you learned about earlier in this chapter? Fireworks adds numerous points along the path in order to account for the fine movements of a cursor when drawing a vector path. Many times, these extra points give the vector path a jagged contour. Using Simplify Paths is an easy way to smooth the contour of a vector path. This command can also be used by selecting Modify ➤ Alter Paths ➤ Simplify.

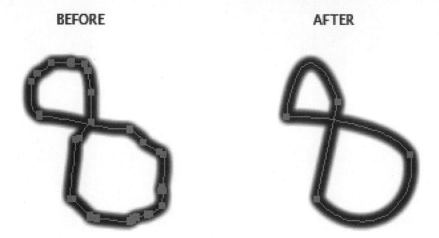

BEFORE   AFTER

Figure 4-23. The Simplify Paths command reduces the number of points in a path.

- The Expand Stroke command allows you to augment the visual weight of a path by increasing the number of points and maintaining control of the stroke as a vector object (see Figure 4-24). Within this command, there are multiple settings that can be adjusted to desired effect: Width, Miter Limit, End Caps, and Corner Radius. This command can also be used by selecting Modify ➤ Alter Paths ➤ Expand Stroke.

BEFORE   AFTER

Figure 4-24. Increasing points and path weight via the Expand Stroke command

- Convert Strokes to Fills **is an easy way to create a separate vector object from the stroke of a shape. In order to use this tool, the selected object must have a stroke. After applying the command, the stroke**—whether 1 px in width or 20 px in width—**will itself become a vector object and will be separated from the object to which it was previously associated, as shown in Figure 4-25.**

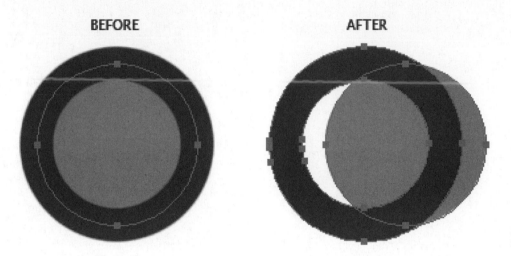

BEFORE   **AFTER**

Figure 4-25. The Convert Strokes to Fills command in action (shapes separated for easy viewing)

- Inset/Expand Paths **can be used to enlarge or shrink a vector object by pushing the path in or out (see Figure 4-26).** Inset Paths **pushes the path in, making the object smaller;** Expand Paths **makes the object larger by pushing path out. Not only does this make an object smaller or larger, but by adjusting a few properties along the way, you can actually change the contour of the object's path as well. Adjustments can be made to the path's widths, corner radius, and miter limit. This command can also be used by selecting** Modify ➤ Alter Paths ➤ Inset Path.

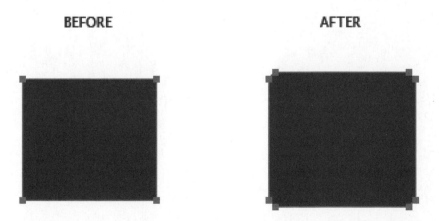

BEFORE   **AFTER**

Figure 4-26. Changing the size of a shape with the Inset/Expand Paths command option

■ The Invert Paths command allows you to reverse the area of an object relative to the Fireworks document. Doing so maintains the shape as an editable vector object, as shown in Figure 4-27.

Figure 4-27. Reversing the area of an object with the Invert Paths command

■ Invert Gradients does exactly what its name suggests—it switches the direction of the gradient fill for a selected object (see Figure 4-28). Likewise, it also maintains the shape as an editable vector object.

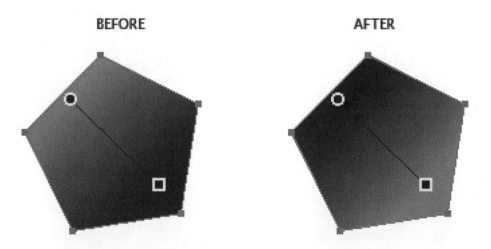

Figure 4-28. The Inverse Gradients command reverses the gradient in a shape.

Earlier in this chapter, you learned about the Knife tool, which can be used to cut a vector object in parts. Doing so results in two separate, independently editable vector objects. If you were to separate the two objects and examine one of them specifically, you'll notice it is not a "closed path." This is easier to see if the shape does not have a fill color.

- Using the Open/Close Paths command will close the gap between the path's two endpoints (see Figure 4-29), so you can treat the path as a vector path.

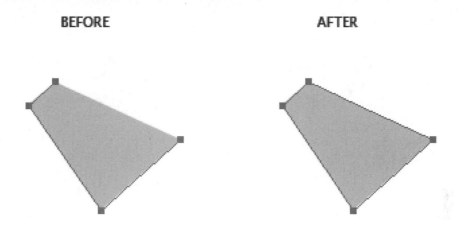

BEFORE   **AFTER**

Figure 4-29. The Open/Close Paths command allows you to close an open path and vice versa.

- Extrude Paths allows you to convert a flat, two-dimensional shape into an object that has three-dimensional qualities (see Figure 4-30). While Fireworks is not a 3D drawing application, this tool can give an object a 3D look. Selecting the Extrude Paths command will bring up a settings panel where you can adjust the Distance, Angle, Taper, and Twist properties of the selected object.

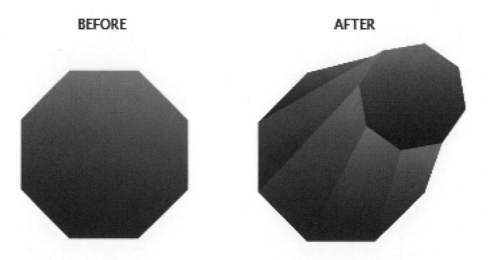

BEFORE   **AFTER**

Figure 4-30. The Extrude Paths command gives your objects a 3D look.

- The Fisheye Paths command changes the contour of a vector object using the shape of an ellipse to guide the distortion. Simply draw a vector object, such as a star. On the next layer above the star, draw an ellipse of any dimension. Select both objects, and then click the Fisheye Paths button. Figure 4-31 shows the result of applying this command. Notice how the path of the star object has been modified according to the shape of the ellipse.

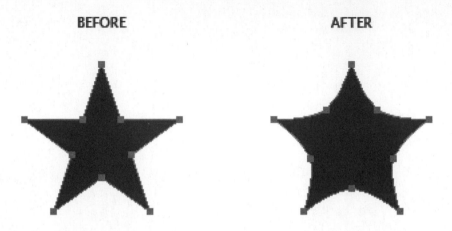

BEFORE   **AFTER**

Figure 4-31. Changing the contour of a vector object with the Fisheye Paths command

- **Deform to Path** requires two vector objects. With both objects selected, clicking the Deform to Path button will take the object on the lower layer and wrap it around the object in the upper layer. This command "deforms" the path of an object based on the path of another object (see Figure 4-32).

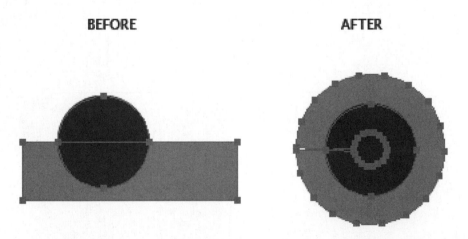

BEFORE   **AFTER**

Figure 4-32. The Deform to Path command at work

Selecting points on a line or path

Fireworks gives the user pixel-precision control over all aspects of drawing vector objects. Points are the "handles" a user can grab hold of to control everything from the curvature of a line to the alignment of endpoints. The ability to modify points along a path demonstrates the power of manipulating vector objects in Fireworks.

Before we can edit the points in a path, we have to be able to select them (see Figure 4-33), which is why we're discussing the options in the Select Points section before those in the Edit Points section of the Paths panel. Selecting points manually can be both time consuming and difficult, and it's not always an exact science. The Paths panel, found in the Workspace panel located to the right of the canvas, contains several commands that make it easy to select exactly the points you need to start modifying a particular object.

Figure 4-33. Visual indication of selected vs. nonselected points

Following are the commands, from left to right, of the Select Points section:

- Select Contour highlights the entire contour of the shape and selects all the points that make up the object.

- Select All Points selects all the points along the path of an object and activates each point for editing with the Subselection tool. This prevents you from having to manually select every point in the path, which can really save some time if you're working with a vector object that has numerous points.

- Select No Points is the inverse of Select All Points. This command will deselect all points regardless of how many points or which points are currently selected.

- Select First Point highlights the first point in the path and activates the associate Bézier handles for editing with the Subselection tool.

- Select Inverse Points deselects the point or points currently highlighted and selects the points that are currently unselected. This can be helpful if you want to select all points except for one specific point. Just select that point and then click the Select Inverse Points button, and all other points will be selected, leaving the one specific point unhighlighted.

- The Select/Deselect Next/Previous Points command along with the Grow Selection and Shrink Selection commands are helpful when trying to make selections along a complex path with numerous points and you'd rather not select them manually.

- The Select Top/Right/Bottom/Lefts Points command speeds up the point selection process by allowing you to select all the points on a given side of a vector object at once. If you have a square-shaped vector object and you'd like to make it a rectangle, just use the Select Right Points command to select the two points on the right of the square. Then move those points to the right using your arrow keys to create a rectangle.

Editing points

Now that you are comfortable selecting points, you can start learning some different techniques for modifying points. Following are the commands, from left to right, of the Edit Points section:

- Straighten Points removes the Bézier handles of a selected point and straightens the lines extending to and from the selected point (see Figure 4-34). This is an easy way to turn an ellipse into a trapezoid, among other uses. This command works on all points along a path or on individually selected points.

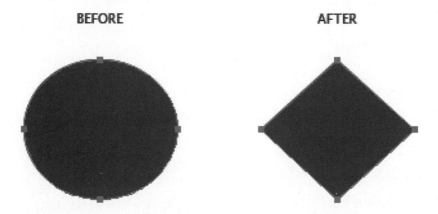

BEFORE **AFTER**

Figure 4-34. The Straighten Points command lets you easily turn an ellipse into a trapezoid.

- Smooth Points is the inverse of Straighten Points. If you were looking to draw a random-looking, organic shape with no straight lines, you might try drawing a shape using the Pen tool. However, your shape will probably have a few hard lines or jagged angles. The Smooth Points command allows you to convert your jagged object into an organic shape with curved lines and a smooth contour (see Figure 4-35).

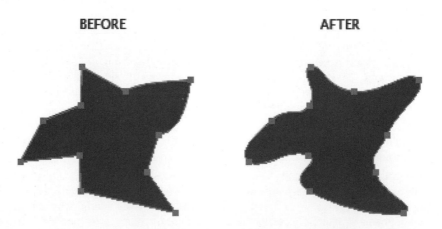

BEFORE **AFTER**

Figure 4-35. Creating an organic shape with the Smooth Points command

- Use the Round Points to Pixels/Round Points to Half-Pixels command for precision control of the anti-aliasing of the path of a vector object. Whereas Rounding Points to Pixels will force an object to the next nearest whole pixel location on the canvas, Rounding Points to Half-Pixels will force an object to move a half-pixel. Doing this will soften the edge of the path but give you even finer precision control over exact placement on the canvas.

- The Move Points command allows you to avoid manually moving a point to a desired location with either the mouse or the arrow keys. Instead, with the desired point selected, click the Move Points button. You will be asked to enter the number of pixels you would like the point to be moved horizontally and the number of pixels you would like to move the point vertically. Figure 4-36 shows the results of applying this command to a shape.

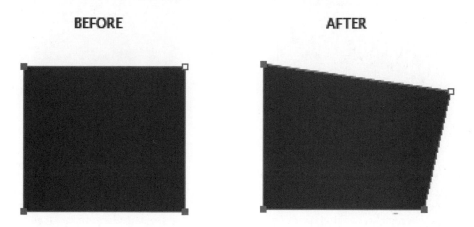

BEFORE   **AFTER**

Figure 4-36. The Move Points command in action

- Scale Points is very similar to Move Points. However, instead of entering values that will move the point horizontally or vertically by a given number of pixels, the Scale Points command allows you to enlarge or decrease the size of the object, expressed in terms of a percentage.

- Rotate Points is a simple command used to rotate a vector object in a clockwise direction. The exact rotation is precisely controlled by entering a value (in degrees).

- Mirror Points is another simple command used to flip a vector object. Select an object on the canvas, click the Mirror Points button, and then select Horizontal or Vertical, which will flip the object accordingly.

- Sharpen Points is similar to the Straighten Points command mentioned earlier, except it will actually remove points in the path in order to make the remaining points sharp (that is, not smooth or curved), as shown in Figure 4-37.

BEFORE   AFTER

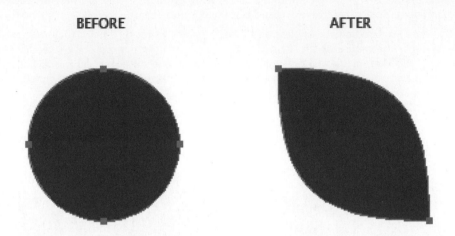

Figure 4-37. The results of applying the Sharpen Points command to a circle shape

- Fillet Points is an extremely useful command used to round the corners of polygons or other shapes (see Figure 4-38). With an object on the canvas selected, click the Fillet Points button, which will then allow you to assign a value to the corner radius of each point of the object. With this command, you can not only round the corners of a square or rectangle, but also round the points on stars or triangles or even text that has been converted to vector paths.

BEFORE   AFTER

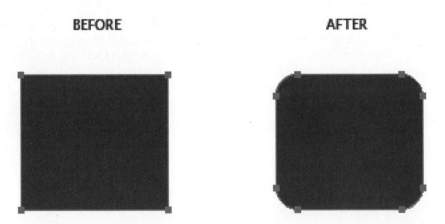

Figure 4-38. The Fillet Points command lets you round a shape's corners.

- The Add Points and Subdivide Points commands allow for the addition of more points and evenly spaces them along the path of a vector object (see Figure 4-39). This is particularly useful if you need more points to more precisely modify the shape of an object. The main difference between the two commands is the Add Points command enables you to add a specific number of extra points, whereas the Subdivide Points command only adds a point exactly between every other point along the path. Similarly, Add Points to Curves will add points to curves based on a threshold value. Adding points to curves allows for further modification points along a path.

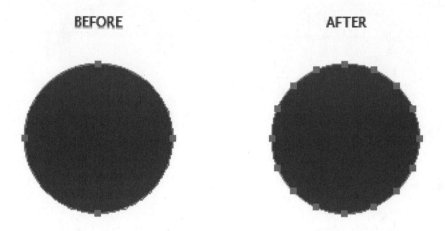

Figure 4-39. Adding a specified number of points via the Add Points command

- Offset Points enables the enlargement of a vector object by entering an offset value. This offset value, which is a threshold, not an exact pixel value enlargement, can apply to all the points in a path or a single point (see Figure 4-40).

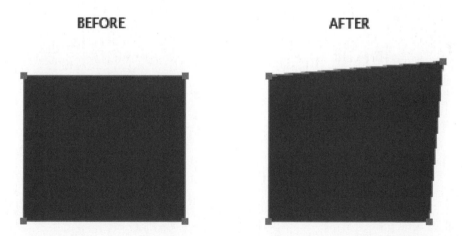

Figure 4-40. The Offset Points command allows you to enlarge an object by offsetting a value.

- The Knife on Points command is similar to using the Knife tool to bisect a path (see Figure 4-41). However, Knife on Points automatically bisects the path at the exact point, preventing the addition of extra points, which would happen if the path was bisected between points. Again, this command can be applied to all the points within an object or a single point.

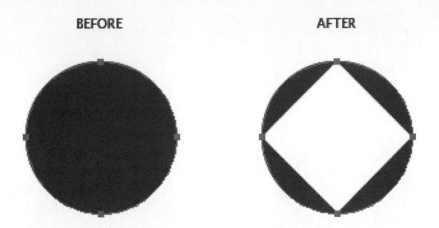

Figure 4-41. Bisecting a path using the Knife on Points command

- Make Handles Tangent and Make Handles Same Length commands are used to adjust the length and proportion of the Bézier handles on a given point. Make Handles Tangent adjusts the handles so they are tangent with the curve the point sits on. Make Handles Same Length evens the length of the handles on a given point. These tools are useful if you have edited the handles at some point, but would like to normalize them with some "automated" placement or positioning.

- Join Points is a handy command used to connect two open endpoints. For instance, consider two straight lines, which are separate vector objects. To connect the two open endpoints of the lines, select each endpoint using the Subselection tool and then click the Join Points button. The two lines are now one vector object (see Figure 4-42).

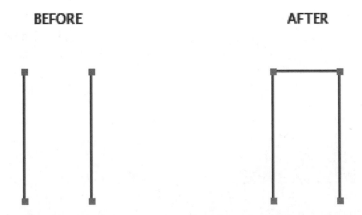

Figure 4-42. Joining lines to form one vector object with the Join Points command

- Weld Points combines two adjacent points along the same contour, making them one, but factors in their position and tangents to reshape the object accordingly (see Figure 4-43). The Weld Points command only works on adjacent points along the same path and can include any number of two or more points.

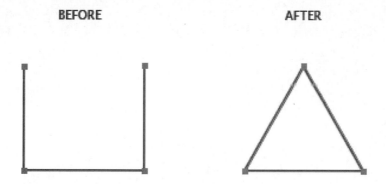

Figure 4-43. The results of applying the Weld Points command to an open path

Summary

In this chapter we've looked at the tools Fireworks offers to draw vector objects. You learned how to draw everything from simple lines and shapes, such as a square, to more complex, free-form shapes. You also learned how to modify the points along a path to change the contour and shape of vector objects.

Now that you are familiar with the vector drawing tools and the many commands that assist in manipulating the objects you draw, you can harness the real power of Fireworks. With the understanding you've gained, you're prepared to take advantage of Fireworks' unique ability to mix vector objects and raster graphics on the canvas together, which will speed up your workflow and help you design more efficiently.

Chapter 5

EXPORTING FROM FIREWORKS TO THE WEB

When we consider all of the functionality of Fireworks and the workflow born out of that functionality, the feature that sets Fireworks apart from its competitors as a superior web design tool is the exporting workflow. The workflow for exporting graphics from Photoshop is complex and time consuming. By comparison, Fireworks' exporting process is elegant—on the order of an Aston Martin to a Ford Taurus. This chapter provides information on file and image optimization and exporting graphics.

File optimization: The tools

Two tools are used for exporting from Fireworks: the Slice tool and the Hotspot tool. Both the Slice tool and the Hotspot tool were created by Adobe to add interactivity to a web page and to export graphics to HTML. Because the Hotspot tool's main utility lies in creating the outmoded image map, most professional web designers these days use only the slice function to export images for use in their custom handwritten (X)HTML and CSS. Much of this chapter will be devoted to optimizing and exporting images from the Slice tool, with brief mention of the functionality of the Hotspot tool.

Slice tool

Slices divide a graphic into multiple pieces for export as smaller, independently optimized files. A slice is created by selecting an element in your graphic and inserting a slice (from the Edit menu or contextual right-click menu), or by choosing the Slice tool and dragging a box around the area to be exported. The Polygon Slice tool is also available, but as with the Hotspot tool, it is used to create a clickable area on an image map, an outmoded method that is not used by professional web designers.

Here are a few tips for you to consider as you create your slices:

- **Slice only the needed graphics, and keep these graphics as small as possible**: Since you won't be using the slice functionality for its original purpose, exporting an entire layout to HTML tables and images, you don't need to slice up the entire layout. You only need to create slices for the pieces of the layout that have to exist in an HTML page as an image, such as logos, textures, and decorative photos.

  In creating your slices, consider repeating patterns, reusable images, and so on, and use as few slices as possible. Make these slices take up as few pixels as possible (e.g., a repeating gradient background only needs to be 1-px wide). Every saved byte counts for page load time and site performance.

- **Name your slices**: As with pages, layer groupings, layers, and states, it is helpful to give your slices smart names for easy reference, regardless of the number of slices in your design. You've probably already experienced (or you will soon if you are in the business long) opening up a file you haven't seen in years and wondering why in the world you have four slices and what each of them are there for. Good slice naming can solve this problem. It will also help other designers who may inherit the project and your source files to understand what is going on.

Hotspot tool

Fireworks provides a Hotspot tool, similar to the Slice tool, for creating interactive image maps. Image maps are an outmoded HTML technology that makes certain areas of an image clickable when viewed in a web browser. As mentioned previously, most professional web designers no longer use image maps, instead utilizing CSS to achieve the same results more easily and flexibly, with greater accessibility and maintainability. We mention this tool here only for completeness.

Hotspots are created in much the same way as a slice. Using the Hotspot tool, highlight a portion of the graphic that you would like to turn into a clickable area, or a hyperlink, on an image map. See Figure 5-1 for an example.

The difference between a slice and a hotspot is that a hotspot is not exported as an individual graphic. When exported as HTML, a hotspot will be converted into an HTML image map.

Figure 5-1. This photo has several hotspots applied to it, which can then be used as links in an image map.

Image optimization

Once you have sliced your graphic file into the desired pieces using the Slice tool, you are ready to export the slices for the Web. Two steps are required in exporting graphics from Fireworks for use on the Web: optimizing and exporting. You should spend some time with this process to make sure you obtain the optimal balance of compression and quality. Every byte you save with optimization will add up to big bandwidth savings, and thus better performance for your users, but you want to make sure you are providing them with a high-quality experience with your images so they continue to come back!

You will need to keep in mind several major factors as you optimize your sliced images for export: file type, compression, and color depth. These factors will determine your file's size and quality. Your goal is to achieve as high quality an image as possible with the smallest file size possible. An acceptable quality/size ratio is often a judgment call, though some companies have strict style guides or regulations for this. Experimentation is the key, and every exported image should be considered individually.

Choosing the right file type

Seven file types are available for use in Fireworks. For web design, we use primarily PNG, JPEG, and the occasional GIF.

GIF (Graphics Interchange Format) is a proprietary format that contains up to 256 colors and can support transparent areas and multiple frames for animation. GIFs are best used for images comprised of solid-color areas such as cartoons or that need transparent areas or animation.

JPEG (Joint Photographic Experts Group) format supports millions of colors (24-bit system). JPEGs were designed for photographs and are best used with them or with images featuring intricate textures. Because the compression algorithm developed for the JPEG format was designed for photographs, it is optimized for images with smooth tonal transitions. Compressing images that have harsh tonal transitions (such as line art) will create what are known as **artifacts** and noise in the areas around the edges of harsh tone transitions.

PNG (Portable Network Graphic) format uses a lossless data compression (known as DEFLATE), a nonpatented method; supports up to 32-bit color depth; can contain transparency, or an alpha channel; and can be progressive. Probably the most versatile image format, usable in many situations, PNG is a great replacement for GIF in many circumstances (hence, the acronym has a recursive "street" meaning: "PNG Not GIF"). Always try compressing an image in PNG format first, with the exception of photographs, which will almost always be better off in JPEG format.

PNG supports RGB and grayscale images. As its name implies, it was created for use on the Internet, not for print graphics, and as such does not support the CMYK color space (or other color spaces besides grayscale and RGB).

It is possible to export three different types of PNG files: PNG8 (for 256-color and grayscale images), PNG24 (for true color or RGB images), and PNG32 (for RGB images with an alpha transparency).

Fireworks has the capability of producing an 8-bit PNG (PNG8) with an alpha channel (semitransparent layer) that degrades nicely in Internet Explorer 6, making the format an ideal replacement for proprietary GIF images.

PNG is the native file format for Fireworks. A Fireworks PNG contains additional application-specific information that is not stored in an exported PNG.

> *Internet Explorer 6 does not support the PNG-native alpha-channel transparency. JavaScript must be employed to fix this, though there is no silver-bullet solution.*

WBMP (Wireless Bitmap) is a 1-bit (black-and-white) format created for mobile computing devices. This format is used on Wireless Application Protocol (WAP) pages.

TIFF (Tagged Image File Format) is used for storing bitmap images, most commonly in print publishing. Fireworks supports three different bit depths for this format: 8, 16, and 32 bits.

BMP (Bitmap) is the Microsoft Windows graphic file format, commonly used to display bitmap images. BMPs are used primarily on the Windows operating system. Fireworks supports two different bit depths for this format: 8 and 24 bits.

PICT, developed by Apple Computer, is a graphic file format commonly used on Macintosh operating systems. Fireworks supports two different bit depths for this format: 8 and 24 bits.

Having selected the appropriate file format, we now determine the appropriate compression and color settings to use.

Compression and color settings

Choosing a compression level is a largely subjective task. Determining how much compression you can apply and still have an image with acceptable quality is done on a case-by-case basis. Art for a finished web site should be carefully considered. Every byte saved by image compression and color setting adds up to large bandwidth savings, and thus saved expenses, in the long run. These settings are chosen in the Optimize panel, as shown in Figure 5-2. You can access this panel by selecting Windows ➤ Optimize or pressing F6.

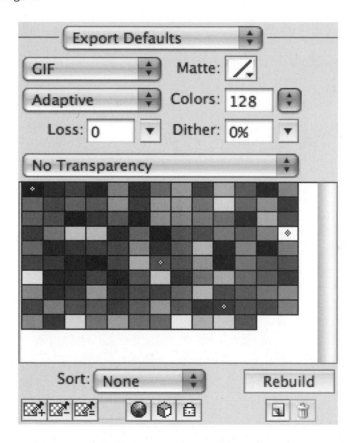

Figure 5-2. In the Optimize panel, you can select file type, compression, and color settings to adjust your exported graphic to the desired quality and file-size level.

There are several settings to consider in this panel, depending on file type, which we'll look at next.

Palette index

The following options are available for color palettes via the palette index:

8-bit image formats contain a color palette of up to 256 colors. Choosing the correct color palette will help you achieve the highest quality image with the smallest file size. You can choose from the following options:

- Adaptive: A custom palette derived from the actual colors in the document. This option, the default, most often produces the highest quality image.
- Web Adaptive: An adaptive palette in which colors are converted to the closest web-safe color. Web-safe colors are those that come from the Web 216 palette.
- Web 216: A palette of the 216 colors common to both Windows and Mac OS computers. This palette is often called a web-safe or browser-safe palette because it produces fairly consistent results in various web browsers on either platform when viewed on 8-bit monitors.

> The "web safe" color palette is an outmoded concept by most standards. Modern computer displays are typically set to millions of colors, so restricting a graphic to these colors is not necessary.

- Exact: A palette that contains the exact colors used in the image. Only images containing 256 or fewer colors may use this palette. Otherwise, the palette switches to Adaptive.
- Windows and Mac OS: Each contains the 256 colors defined by the Windows or Mac OS platform standards, respectively.
- Grayscale: A palette of 256 or fewer shades of gray. Choosing this palette converts the image to grayscale.
- Black and White: A two-color palette consisting only of black and white.
- Uniform: A mathematical palette based on RGB pixel values.
- Custom: A palette that has been modified or loaded from an external palette (ACT file) or a GIF file.

Loss

Lossy compression lets you squeeze more bytes out of your GIFs and PNGs by increasing identical pixel patterns to improve compression in indexed-color images. You can increase the level of the Loss setting for smaller file sizes.

Matte

Not specifically an optimization option, Matte lets you choose the background color against which you want to anti-alias your image for any format. Match this color as closely as possible to the background on which the anti-aliased image will appear.

Colors

8-bit images contain anywhere from 1 to 256 colors. You can specify the exact number of colors your image will contain in the Colors field for images in the GIF, PNG8, TIFF8, PICT8, or BMP8 format. A lower number of colors means a smaller file.

The color table

The color table displays the colors of a slice you are previewing if you are working with an 8-bit (or less) color format. The color table allows you to edit the colors in your image by modifying, adding, and deleting colors from the palette. The color palette also allows you to make certain colors in the image transparent (in a format that supports transparency), change a color to a close web-safe alternative, or lock a color from being edited.

You may also see symbols on some color swatches indicating the specific properties of that color. Table 5-1 describes these symbols.

Table 5-1. Symbols indicating the properties of a color in a slice's color palette

Symbol	Description
	An edited color. This edit only affects the exported file; it will not change the source image.
	A locked color.
	A transparent color.
	A web-safe color.
	A color with multiple properties (here, an edited, locked, web-safe color).

Dither

Dithering is the placement of two colors to create the illusion of a third color. It is a way to reduce a large range of colors down to the 256 (or fewer) colors contained in 8-bit image formats. Dithering can give the illusion of the presence of colors that are not in the current palette, which is especially useful for exporting photographs and graphics with complex blends and gradients to 8-bit formats. With the Dither setting, we select a percentage of dithering, which can increase the fidelity of the dithered image to the original. Higher dither percentages will mean a larger file, so as with overall optimization, you must decide on the appropriate balance.

Transparency

The Transparency property, as its name implies, allows the area of a web page behind the transparent areas of an image to show through.

There are two types of transparency that can be used: index transparency, which makes pixels with a specified color value transparent, and alpha transparency, which can be used for semitransparency or total transparency. Semitransparency only works in the PNG format. Nearly every modern browser supports alpha transparency (translucency). Internet Explorer 6 (a nonmodern browser that is lingering on the Web like a bad habit) does not. If you choose to support this browser, special measures must be taken to ensure that your semitransparent images are accounted for.

In Fireworks, transparent areas of an image are shown as a gray-and-white checkerboard. Note that by default, GIF images are exported without transparency. You must specify the transparency setting in order for the image to be exported with transparency. By default, it will be exported with a white background.

Specifying a color as the index for transparency only affects the exported image and not the source file.

JPEG compression options

The following JPEG compression options are available in the Optimize panel.

Quality

JPEG uses a lossy compression algorithm, meaning that some data is discarded from the original file as it is compressed. This reduces the quality of the final image but also reduces the file size. The lower the quality percentage, the higher the compression and the lower the file size. The higher the quality percentage, the lower the compression and the higher the file size. Experiment and find the balance that is right for your situation.

Selective quality

A way to further compress a JPEG image and retain a high degree of quality is to select certain areas of an image to be compressed at a higher quality and others to be compressed at a lower quality. For example, you might select the subject of a photograph for lower compression and compress the background of the photo at a higher level as in Figure 5-3. This can be accomplished using selective compression, as outlined in the following steps:

1. In the image's original view, use one of the Marquee tools to select the area you would like to keep at a higher quality.

2. Once it is selected, choose Selective JPEG from the Modify menu and select Save Selection as JPEG Mask.

3. In the Optimize panel, edit the Selective Quality settings as follows:

   - Enable the Selective quality option.
   - Choose a compression quality for the selected area. Here you may also choose to preserve the quality of all text and/or button symbols to be exported with the image.

Figure 5-3. This photograph is being compressed using a selective JPEG mask. The boat has been highlighted with a Marquee tool, allowing it to be compressed at a higher quality than the background of the photo.

Smoothing and sharpening

As noted previously, hard tonal transitions, usually from edges of graphic elements, do not compress well in JPEG's compression algorithm, causing "noise," distortion, artifacts, or pixelization. The Smoothing setting applies blurring to the hard edges in the graphics, reducing this pixelization and allowing for higher-quality compression and usually smaller file sizes.

To help preserve detail around edges in graphics, you may select Sharpen JPEG edges from the Optimize panel's options menu. This setting can increase image quality but will increase file size.

Side-by-side comparison

When optimizing images, it is helpful to have the original graphic in view at the same time as the optimized graphic so you can get a sense of how much quality loss is acceptable when selecting compression settings. Fireworks provides two split-views for the preview area: 2-Up (see Figure 5-4) and 4-Up (see Figure 5-5). You can split the preview area into two or four to examine different compression settings and see the approximate exported file size, all at the same time on the same screen.

Figure 5-4. Viewing the image in 2-Up preview mode allows you to adjust compression settings and immediately see the effect those settings would have.

It is possible to give general guidance on exact compression settings, but each graphic is unique and so should be treated individually. It is well worth your time to experiment with a wide range of settings to save as many bytes as possible. Experiment with your graphic and try many different settings out. Adjust percentages in very small increments to shave off as many bytes as possible and arrive at the optimal compression/quality ratio.

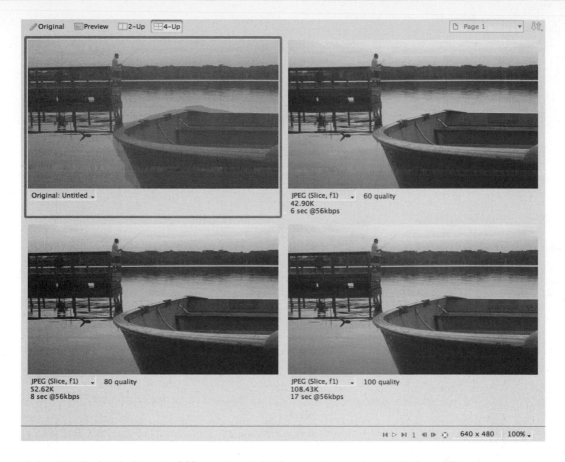

Figure 5-5. Viewing the image in 4-Up preview mode allows you to experiment with three different compression settings and compare them all with the original graphic simultaneously.

Using the Export command

Once you have your graphic sliced appropriately and have all of your compression settings optimized, it is time to export your graphic.

The Export dialog

The simplest way to export a graphic is to simply right-click a slice and select Export Selected Slice (or choose File ➤ Export from the menu). This will bring up the Export dialog, shown in Figure 5-6, where you can choose the type of export you want to perform. You can export a document or parts of a document as a single image file, multiple images, Adobe PDF files, a Dreamweaver library, or as HTML with CSS and images

Exporting to Adobe PDF

During a design review process, it may be very useful to export your design to PDF format for distribution and commentary. Fireworks has a built-in PDF export option, show in Figure 5-6, so that you can export a single page, or all pages of your document, to this format.

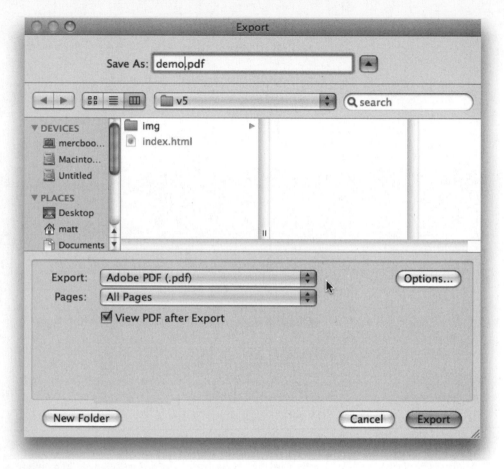

Figure 5-6. Use the Export dialog to select the location you want the file to be saved to and to name the file.

To customize the PDF, click Options in the Export dialog. The Adobe PDF Export Options dialog box appears. You will be able to adjust the following settings in this dialog, as shown in Figure 5-7:

- Compatibility determines which version of the Adobe PDF application can read the file.

- Compression sets the type of image compression. Choose JPEG or JPEG2000 for designs with photographic elements or intricate textures and ZIP for illustrations or designs with large areas of solid colors.

- Quality adjusts image quality settings for the JPEG formats. Higher qualities produce a larger file size.

- Convert to grayscale will create a smaller file size, without color.
- Check the Enable text selection option if you want to be able to copy text from your exported file. This will greatly increase file size.
- Bleed Value sets a border of the specified pixel width around your file.
- Use password to open document and Use password to restrict tasks set your password options.

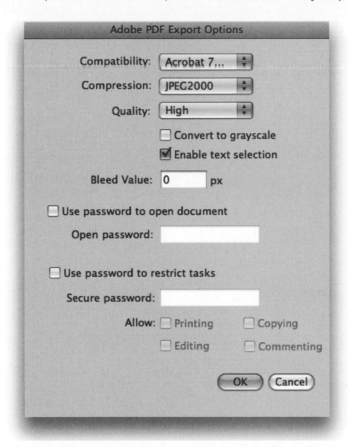

Figure 5-7. The Adobe PDF Export Options dialog enables you to select PDF version compatibility, compression type, quality level, and password options.

Images only

This is the most commonly used export function for professional web designers, allowing you to export your selected area (or all areas), pages, layers, and states, as image files. Figure 5-8 shows the images-only Export dialog. There are many options available here. See the case studies in Part 3 of this book for examples of the power of this functionality. The file format and the optimization settings used for the image are specified in the Optimize panel, which you access by selecting Windows ➤ Optimize or pressing F6.

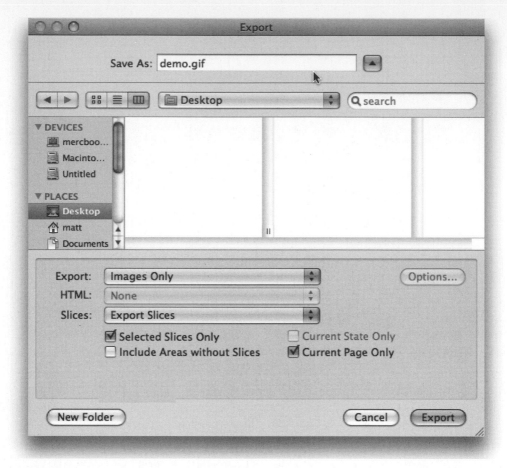

Figure 5-8. The images-only Export dialog allows you to choose which slices, pages, and states you want to export.

Slices

The Slices select box lets you decide how you want your slices to be treated:

- None ignores your slices and exports the entire document.
- Export Slices uses your defined slices as the exported area.
- Slice along Guides exports your entire document in pieces along slice guides, rather than your defined slices.

Selected Slices Only

Check the Selected Slices Only option to export only the highlighted slices. You can select multiple slices by Shift-clicking the desired slices.

Include Areas without slices

Checking the Include Areas without Slices option will export the entire document, including areas outside of your defined slices.

Current State Only

Check the Current State Only option to export slices from the current state visible in the preview window. Deselect this to export multiple versions of your defined slices (one version for each state). This is very useful for simultaneously exporting graphics to show different hover states in an HTML document, such as those used for buttons.

Current Page Only

Check the Current Page Only option to export slices from the current page visible in the preview window. Deselect to export multiple graphics from your defined slices (one graphic for each page).

Dreamweaver Library (.lbi)

A Dreamweaver library file (LBI) is a library object for Adobe Dreamweaver. It is a section of HTML code that can be referenced from multiple files within Dreamweaver. When a change is made to the library object, all referencing pages are automatically updated.

With the Dreamweaver Library (.lbi) option in the Export drop-down, you can create a new Dreamweaver library using the graphics you have created, and HTML is automatically generated by Fireworks.

HTML and Images\CSS and Images (.htm)\Director (.htm)

Fireworks has the ability to export your design as an entire web page (HTML file) with HTML, CSS, and images created for you. This is useful for a quick-and-dirty export to code for showing off a semifunctional prototype of a design. This could also be useful for graphic designers who have a desperate need to create a web page but no working knowledge of HTML or CSS; however, this is not a recommended solution for professional web designers.

Because Fireworks needs to cover all possible scenarios when creating HTML and CSS, the code is very generic, bloated, nonsemantic, and difficult to maintain. It is far better to utilize someone skilled in HTML and CSS, or take advantage of one of the many "graphic to markup" services now available on the Web to achieve professional results. Better still, take the plunge and learn HTML and CSS, which are very easy to use. Fireworks can export table-based HTML layouts, CSS and HTML, and markup specific to Adobe Director and Adobe Dreamweaver (see Figure 5-9). Under any of these options, click the Options button to access the HTML Setup window (see Figure 5-10) to configure your HTML output.

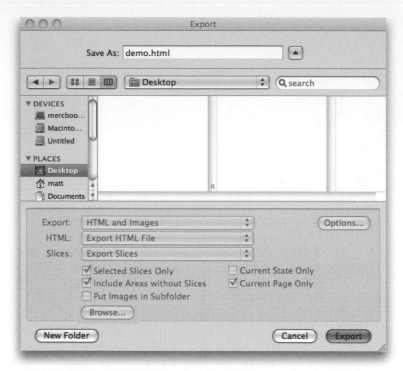

Figure 5-9. Use the Export drop-down option HTML and Images or CSS and Images (.htm) for a quick buildout of a working prototype site.

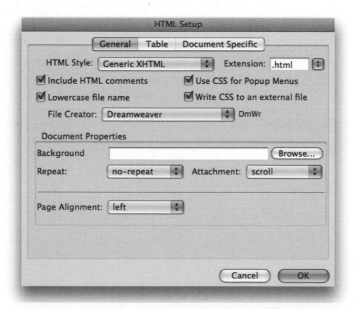

Figure 5-10. Customize your HTML export using the HTML Setup window, accessed via the Options button when exporting to HTML via the Export dialog.

Using the Export Wizard

We presented the "Compression and color settings" section earlier so that you could hand-select the best export settings for your graphic. We recommend customizing the export settings by hand for the best results. However, Fireworks does provide an Export Wizard, which will ask you a series of questions to help you arrive at those settings. The process is as follows:

1. Select File ➤ Export Wizard to bring up the Export Wizard, beginning with the screen shown in Figure 5-11. Here you are allowed to specify a target file size for your exported image. Enter this if you have an idea of what size you'd like to arrive at.

Figure 5-11. Step 1 of the Export Wizard asks you to select an export format or target file size.

2. Click Continue on the first screen to go to the screen shown in Figure 5-12. If your document has states, it will ask you what you would like to do with them:

   ■ Selecting Animated GIF will bring up a preview window where you can choose settings for your animation (see Chapter 8).

   ■ Selecting JavaScript rollover will take you directly to Step 4, with GIF and JPEG as recommended file formats.

   ■ Selecting Single image file will take you to Step 3.

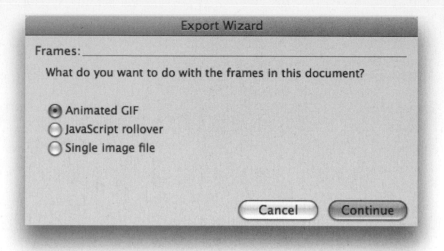

Figure 5-12. Step 2 of the Export Wizard asks you what you'd like to do with the frames (states) in your document.

3. Selecting Single image file and clicking Continue will bring you to the screen shown in Figure 5-13. Here you are asked where you will be using your exported graphic.

- Selecting The web or Dreamweaver will take you to Step 4, with GIF and JPEG as recommended file formats

- Selecting An image-editing application or A desktop publishing application will take you to Step 4, with TIFF as a recommended file type.

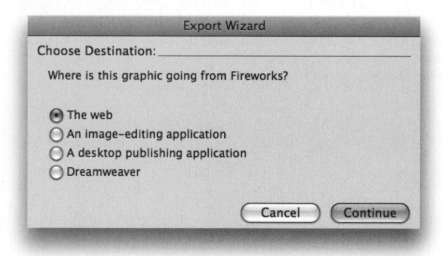

Figure 5-13. Step 3 asks you about the final destination of this graphic.

4. Depending on the options you chose in Step 2 or Step 3, you are taken to one of the screens in Figure 5-14. Click Exit to move on.

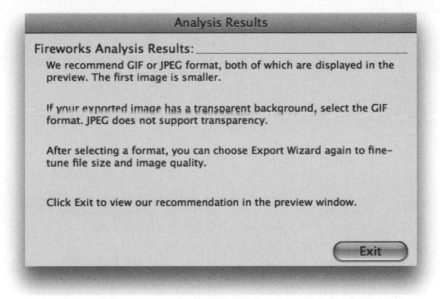

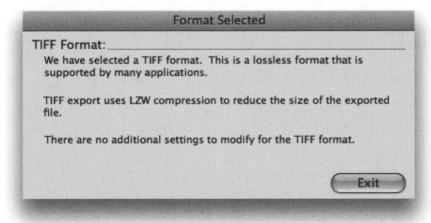

Figure 5-14. Step 4 gives you Fireworks' recommendation for a file format.

Step 4 simply tells you Fireworks default recommendations for the settings you have selected. This is the most limiting part of the process because it only ever recommends GIF and JPEG for web usage. This is based on an outdated premise that most browsers do not properly support PNG files. Modern web browsers properly support PNG files, making them a very viable, and perhaps the best, image format for most graphics needs on the Web.

The Preview window

Clicking Exit in the last screen of the Export Wizard will take you to the preview window with Fireworks default file setting recommendations. We highly recommend that you customize these settings to your particular graphic and application. See the "Compression and color settings" section earlier. You will be taken to one of three preview windows, depending on your selections in the previous steps.

In JPEG or GIF preview mode (see Figure 5-15), you can select between JPEG or GIF file formats and view the output results of either.

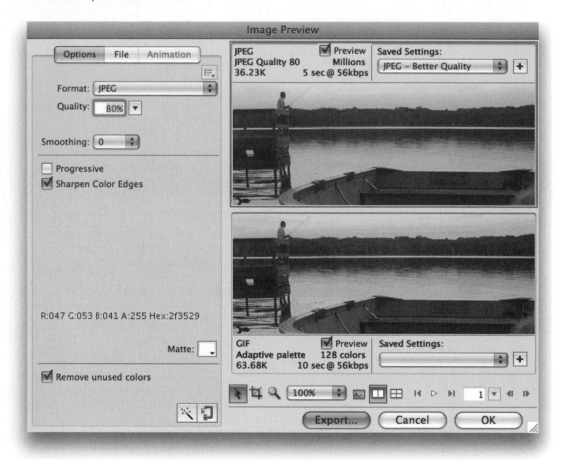

Figure 5-15. The JPEG/GIF preview window gives you customization settings specific to these formats.

In the animated GIF preview window (see Figure 5-16), you can customize the compression and color settings for the whole animated GIF and preview the animation.

Figure 5-16. The animated GIF preview window gives you customization options specific to this format and lets you play or page through each frame of the animated GIF.

Finally, the TIFF preview window (see Figure 5-17) allows you to customize and preview the settings and output of your graphic saved as a TIFF file.

Figure 5-17. The TIFF preview window allows you to see the results of your customization settings for the TIFF format before export.

Once you have customized your compression settings (or have decided to use the defaults), clicking Export will take you to the Export options window as discussed previously.

Summary

In this chapter, you learned about the powerful, flexible, and simple file optimization and export functionality and workflow of Fireworks. The export functionality allows you to save highly optimized images for use on a web page, as a PDF file for preview, as a Dreamweaver or Director library, as a working web site prototype, or even as production print graphics. The simple workflow means huge gains in productivity, allowing you more time for focusing on the actual design and build of your graphic, rather than spending tedious hours slicing and exporting graphics.

Part 2

USING FIREWORKS

In Part 1 of this book, you were introduced to the individual tools that make up Fireworks CS4. You learned about the bitmap tools and the vector tools, and how they play together. You also learned how to export your layouts and designs to the Web. With these core concepts out of the way, it's now time to move on to more advanced concepts.

Fireworks is an extremely flexible tool that can be used to achieve a wide range of goals, and we'll touch on a number of those goals in the chapters that follow. You'll see how the core concepts previously covered can be combined to create a variety of sophisticated effects. You'll learn about animation, Flex component skinning, and Adobe AIR prototypes. You'll also be introduced to the big, wide world of Fireworks extensions—application add-ons that enhance the power of Fireworks. The final chapter of this part introduces you to creating your own extensions—an advanced but rewarding chapter for you technical designers out there.

Chapter 6

CREATING VISUAL EFFECTS

Fireworks provides all of the tools you need to create advanced, sophisticated, wow-your-audience visual effects. In fact, because of the flexibility of the Fireworks toolset, we think you'll find that creating effects in Fireworks is much faster and flexible than in other design tools. Every object, every gradient, every filter, every *everything* in Fireworks is infinitely editable and tweakable, giving you the ability to try, change, and remove until you're satisfied (or exhausted).

Because the term "visual effect" can mean different things to different people, we should probably frame the term and the conversation we're going to have in this chapter. For this conversation, a visual effect can be something as simple as a simulated reflection to something as complicated as magical glowing particle trails. An effect is really just a combination of techniques that result in a perceptively sophisticated result.

In this chapter, we'll first look at the building blocks used to create effects and then combine these building blocks to re-create a number of popular effects seen across the Web, print, and modern RIAs or desktop applications. By the end of the chapter, you'll be creating glassy buttons and headers, reflections, and magic effects like a pro!

Building blocks

Building sophisticated effects is easier than you think—you just need to understand the fundamental building blocks provided by Fireworks. The effects we're going to create in this chapter rely on gradient fills, texture fills, layer blend modes, filters, and styles. Let's step through each of these basics quickly, and then move on to the fun stuff!

Gradient fills

Gradient fills are at the heart of most effects and sophisticated user interface skins. The Fireworks Gradient tool is actually one of the features that have made Fireworks the go-to tool in many visual designer's arsenals. In addition to setting color stops on the gradient, you can specify opacity stops as well. It's the ability to specify opacity stops independently of color stops that sets the Fireworks Gradient tool apart from gradient tools in other applications. Further, with the introduction of Fireworks CS4, gradients are now updated in real time on the design surface as you adjust gradient handles.

Selecting a gradient type

Changing the gradient type and editing gradients is all achieved through the Property inspector. Figure 6-1 demonstrates how to specify a gradient fill type. The most commonly used gradient types are Linear, Radial, and Ellipse, and these are the types we'll show you how to use in the tutorials that follow.

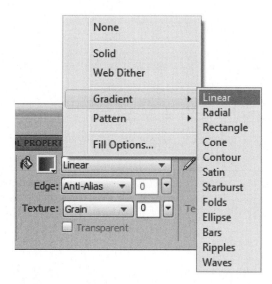

Figure 6-1. Setting the gradient fill type

Editing gradient nodes

Once you've selected a gradient fill type, click the Fill swatch to launch the gradient editor. Figure 6-2 shows the gradient editor expanded with an opacity editor launched for the rightmost opacity node.

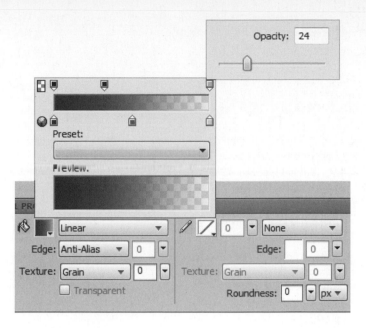

Figure 6-2. Editing opacity nodes

The top row of nodes represents opacity nodes, while the bottom row represents color stops. Drag nodes horizontally to change their position, drag nodes vertically to remove them, and click between existing nodes to add new nodes. Click a node to launch either the color editor or the opacity editor (depending on the node type). This node-editing interface is the same regardless of the type of gradient you have chosen.

Adjusting the gradient direction

Unlike editing gradient stops, editing a gradient's direction is not done via the Property inspector. Instead, direction editing is performed on the design surface itself. Figure 6-3 shows a rectangle on the design surface with a linear gradient applied. Notice the vertical black adorner, anchored by the circle glyph and the square glyph. This is the gradient direction editor. The circle indicates the start of the gradient, while the square indicates the end of the gradient.

Figure 6-3. Gradient direction editing

Reposition the gradient by dragging the start point (circle), change the direction freely by dragging the end point (square), or rotate the gradient by mousing over the connector line and dragging when the cursor changes to a rotation indicator.

You can snap the rotation to 45-degree intervals by holding down the Shift key while dragging.

Advanced gradient editing

The default Fireworks gradient editor is fast and easy to use, and is excellent for simple gradients. However, for more complex gradients that employ a large number of gradient stops, it becomes difficult to select the exact stop that you want, especially if you want the stops to be practically on top of each other. This is a common technique for creating sharp, glass-like gradient effects. I created the Gradient panel for Fireworks to address this limitation in the default editor. You can download the Gradient panel from my web site, www.granthinkson.com/tools/fireworks, and install it using the Adobe Extension Manager. Once installed, launch the editor from the main Fireworks menu (Window ➤ Gradient Panel).

Figure 6-4 shows two states of the Gradient panel. The leftmost state is the zoomed out, default view of the panel. The positioning of the nodes here is the same as it would be if you launched the default Fireworks gradient editor. In the rightmost panel, we have zoomed in on the two center color nodes by dragging the zoom slider all the way to the right and the offset slider to the middle. Zoomed all the way in, we can now accurately position these two stops that appear to be right on top of each other in the nonzoomed view.

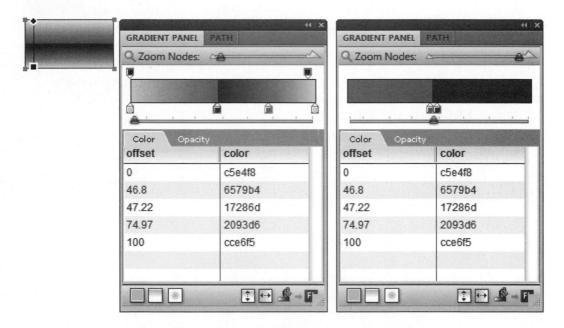

Figure 6-4. Advanced gradient editing with the Gradient panel

For even more precise editing, you can manually enter the offset, color, or opacity in the supporting Color and Opacity grids directly beneath the live preview.

Texture fills

Fireworks ships with a number of textures that are sure to look familiar to you if you've paid attention to the artwork used on modern Web 2.0–style web sites. Built-in textures, such as Line-Diag 1 and Line-Horiz 1, are used in subtle ways on a vast array of sites to provide an extra dimension to layouts. The familiarity of these textures stands as a testament to the widespread usage of Fireworks in the world of web design. Figure 6-5 shows how to apply the texture named Line-Diag 1 to a selected rectangle on the canvas.

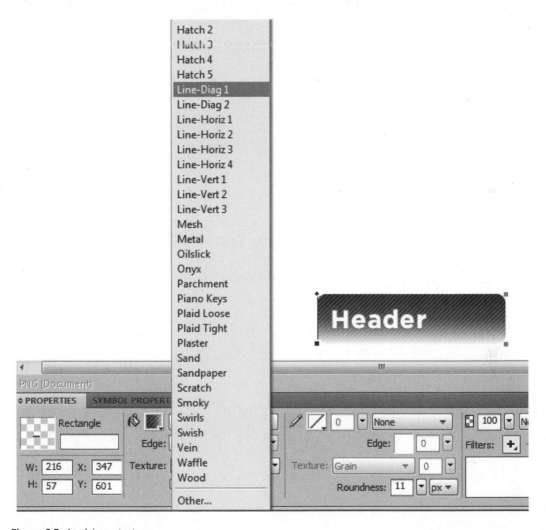

Figure 6-5. Applying a texture

These textures are simply a collection of bitmaps stored in the Configuration\Textures folder of your Fireworks CS4 installation directory. You can add your own textures to this folder to have them appear in this list, or you can simply click Other at the bottom of the menu to browse to a custom bitmap.

Blend modes

Blend modes are often confusing to many designers. The Blend mode names (like Color Dodge, Color Burn, Screen, etc.) are based on predigital photo development techniques that few people are familiar with anymore. However, once you get a taste for the power that blend modes offer, you'll forget you ever had a problem with their weird names.

You can change a blend mode in two places: in the Layers panel and in the Property inspector. Figure 6-6 demonstrates how to change the blend mode via the Layers panel, while Figure 6-7 demonstrates how to change the blend mode via the Property inspector.

Figure 6-6. Changing the blend mode from the Layers panel

Figure 6-7. Changing the blend mode from the Property inspector

Blend modes affect the way objects are blended with other objects *beneath* them in the Layers panel. Draw two red rectangles side by side, and then draw a gradient-filled rectangle and position it beneath the first two. Change one of the rectangle's blend modes to Lighten. Step through the various blend modes available and observe how the resulting visual changes. And remember, the blend mode applied to an object affects the way that object is blended with the pixels *beneath* it. In the sections that follow, you'll see how these seemingly mysterious modes can enable some beautiful visual effects.

Filters

Filters, or plug-ins as they're also known, allow you to create visuals that cannot be achieved with the standard design tools alone. (If you've worked in Photoshop, you know these as Live Effects.) Filters are applied to their underlying objects at the pixel level and can be used to add a level of photorealism to standard vector-based or bitmapped artwork. Soft glows and drop shadows are filter based, for example. In Fireworks, you can apply any combination of a number of built-in filters (such as Drop Shadow or Gaussian Blur) to objects on the canvas, and then tweak those effects infinitely, all while your underlying object is preserved. If you don't like a particular effect, you can simply remove the filter.

Fireworks pioneered this concept, known as Live Filters. Prior to Fireworks, tools like Photoshop forced you into a very linear pattern, rendering the effect directly to the target object. In order to test variations of the effect, you had to undo the effect, and then reapply with different settings. Changing your mind several steps later was not an option. Fireworks changed the paradigm, introducing the concept that filters are attached to an underlying object. Much to the delight of designers everywhere, most tools (like Photoshop) have followed Fireworks' lead and now support the Live Filters concept.

Why use filters?

It's actually amazing what can be achieved *without* filters. You can create surprisingly complex visuals and layouts using a combination of techniques, relying purely on different fill types (solid, linear gradient, radial gradient, etc.) and varying degrees of opacity. Filters, however, bring an entirely new dimension of possibilities to the table. Filters like Gaussian Blur can be used to create a sense of depth or make an object feel "soft" in a way that cannot be achieved purely with a fill. The Drop Shadow effect can quickly give your object a 3D appearance and adds an element of pseudo-reality that is common in modern design. The color filters, such as Brightness/Contrast and Hue/Saturation, give you the power to alter the color of the underlying object in a way that is difficult (or impossible) using the fill tools alone.

Applying filters

Instead of diving headfirst into a complex filter-based effect, we'll first cover the basics of filters in Fireworks. Like the majority of property editing, filter-editing takes place in the Property inspector. Figure 6-8 shows the Add Filter menu, available in the Property inspector when an object is selected on the canvas.

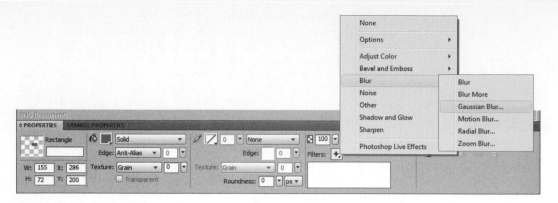

Figure 6-8. Adding a filter

Fireworks filters are divided into a number of categories on the fly-out menu. In Figure 6-8, we've selected the Gaussian Blur filter from the Blur category. Once selected, we immediately get a Gaussian Blur dialog, as shown in Figure 6-9.

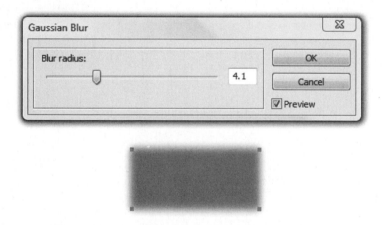

Figure 6-9. Adjusting the Gaussian Blur filter

After adjusting the Blur radius setting and clicking OK, a Gaussian Blur entry is added to the applied filters list. As you apply more filters to your object, you'll see those filters added to the list as well. Figure 6-10 shows the filter list for an object that has the Gaussian Blur, Drop Shadow, and Hue/Saturation filters (obscured from view) applied.

Figure 6-10. Applied filters list

At any point in time you can modify the filter settings by clicking the blue information icon next to the filter. Toggle the visibility of a filter by checking and unchecking its check box, or remove a filter completely by selecting it in the list and clicking the Delete button next to the Add button (the minus sign currently grayed out). Reorder filters simply by dragging them in the list.

Figure 6-11 shows a number of basic filters applied to the same rectangle. Experiment with the base filters to get a feel for their flexibility and limitations. Try combining them now to see how they play together.

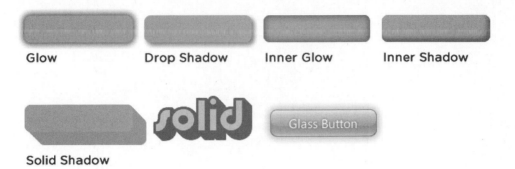

Figure 6-11. Basic filters

The ability to infinitely modify, reorder, add, and remove effects to an object is just one of the many reasons Fireworks users are passionate about their tool. This flexibility is going to come into play as we step through creating a number of popular effects.

Styles

Styles in Fireworks CS4 are similar in concept to CSS classes, only much more powerful. A style in Fireworks can represent all of the settings that can be applied to an object, including the fill settings, stroke settings, text settings, and effects. Fireworks CS4 actually ships with a large number of prebuilt styles that can both speed up your design process and serve as excellent teaching tools.

Open the Styles panel (Window ➤ Styles) and select Plastic Styles from the list of libraries. Figure 6-12 shows the Styles panel with the library selector expanded.

Once you've selected a prebuilt library, first select a target object or set of objects on the canvas, and then select one of the styles from the library. When you apply a style, two things happen:

Figure 6-12. Selecting a style library

- The style is copied to the current document's style library.
- A reference to the style is added to the target object.

Instead of simply applying the settings housed in the style to the target object, a reference to the style is added to the object. This means that any time the style is changed, all objects referencing that style are updated. Figure 6-13 shows a rectangle that has the Plastic 011 style (from the Plastic Styles library) applied. Change the library in your Styles panel to Current Document, and you'll see that the Plastic 011 style has been copied to your document, along with all other styles present in Current Document.

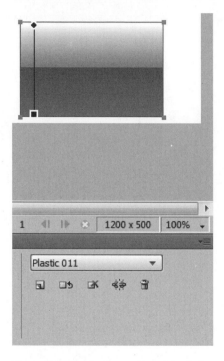

Figure 6-13. Reviewing applied styles in the Property inspector

Creating popular effects

With the basics out of the way, it's now time to move on to the fun stuff! Let's start by creating a popular effect that doesn't appear to be going away anytime soon—the glass effect.

Creating glass buttons

Glass buttons were made popular years ago with their introduction on Apple's web site and in Mac OS X. If you search the Web, you'll still find countless tutorials for creating Mac OS X–style buttons. However, since that introduction years ago, the glass effect has become so pervasive that its relationship to Mac OS X has almost been forgotten. Where you once may have been accused of copying the

"Apple look" by adding glass buttons, you're now just adding a key element in modern graphic design. Glass is no longer an add-on feature, it's an expected practice.

You can employ a number of techniques to achieve the glass look. Most involve laying down either a base solid or base gradient, and then applying a white-based gradient in the foreground to create the appearance of refracted light. We'll start by creating the basic two-piece glass button.

Draw a rectangle 160 px (pixels) wide by 40 px tall. Apply a linear gradient that starts with a shade of blue and ends with a slightly lighter version of that blue. In Figure 6-14, you can see that we added a highlight color at the end of our gradient to give the resulting button a little more depth. We've also set the rectangle roundness to 11 px.

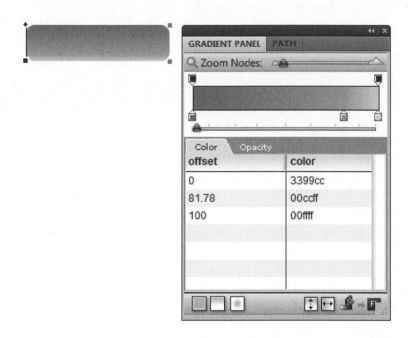

Figure 6-14. Defining the glass button base

Now to catch the light, draw another rectangle in the foreground that is roughly 50% of the height of the base rectangle. It should be inset by 1 px on the left, top, and right. Apply a linear gradient with white color stops at the beginning and end of the gradient. The opacity stops are what we're concerned with at this point. Figure 6-15 shows the Opacity tab of the Gradient panel selected. You can see that we've set the opacity of the first (topmost) node to 90% and the opacity of the second node to 20%. Adjust these values to achieve the desired amount of "glass."

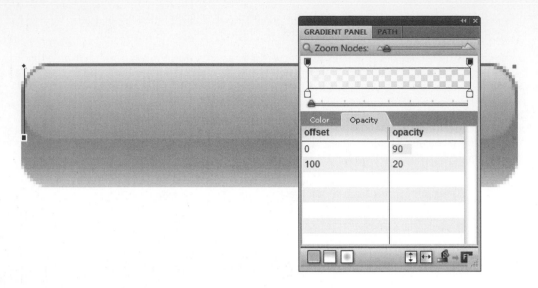

Figure 6-15. Adjusting the highlight rectangle

Generally, for the effect to work well, you need a base object that goes from dark at the top to a lighter color at the bottom, or a solid base color. In our base object, we added an extra highlight color at the very bottom of the base object, simulating another light source. This technique can give your object even more depth.

Before adding text, we want to help the button stand out from the background just a bit more. We can achieve this by applying a Glow filter to the base rectangle. Figure 6-16 shows the settings we used for the Glow filter. We chose a color toward the lighter end of the base rectangle's gradient fill. This is another area where you can refine your settings infinitely to achieve the look you're after.

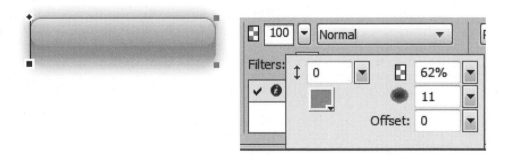

Figure 6-16. Adding a Glow filter to the base rectangle

With the body of the button complete, it's now time to add the final element—the text. Center your text in the button horizontally and vertically, and set the fill color to white. To increase the legibility of your text and create additional depth, you can once again take advantage of the Glow filter. Figure 6-17 shows the settings we used for a Glow filter applied to the text object. This time we chose a color from the darker end of the base rectangle's gradient fill.

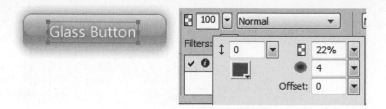

Figure 6-17. Adding a Glow filter to the foreground text

As we mentioned at the beginning of this section, there are a number of variations on this technique. Apply some of the styles from the Plastic Styles library to see how glass can be created using a single object. Instead of using a foreground rectangle to create the highlight, a single gradient is used to create a similar effect. The single gradient technique is useful when you need to resize your glassy objects frequently. Instead of having to adjust both your base rectangle and highlight rectangle every time you resize, you can simply adjust the gradient handles.

Creating reflections

Reflection effects, like glass effects, are not going away anytime soon. And again, like glass effects, the judicious use of simulated reflections in your layout can lend a polished, contemporary look to your design. We won't attempt to define the parameters of judicious though; we'll just show you *how* to create this effect and leave the judgment of *when* to use this effect up to you.

Let's create a reflection of the glass button we just created. Start by removing the Glow filter from the base rectangle. We think the glow will interfere with the reflection. Next, select all of the elements used to make the button and press F8 to create a symbol. Name the symbol GlassButton in the Convert to Symbol dialog that appears. (We're having you create a symbol so that you only have to update the text in one place once your reflection is in place.)

With the symbol created, copy and paste the button and position the copy directly beneath the original, leaving a 1- to 2-px space between the two objects. Flip the copy by selecting Modify ➤ Transform ➤ Flip Vertical from the main menu. Your canvas should look like Figure 6-18 at this point.

Figure 6-18. Reflection object flipped

With the object positioned and flipped, it's now time to add a linear gradient opacity mask. The fastest way to do this is via the Commands menu. With your reflected object selected, select Commands ➤ Creative ➤ Auto Vector Mask from the main menu. Select the preset from the lower-left corner of the resulting dialog, as shown in Figure 6-19.

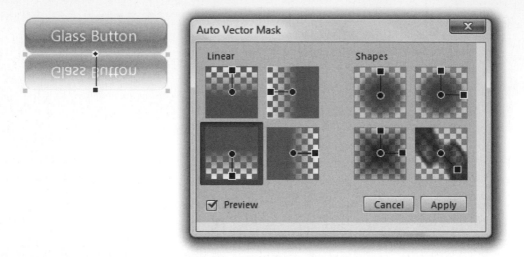

Figure 6-19. Applying an auto vector mask

After clicking Apply, a new vector mask is added to the selected object. When selected, we can adjust the gradient handles just like adjusting any other gradient fill. The mask remains editable even after moving on to other things. Simply click the mask icon next to the object preview in the Layers panel, as shown in Figure 6-20.

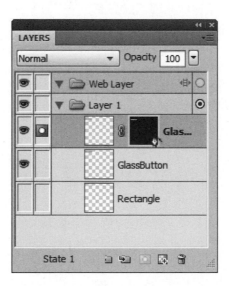

Figure 6-20. Selecting an object's mask

The Auto Vector Mask command got us close but not all the way. We *do* need to adjust the mask a bit to create an acceptable reflection effect. In Figure 6-21, we've moved the start handle of the gradient above the reflected object itself, set the reflected object's opacity to 70%, and changed the background from white to black.

Figure 6-21. Final reflection

As with the reflection effect, you may want to tweak this effect for your personal needs and design goals: the opacity of the reflection, the point where the reflection fades out completely, and the amount of space between the source object and reflection object are all areas of customization. Further, these settings generally change as the color of your background changes. This same approach works for any object on the Fireworks design surface, including plain text objects and bitmaps.

Creating web headers

When designing web layouts, most start by focusing on the design of the header. The header is the first thing site visitors encounter. It defines both the brand (even if it's a personal blog) and personality of the site, and it serves as an anchor for the page. We're going to teach you how to replicate a common look seen across many commercial and powerful sites. You'll see how the Fireworks foundational tools we looked at in the beginning of this chapter make this exercise a cinch. First, let's take a look at where we're going. Figure 6-22 shows the final header for "My Web Site."

Figure 6-22. Final web header

The style of the header should be familiar, just as the glassy button and reflection effect before it were. This header includes a number of popular techniques: diagonal textures of varying degrees of thickness; a sharp, glass-like foreground effect; the Helvetica Rounded font, with a double-stroke and subtle glow applied; and additional text-based textures. The palette was chosen from among thousands at the kuler site (http://kuler.adobe.com), a great resource and tool you'll want to use if you don't know about it already.

Finding the right color palette

Figure 6-23. The header color palette

Before you dive into your layout, it's important to start with a color palette. The header in Figure 6-22, as we just mentioned, is based on a color palette we found on kuler. Figure 6-23 shows the five swatches of this palette.

We used the bright blue as the starting color for the header, and then applied the lime green as our "pop" color—the result is a text treatment that really stands out from the background.

The color palette values are as follows:

- #13140F
- #D4FF00
- #E4FFE6
- #68776C
- #00D6DD

Creating the thick diagonal background texture

Figure 6-24. 10×10 px custom texture

As you've already seen, Fireworks ships with a number of textures, including a few diagonal line textures. However, those diagonal line textures are just 1-px thick; to achieve the look we're going for (and the look you've seen on countless sites), we need a heavier line. Fortunately for us, creating additional textures is easy. Figure 6-24 shows a 10×10 px black-and-white image that we created in just a few minutes.

When creating custom textures, it's important to remember that the white areas are opaque and the black areas are transparent. It's a little confusing at first, but with a little practice, you'll get the hang of it. With your custom texture created, export it as a 32-bit PNG to a location of your choosing before moving on to the next step.

Defining the container rectangle

Start by creating a new document approximately 700×200 px in size. Set the document's background color to black, and then draw a rectangle 600×128 px in size. Now, set the rectangle roundness to 14 px. We applied the darker of the two blues from the color palette to this rectangle (solid fill #68776C).

With the shape defined and the fill color set, it's now time to apply our custom texture. Click the Texture button, and then select Other from the menu that appears. Browse to the texture you saved in the previous step and click OK. Your custom texture should now be applied. We're almost finished with this element—just a couple of additional settings to make before we move on. Check the Transparent check box option beneath the texture list and set the opacity of the texture to 100%. This ensures that the texture and only the texture is seen when the rectangle is drawn. Finally, change the opacity of the rectangle itself to 45. Your rectangle should look like the rectangle in Figure 6-25.

Figure 6-25. Container rectangle in place

Defining the primary rectangle

With the container rectangle in place, draw another rectangle inside the bounds of the previous rectangle (you may want to lock the previous rectangle to prevent accidental selection). It should be 16 px smaller on both axes to create an 8-px border all the way around. Final dimensions: 644✕112 px. Reduce the roundness on this rectangle to 12 px to ensure symmetry with the larger container rectangle. Now, apply a vertical linear gradient based on the primary blue color of our palette. Figure 6-26 shows our final gradient applied. The primary blue has been positioned at approximately 60%, and we've set the first color stop to a slightly darker version of the same color.

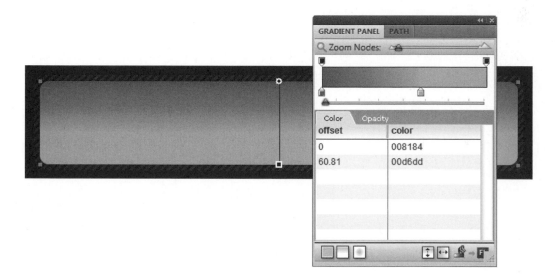

Figure 6-26. Primary rectangle in place

Adding texture to the primary rectangle

Let's take this diagonal theme a little further and apply a finer-grained diagonal texture to the foreground of our primary rectangle. Start by copying and pasting the last rectangle. Now apply the Line-Diag 1 texture, again checking Transparent and setting the texture opacity to 100%. Finally, apply a vertical linear gradient that goes from 60% opacity at the top to 0% opacity at the bottom. Both color stops should be white. Your latest layout should look like Figure 6-27.

117

Figure 6-27. Fine-grained diagonal texture applied

Adding a highlight border

You may not have noticed it when you first saw the layout at the beginning of this section, but the container has a 4-px-thick white border that fades vertically from opaque to transparent. Once again, create a copy of the last rectangle and paste it in the foreground of the other rectangle. Clear the rectangle's fill and apply a 4-px white stroke. Select the Basic ➤ Soft Line preset from the Stroke category menu in the Property inspector. Now, click the Stroke category button again and select Stroke Options from the menu, as shown in Figure 6-28.

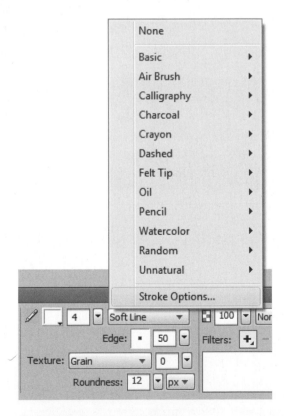

Figure 6-28. Accessing stroke options

From the Stroke Options dialog, change the location of the stroke to Stroke Inside, as shown in Figure 6-29.

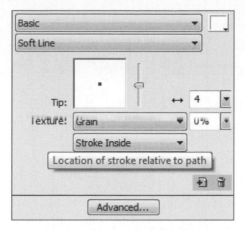

Figure 6-29. Setting the location of the stroke

The stroke is now drawn from the edge of the rectangle in. This prevents the stroke from overlapping the background texture we created in the first step. With the rectangle still selected, select Commands ➤ Creative ➤ Add Vector Mask from the main menu, and, as before, select the vertical gradient pre-set in the lower-left corner of the dialog. Your border should now fade from the top to the bottom. To prevent the border from fading out completely, change the value of the black opacity stop to #313131 so that a touch of the border is still along the bottom edge. Your layout should now look like Figure 6-30.

Figure 6-30. White border in place

Adding text elements

Are you sick of rectangles yet? Now's your chance for a brief break as we focus on the text elements of the header. Using the Text tool, add the name of your site to the header. The font settings are shown in Figure 6-31; of note are the position (41,54) and font size. You also need to apply green as the foreground (#D4FF00).

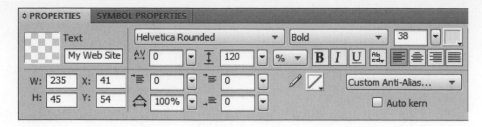

Figure 6-31. Text settings

We're now going to add a stroke to the text, but on a copy of the text block, not on the current text block. Copy and paste the current text block, and then either select the original from the Layers panel or move the currently selected copy behind the original by pressing Ctrl+down arrow (Cmd+down arrow on a Mac). Now apply a 2-px stroke to the text block using the darker blue in our color palette (#68776C). To set the stroke thickness on a text block, you have to launch the Stroke Options dialog like we did earlier to set the location of the stroke.

Now, copy and paste the text block one more time, and move the copy behind the previous two text block instances. Apply a white stroke that is 4-px thick. Also apply a white glow with a width of 0 px, opacity of 54%, and softness of 9. The final result is shown in Figure 6-32.

Figure 6-32. Creating the main title

The subtitle "a me production" is created using the same technique, only you start with the darker blue text and apply a white stroke. You also need to add the text "2009" to the lower-right area of the primary rectangle. Use the light blue from our color palette (#E4FFE6), set its opacity to 40%, and bump the font size to 50.

Adding foreground glass

See, we told you glass was pervasive! We also told you that there are a number of techniques and variations of approaches employed when creating the glass effect. This header employs a technique slightly different from what you saw with the glass button previously. Start by drawing a rectangle that is approximately 50% of the height of the primary rectangle; ours is 55-px tall. Now apply, you guessed it, a white-based vertical gradient. This time, however, we'll go from transparent at the top to slightly opaque at the bottom. Because pictures tell a thousand words, take a look at Figure 6-33 to see exactly how we positioned the gradient handles on the design surface and the opacity stops in the gradient definition.

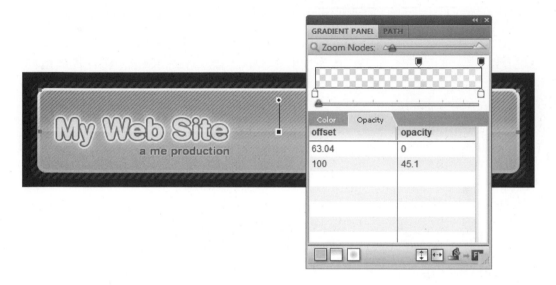

Figure 6-33. Defining the glass rectangle

With the addition of this last rectangle, we have achieved the look of a modern, Web 2.0–style header. As with the previous effects, there were countless steps along the way that introduce the possibility of customization and personalization.

Adding "magic"

You've undoubtedly seen visuals online that look like they have been rendered by some sophisticated 3D particle generator but have, in fact, been created in a 2D program like Fireworks. In the exercise the follows, we'll employ the use of layer blend modes, blur effects, and the advanced stroke options (Edit Stroke) dialog to create a layout that looks much more difficult to create than it really is.

Start by creating a document approximately 600×400 px with the canvas color set to black. Now, draw a rectangle the same dimensions as your document and set its fill mode to Linear. With the rectangle selected, launch the Fill Options dialog as shown in Figure 6-34.

From the Fill Options dialog, select the Spectrum preset from the gradient presets list, as shown in Figure 6-35.

Figure 6-34. Launching the Fill Options dialog

Figure 6-35. Applying the Spectrum gradient preset

With the spectrum applied, change the orientation of the gradient to be horizontal (you can adjust this later), and drag the gradient handle so that only the first three colors are visible on the canvas (red, magenta, and blue). Your canvas should now look like Figure 6-36.

Figure 6-36. Base gradient defined

Now the fun begins. Change the rectangle's Blend mode to Multiply and lock the rectangle. Select the Vector Path tool, draw a quick shape similar to the one shown in Figure 6-37, and position it beneath the locked rectangle. Set the stroke color to white.

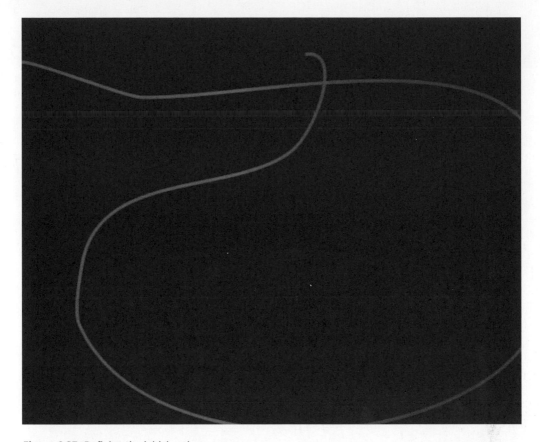

Figure 6-37. Defining the initial path

With the path selected, change the stroke setting to Random ➤ Dots from the Stroke category menu. Launch the advanced stroke options (Edit Stroke) dialog and change the Tips setting to 2 on the Options tab. Select the Shape tab, uncheck the Square check box if it's checked, and change the Size setting to 15. Select the Sensitivity tab and select Size from the Stroke property combo box. Now adjust the value of Speed. By adjusting this value, the size of the stroke is altered along the path depending on the speed at which you drew the path. Take a few minutes to play with this value and draw and redraw the path at varying rates to see how this setting can affect your final visual. Figure 6-38 shows our final stroke settings.

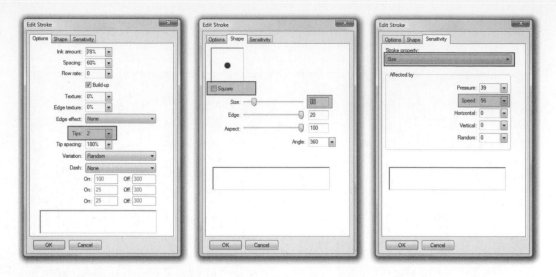

Figure 6-38. Setting stroke properties

With your stroke options in place, your path should now look like the one in Figure 6-39.

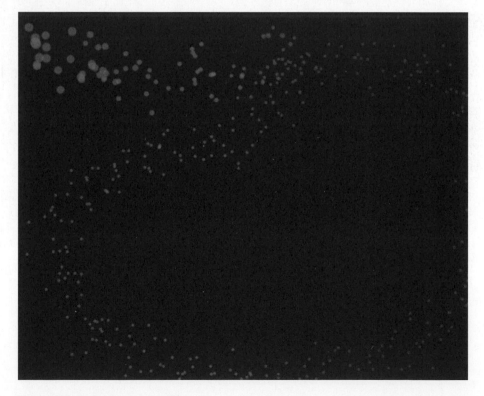

Figure 6-39. Path with particle effects

The magic is already starting to happen. You can see more clearly now the effect of the gradient on the underlying objects. The white of the path is acting like a mask, revealing the gradient fill of the rectangle. We'll use several instances of this path to make the effect more dramatic. Copy and paste two instances in the foreground of the original. Now, select the original and apply a Gaussian Blur filter with a radius of 7.8. You should now see a soft glow around the dots, almost as if they're emitting light.

Copy and paste two more instances of this blurred path, and again select the bottommost path. All of the previous paths have remained directly on top of each other. Offset this path so that it feels almost like a nebula of light. Figure 6-40 shows the result after adding these numerous copies.

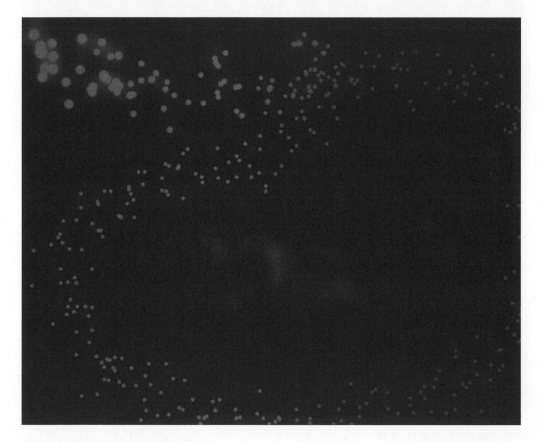

Figure 6-40. Evolving the particle effect

The particle effect looks nice as is, and you may feel inclined to stop here, but we're going to create one more copy of the original path and paste it in the foreground of the rectangle. Pasting it in the foreground of the rectangle excludes the path from the effects of the Overlay blend mode applied to the rectangle and makes the particles look more like light sources.

Before adding text elements to this layout, we're going to add some depth to the background by incorporating a few strategically placed circles. Figure 6-41 shows our final background with these circles in place. Each is placed beneath the gradient-filled rectangle, and has a fill of white and an opacity of 46%.

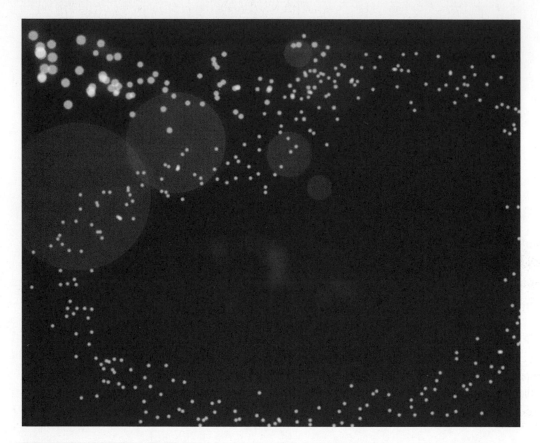

Figure 6-41. Final background texture

With the background texture complete, we're now going to employ the same technique you just saw, only this time with text. We'll add text both behind the rectangle and in the foreground of the rectangle. The text in the foreground is simply white with no effects, while the text behind the rectangle has a Gaussian Blur applied to create a nice glow. Try experimenting with the number of copies you create for the glow effect, adjusting the amount of blur applied to each layer. Figure 6-42 shows the final layout with the text effects added.

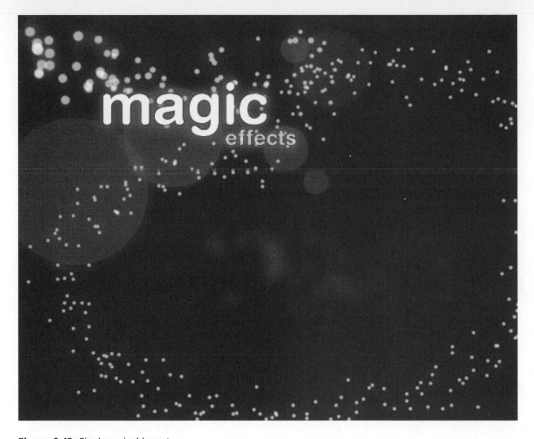

Figure 6-42. Final magical layout

Summary

You've now seen how to create a number of popular effects using Fireworks and Fireworks alone. While we've in no way covered every effect possible, we've covered the core set of techniques within Fireworks required to achieve the majority of visual effects possible with the tool. With these core techniques under your belt, you should now be empowered to tackle and understand practically any tutorial you find online.

The same flexibility that makes Fireworks great for layout (e.g., infinitely editable paths and rectangles) makes Fireworks great for effects. Your choices are always reversible and tweakable, which is a very comforting thing. Now, go create something amazing!

Chapter 7

THE INS AND OUTS OF ANIMATION

In this chapter, you will learn the ins and outs of animation states, formerly called frames, in Fireworks CS4. Then, you will see how to create two unique animations using different techniques by following step-by-step instructions. Finally, you will learn about exporting your animations in both GIF and SWF (Adobe Flash) formats.

An animation is a series of different static states of a graphical set. Running the states simulates the effect of the graphical set performing some action. Each of the static states of an animation can be created and edited in the Fireworks PNG document before exporting it as an animated GIF. By allowing the states to be independently accessed and edited, Fireworks provides you with higher fidelity while working on the designs.

The States panel

The States panel, shown in Figure 7-1, is the control center for all things related to animation in Fireworks. Formerly called the Frames panel, Adobe decided to rename the panel for the CS4 release since Fireworks is now geared more toward rapid prototyping. You can use states on practically anything, but they are most commonly applied to animation frames, user interface view states, and multipage web site mockups. The CS4 release added the provision of right-clicking inside the panel, making panel menu accessibility and discoverability better for new users. The right-click menu options are the same as those shown in Figure 7-1 except for the Help option.

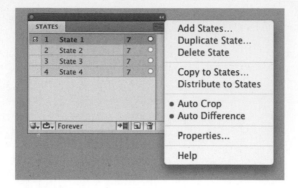

Figure 7-1. The States panel with its options menu open

Next, we'll dissect the States panel so you can familiarize yourself with all of the icons, buttons, and menu options.

Quick onion skinning

Near the top left of the States panel, you'll notice a small triangular icon. This slider is used to quickly adjust how many states you would like to overlay on your current state. **Onion skinning** allows you to view semitransparent versions of surrounding states in your animation. By default, **multistate editing** is enabled, which you can change via the Onion Skinning button at the bottom left of the States panel.

State position and name

To the right of the onion skinning view adjuster, you will see a number and a state name. The number corresponds to the state order, which is sequential and always starts with 1. To the right of the number is the state name, which will be autogenerated by Fireworks. By double-clicking any state name, you can rename the state for organization's sake. You can also change the order of the states by dragging a state name to any position you like.

State delay

To the right of the state name is a column that indicates state delay by number. This number represents the delay, in 1/100 seconds, between states when the animation is playing. So, a delay of 100 would be one second, and a delay of 7 would be seven-hundredths of a second. You can change the delay by double-clicking the number and typing in your own value. You can also select multiple states while holding down the Shift key and then double-clicking any delay number to change all of the selected state's delay properties at once.

Quick glance

The icon to the right of the delay number lets you quickly see which states contain graphical data and which do not. States with bitmap or vector objects in them will display a fully opaque circle icon, while empty states will show a ghosted or semitransparent circle icon in this column. When a state contains some objects selected within it, a dot appears in the center of the circle icon. If the state contains an object or objects but none of them are selected, the circle icon will be fully opaque.

You can use the circle icon to move selections between states, a feature new to the CS4 release. When the circle icon for a particular state contains a dot within it (i.e., an object or objects are selected), you can drag that icon to any other state, and the selected object(s) will be moved from the source state to the destination state.

Onion skinning options

Moving down to the lower right of Figure 7-1, you will see a button sporting a tiny onion icon. This Onion Skinning button is used to change the onion skinning view options, such as the multistate editing default mentioned previously (see Figure 7-2).

Figure 7-2. Onion skinning options

GIF animation looping

To the right of the Onion Skinning button is the GIF Animation Looping button, which is used to adjust the loop setting for exported GIF animations. By default, GIF animations loop forever, but you can change the looping number to 1, 2, 3, 4, 5, 10, or 20, or select No Looping, as shown in Figure 7-3.

No Looping
1
2
3
4
5
10
20
✔ Forever

Figure 7-3. GIF animation looping options in the States panel

131

Distribute to states

To the right of the GIF Animation Looping icon is the Distribute to States button. You can use this command to transfer single or multiple objects to their own individual frames. Later in this chapter, we will use this feature to create an animation with as little effort as possible.

New/Duplicate state

To the right of the Distribute to States icon is the New/Duplicate States button. By clicking this button, you can add states to your animation, or you can drag existing states to this button to duplicate them. Later in this chapter, we will use this feature to duplicate a series of states to save us time and effort.

Delete state

To the right of the New/Duplicate States icon is the Delete State button. By clicking this button, you will delete the currently selected state. You can delete multiple states by selecting more than one and either clicking the Delete State button or dragging the selected states to this button.

Building an animation

In this first example, we will build an Ajax-style loading spinner. Figure 7-4 shows what the first state of the finished animation will look like.

Figure 7-4. The first state of the finished animation example zoomed to 800%

1. Create a new 32×32 px (pixel) document with a white canvas color, as shown in Figure 7-5.

New Document
Canvas Size: 4.00 K

Width: 32   Pixels   W: 32

Height: 32   Pixels   H: 32

Resolution: 72   Pixels/Inch

Canvas Color

◉ White

◯ Transparent

◯ Custom:

Cancel   OK

Figure 7-5. Creating a new document

We'll be building this animation using vector objects, so if we need to scale it up to a larger size, we can do so without image degradation.

2. Using the Rectangle tool, create a single rectangle, and set W to 2, H to 7, X to 15, Y to 2, Fill to #CCCCCC, and Stroke to None.

3. Duplicate this object by using the Edit ➤ Copy and Edit ➤ Paste menu commands or pressing Ctrl/Cmd+C and then Ctrl/Cmd+V.

4. Set the X coordinate of this new object to 15 and the Y coordinate to 23.

5. Select the Arrow tool, hold down the Shift key, and click both rectangles to select them.

6. Group the rectangles together by using the Modify ➤ Group menu item or pressing Ctrl/Cmd+G (see Figure 7-6).

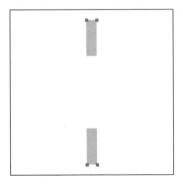

Figure 7-6. Two rectangles grouped together

Manipulating objects

Continuing on with this exercise, you'll see how to manipulate your objects in the following steps:

7. With this object group still selected, duplicate it five times using the Copy and Paste commands, or just press Ctrl/Cmd+C once and then press Ctrl/Cmd+V five times.

8. Move over to the Layers panel and click the bottommost layer group if it isn't already selected.

9. Select Modify ➤ Transform ➤ Numeric Transform or press Ctrl/Cmd+Shift+T to bring up the Numeric Transform dialog box.

10. Choose Rotate from the drop-down menu and enter 30 in the Angle field. Click OK.

11. Move back over to the Layers panel, and click the fifth group in the layer (the second-to-last one).

12. Bring up the Numeric Transform dialog again, but this time enter 60 in the Angle field.

13. Move back over to the Layers panel, and click the fourth group in the layer. Rotate this group 90 degrees.

14. Click the third group, and rotate it 120 degrees.

15. Rotate the second group 150 degrees.

16. Rename the layer to AJAX Spinner (see Figure 7-7).

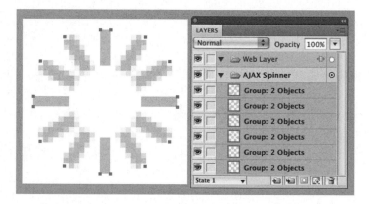

Figure 7-7. Six groups, each rotated at 30-degree increments

Fading around the circle

We're almost there now. Let's create some color differences on a few of the vector objects so that when we animate the spinner, it looks like it's actually spinning.

17. Using the Subselection tool, click the top-middle rectangle and change the color to black (#000000).

18. Click the rectangle to the left of the top-middle rectangle and change the color to #333333.

19. Change the color of the object to the left of the rectangle you just altered to #666666.

20. Change the color of the leftmost rectangle to #999999.

Figure 7-8 shows the results of the preceding steps.

Figure 7-8. Top-left quadrant objects colored from black to medium gray

Creating the animation frames

All we have left to do is change our spinner into a Fireworks animation symbol.

21. Select all of the objects on the canvas by clicking the AJAX Spinner folder in the Layers panel, or just press Ctrl/Cmd+A.

22. Select Modify ➤ Animation ➤ Animate selection.

23. In the dialog that appears, set Frames to 12, Move to 0, Direction to 0, Scale to 100, Opacity 100 to 100, and Rotate to 330, and make sure that CW is selected (see Figure 7-9).

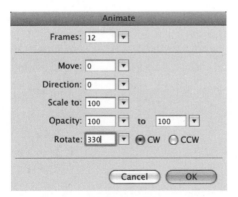

Figure 7-9. Animation settings for the spinner

24. Click OK, and your animation will automatically be created.

You might get a dialog box stating that Fireworks needs to increase the number of states in order to create an animation symbol. Click OK to proceed.

Why did we choose 12 frames? Well, if you count the total number of vector objects on the canvas, you'll see it equals 12.

Why did we create 12 objects? We want to rotate our animation in a complete circle, and a circle contains a total of 360 degrees. 360 is equally divisible by 12 with a quotient of 30. So, 360 divided by 12 equals 30 with no remainder.

Why did we rotate 330 degrees? If we would have rotated our object 360 degrees rather than 330 degrees, our first and last state would have the exact same information in them. During preview, you would see a hiccup or slight pause on the last state. To prevent this from happening, we just rotate the animation one increment less: 360 minus 30 equals 330.

Previewing the results

If you'd like to see what your animation looks like without actually exporting it, just use the player controls located at the bottom right of the document window. Click the triangular button to play the animation, and click the square button to stop the animation.

Let's try one more animation before we get into the details of exporting. This tutorial will use some of the built-in Fireworks commands to leverage all state creation.

Morphing an animation

The purpose of this tutorial is to show how to create an animation without actually managing any states. We'll have Fireworks create our individual state objects and use the Distribute to States command to automatically create the animation. Then, we'll issue some extra commands to duplicate multiple states and reverse the order of a range of states.

Preparing the document

To begin, create a new document with dimensions of 300×200 px with a white canvas color (see Figure 7-10).

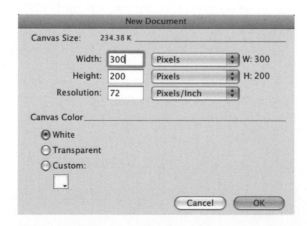

Figure 7-10. Creating a new document

Making some shapes

Now that you have your canvas set up, it's time to add some shapes.

1. Using the Ellipse tool, create a 50✕50 px ellipse and place it in the upper-left portion of the canvas.

2. Change the color of the ellipse to #999999.

3. Using the Polygon tool, create a 100✕100 px polygon and place it in the lower right of the canvas.

4. Change the color of the polygon to #666666.

Your canvas should appear as shown in Figure 7-11.

Figure 7-11. Adding an ellipse and a polygon

Applying a morph effect

Follow these steps to morph the shapes on your canvas:

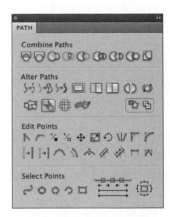

5. Select both the ellipse and the rectangle by using the Arrow tool, hold down the Shift key, and click both objects.

6. Open the Path panel by selecting Window ➤ Others ➤ Path.

7. Under the Alter Paths area in the Path panel, click the Blend Paths icon, which is the second icon in the second row (see Figure 7-12).

8. When prompted for the number of steps, enter 5 and click OK.

9. When prompted to flatten blended portions, choose No.

Figure 7-12. Blend Paths command from the Path panel

Separating the groups

Now you should have a series of objects that seem to morph from an ellipse to a polygon. In order to transfer these objects to their own individual states for animation, we need to ungroup them.

To ungroup all of the objects, first select Edit ➤ Select All or press Ctrl/Cmd+A to select all of the objects on the canvas. Then issue the Modify ➤ Ungroup command two times or press Ctrl/Cmd+Shift+G two times. You canvas should now look similar to Figure 7-13.

Figure 7-13. Ungrouped objects in our morph animation

Creating the animation states

With all of the objects still selected, open the States panel and click the Distribute to States icon in the lower-right corner (it looks like an arrow pointing right into a filmstrip).

And with that, we have an animation that morphs a dark gray polygon in the lower right of the canvas into a medium gray ellipse in the upper left of the canvas.

Preview the animation using the controls in the lower-right portion of the document window. It looks pretty decent considering we only spent a few minutes creating it, but it would look much better if there wasn't a very noticeable skip in the loop from State 7 to State 1. We can remedy this by creating a seamless loop using a couple of built-in Fireworks commands and a little bit of ingenuity.

Duplicating and reversing states

To create a seamless loop for your animation, follow these steps:

1. Using the States panel, click State 2, hold down the Shift key, and click State 6.
2. Now, drag these states to the New/Duplicate State icon in the lower-right portion of the States panel.

All we need to do now is reverse the order of these newly duplicated states.

3. Select Commands ➤ Document ➤ Reverse States to bring up the dialog shown in Figure 7-14.

Figure 7-14. Reverse states

4. Choose Range of states.

5. Specify 8 for the start state.

6. Specify 12 for the end state.

7. Click OK.

Try previewing the animation now, and you'll see a smooth transition starting from the polygon, morphing into the ellipse, and then morphing back to the polygon.

Exporting animations for the Web

There are two options for exporting animations in Fireworks CS4: GIF or SWF (Flash format). An animation created in Fireworks is a default PNG file, which will not function as expected in a browser. Thus we will have to export the design in one of the two animation formats mentioned.

GIF animations

The GIF animation format is the most widely supported as far as browsers are concerned. If you export as a GIF animation, you are pretty much guaranteed that all of your viewing audience will be able to see the animation. However, GIF suffers from a 256-color palette limitation as well as only a single index color for transparency. High-color animations with many states could look severely color muted or dithered.

This method of creating animation is growing old, what with the growing popularity of Flash. However, almost all browsers have good support for animating GIFs, and you can be assured of your audience having a consistent user experience with this format.

To export your animation as a GIF file, open the Optimize panel, and choose the Animated Gif Websnap 128 preset in the top drop-down menu, as shown in Figure 7-15.

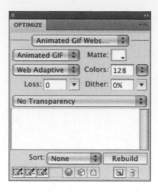

Figure 7-15. Optimizing as a
GIF animation

Flash (SWF) animations

Saving your document as a Flash animation will create a Flash SWF movie file. In order for your animation to be viewed, you will need to embed some proprietary Adobe code in an HTML document as
well as make sure that users have the Flash plug-in installed on their system. Flash animations are far
less limited when compared to GIF animations in that they have no color palette restrictions and they
have much more flexibility with frame rates.

To export your image as a Flash animation, select File ➤ Save As or press Ctrl/Cmd+Shift+S.
When prompted, choose Adobe Flash (*.swf) from the Save copy as drop-down menu, as shown in
Figure 7-16.

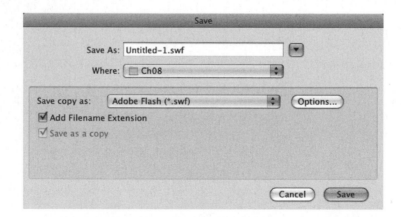

Figure 7-16. Saving as an Adobe Flash animation

This format is gaining popularity, becoming the standard format for animation as it provides a rich
user experience. The Flash Player plug-in required to play these animations is present on almost all
machines now.

You can add or change Flash-specific export options by clicking the Options button in the Save As dialog. This brings up the dialog shown in Figure 7-17.

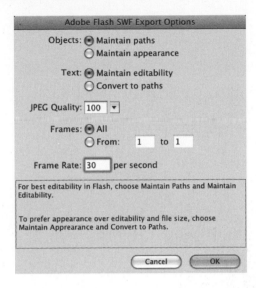

Figure 7-17. Flash export options

Summary

This chapter explains the fidelity of Fireworks CS4 in creating animations. Animations can be exported as GIF files or advanced SWF files. The fine control of optimization settings allows designers to strike the right balance between graphic quality and file size. The flexibility of states present in the application makes it easier to tune individual states, resulting in crisp transitions.

The examples presented in this chapter give you just a sneak peek into the animation capabilities of Fireworks. It is now left to your imagination to create some engrossing ones without getting caught up in the complexity of application functionality.

Chapter 8

SKINNING FLEX COMPONENTS WITH FIREWORKS

The Adobe Flex framework (also known as the Flex SDK) is a powerful foundation upon which many sophisticated Rich Internet Applications (RIAs) are built. One of the core features of the Flex framework is the set of user interface components that it ships with. These components range from simple buttons, check boxes, and radio buttons to complex data grids, combo boxes, and text editors. If you've seen a large number of Flex applications, you may have started to recognize them as "Flex applications." We added the quotation marks because the use of the default component skins tends to give Flex-based applications a similar look. This is fine if you want to create a quick application that has a nice look and feel (the default skins are clean and aesthetically pleasing), but not so fine if you want to create a branded experience that stands out among the crowd.

Fortunately, all of the Flex components can be reskinned using images and a custom form of CSS specific to the Flex framework. If the terms "custom" and "CSS" just scared you, don't worry! Fireworks and Flex Builder do the heavy lifting, generating the custom CSS for you automatically. In fact, Fireworks CS4 takes pretty much all of the guesswork out of the process, leaving you to what you do best—design!

Most Flex applications are created using Adobe's Flex Builder software, and you'll use this application briefly toward the end of the chapter to import your Fireworks-generated artwork. While it's primarily a development tool, we think you'll see that with a little guidance, you can navigate its many panels and menus just fine.

In this chapter, we'll start by loading the default Flex skins in Fireworks using the New Flex Skin menu command. We'll then update a simple control (Button) and export our changes using another built-in command. With our skin files exported, we'll create a new Flex project using Adobe Flex Builder 3 (go to www.adobe.com/flex to download a free trial) and import our artwork. Finally, we'll tweak the nine-slice scaling of our images using Flex Builder and publish a test SWF. So, let's get started!

Creating a new Flex skin in Fireworks

Start by selecting Commands ➤ Flex Skinning ➤ New Flex Skin from the main menu. Figure 8-1 shows the New Flex Skin dialog that is launched when this command is executed.

Figure 8-1. The New Flex Skin dialog

You first need to choose whether you want to reskin all of the Flex components or just a single component. For this exercise, let's go with the default and select Multiple components. After you click OK, a new document will be created that contains all of the Flex components and their states. Figure 8-2 shows a partial view of this layout.

If you just want to skin a specific component, select the Specific components *radio button. You can then choose the component type you're interested in and optionally give your skin a specific style name. If you don't give your skin a name, it will be imported into Flex Builder as the default skin for the component type you've selected. This is perfect if you want to reskin all* Buttons *in your Flex application. However, if you have several different types of* Buttons *in your app (like a play button, a pause button, etc.), you will want to give your skin a name, like* PlayButton. *When your artwork is imported into Flex Builder, a new style will be created with the name you specify here. You can then manually assign your style name to unique* Button *instances to see your skin applied.*

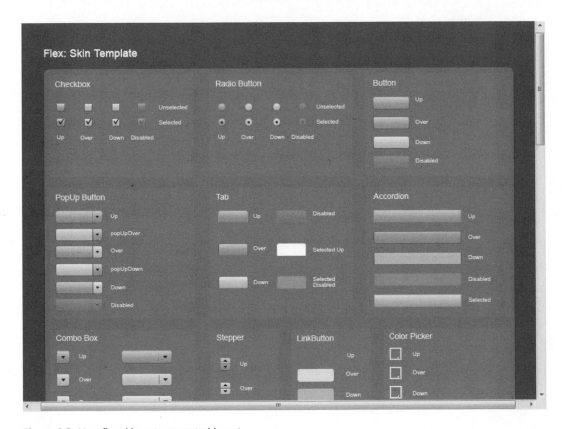

Figure 8-2. New flex skin autogenerated layout

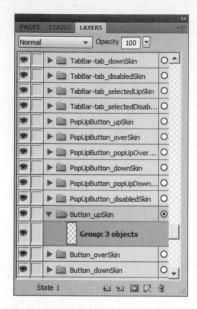

Figure 8-3. Flex skin Layers panel

This document is actually twice as tall than it is shown in Figure 8-2. If you're new to skinning, this may be a little overwhelming. If you're an old skinning pro, this should put a smile on your face! Instead of having to guess what states are available and dig through folders of images, all of the target elements are neatly organized and ready to be tweaked. Figure 8-3 shows a section of the Layers panel that supports this document.

There are unique layers for each state of each component, and each layer is named using the following formula: ControlName_stateSkin. All of the nonskin artwork (background, control, and state labels) is defined in the layer named _BASE.

> *Do not rename any of the layers. The layer names are used by the* Export *command to generate Flex-ready artwork.*

Reskinning the button

With the new template document created, the reskinning phase is really no different from any other design exercise in Fireworks. We're just going to update artwork in the control-specific layers that we're interested in (in this case the Button_state layers) and export. Since this chapter is more about *how to skin* than *how to create a highly polished skin*, we're going to focus on getting you through the steps rather than on the details of artistry. We'll show you how to quickly apply some of the default styles that ship with Fireworks CS4 so you can create your first custom Flex skin.

Start by selecting the Button_upSkin layer. It's a good idea to lock all of the other layers so you don't accidentally create artwork in a different layer (remember, layer names are used by the Export command when generating your skin). You

Figure 8-4. Paths that make up Button_upSkin

can quickly lock the other layers by selecting Commands ➤ Document ➤ Lock Other Layers from the main menu. When you expand the Button_upSkin layer, you should see a group of three objects. Ungroup those objects to reveal three paths. Figure 8-4 shows the three paths selected on the canvas.

The base path is used to define the outer border, the middle path is used to define the fill, and the topmost path is used to define a highlight. We really want to talk about how partially transparent gradients, which are used as the fill, are a great way to create skins that are flexible enough to work in multiple layouts, but that's really a discussion for another chapter (and possibly another book). What we really *need* to do is apply a new fill to each state of the button and get on with the exercise. So, let's do it.

Launch the Styles panel (Window ➤ Styles) and select Plastic Styles from the combo box. Now, select the middle path and apply any style that makes you happy. We chose a lime green glassy gradient (Plastic 095). Now, step through each of the other three Button skin layers (Button_overSkin, Button_downSkin, and Button_disabledSkin) and do the same thing, making sure you apply a different style for each state.

Exporting the skin

When you're ready to export your artwork, select Commands ➤ Flex Skinning ➤ Export Flex Skin from the main menu. You will be prompted to select a destination folder for your exported artwork. Once you select a folder, each layer will be individually exported to a unique, flattened PNG file. Figure 8-5 shows a snapshot of an exported skin in Windows Explorer.

With the artwork generated, it's now time to switch gears and jump into Flex Builder. If you didn't catch the link earlier when we mentioned it, visit www.adobe.com/flex to download a free trial.

Figure 8-5. Exported skin artwork in Windows Explorer

Importing the skin in Flex

If the idea of using Flex Builder frightens you, don't worry! We're going to stay in the designer-safe zone and avoid the coding aspects of Flex (aside from viewing a little CSS).

Creating a new Flex project

Start by creating a new Flex project (select New ➤ Flex Project from the main menu). The New Flex Project dialog is shown in Figure 8-6.

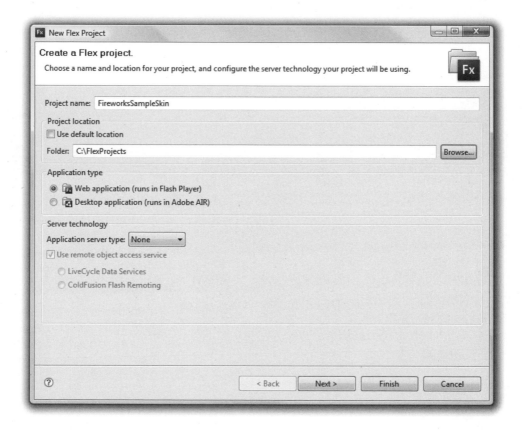

Figure 8-6. New Flex Project dialog

Give your project a name, and then select a folder for the project location. A subfolder will be created in the project location folder with the name of your project (e.g., folderName\projectName). Select Web application (runs in Flash Player) as the application type, and click the Finish button at this point. When the wizard has completed generating the default project files, an MXML (Macromedia Extensible Markup Language) file should open in the IDE. Click the Design button to switch from the markup (source) view to the design view.

Adding a Button component

We're now going to add a Button to the design surface. Find the Components panel (select Window ➤ Components if it's not already open) and expand the Controls folder. Now, drag an instance of the Button component onto the stage. Figure 8-7 shows the Controls folder expanded with a Button component already dragged to the stage.

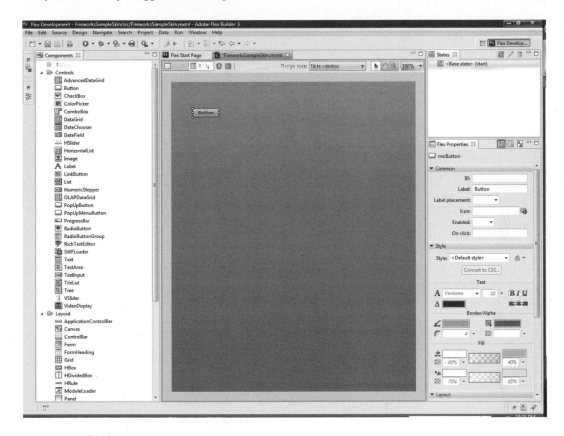

Figure 8-7. A Button component on the stage in Flex Builder

See, that wasn't too bad! A simple drag and drop, and you've added a Button to the design surface in a professional development tool.

Importing the skin images

It's now time to make use of the images Fireworks generated for us before we switched to Flex Builder. From the Flex Navigator panel in Flex Builder (Window ➤ Flex Navigator) right-click your Flex project and select Import from the context menu that appears. In the Import dialog, expand the Flex Builder folder and select Artwork, as shown in Figure 8-8.

Click Next to proceed to the Import Skin Artwork dialog shown in Figure 8-9.

149

Figure 8-8. Artwork Import dialog in Flex Builder

Figure 8-9. Import Skin Artwork dialog

Start by browsing for the destination folder you selected in Fireworks when you exported your Flex skin. Flex Builder will automatically fill in the Copy artwork to subfolder and Create skin style rules in fields for you after you've selected the source folder. Notice in Figure 8-9 that the artwork subfolder and CSS file name both match the name of the source folder of images. You can now click Next to move on to the final dialog of the import process, as shown in Figure 8-10.

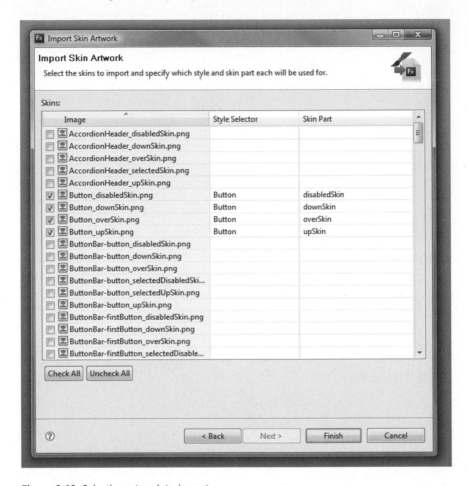

Figure 8-10. Selecting artwork to import

In this final dialog, you have to select which files you want to import. By default, all of the files are checked. We clicked the Uncheck All button and then manually checked all files that start with Button_ since those were the only ones we modified in Fireworks. Note that Flex has matched the Style Selector and Skin Part columns of this dialog to the images perfectly! We don't have to manually match images to components or states because Fireworks has named all of the files in a way that Flex recognizes. Click Finish to complete the artwork import process.

Switch back to the Flex Navigator panel to see the new CSS file and artwork folder that have been added to the src folder of your project. The new CSS file is automatically opened in the IDE, as shown in Figure 8-11.

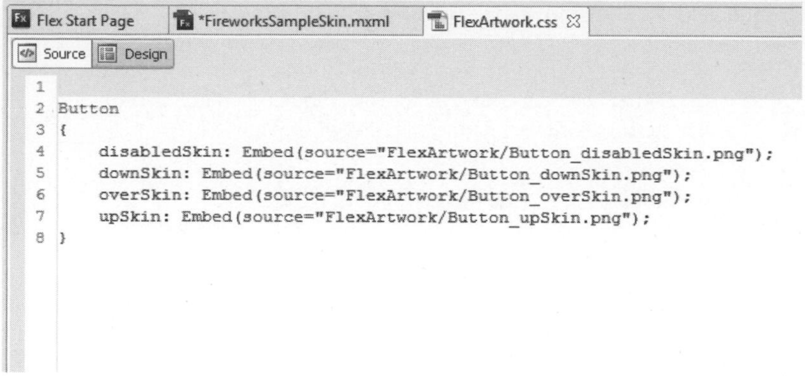

Figure 8-11. The autogenerated CSS file open in Flex Builder

As we mentioned at the beginning of the chapter, Fireworks and Flex do the heavy lifting for you. You didn't have to know any of the custom CSS syntax; it was generated for you automatically. You should now be able to switch back to your MXML file and see your new skin applied to the Button you created earlier. If you don't see your skin, try clicking the Refresh button (next to the Design button), or try clicking the Play button if that doesn't work. When you click Play, the Flex application is compiled, and a sample HTML page is launched. Your SWF-based Flex application is loaded in the HTML page for you to play with and test.

Modifying the nine-slice scaling

If your artwork includes rounded corners, and a very high percentage of modern user interface artwork does, you'll likely want to tweak the nine-slice scaling settings that will be applied to your underlying artwork at runtime. The nine-slice grid in Flex behaves exactly as it does in Fireworks: the underlying image is divided into a 3×3 grid. When resized, the corner artwork is preserved, while the artwork in the other sections is stretched.

To edit the nine-slice scaling in Flex Builder, open the CSS file that was just generated, switch to design view, and then click the Edit Scale Grid button in the upper-right corner of the design surface. Figure 8-12 shows our custom Button skin in Edit Scale Grid mode.

Simply drag the dashed lines to redefine the scaling grid, exactly like you do in Fireworks. When you're satisfied with your changes, switch back to source view to see how the CSS has been modified to support this scaling mode. The following code shows the addition of the scaleGridLeft, scaleGridTop, scaleGridRight, and scaleGridBottom attributes:

```
upSkin: Embed(source="FlexArtwork/Button_upSkin.png", ➡
scaleGridLeft="7",scaleGridTop="1",scaleGridRight="56", ➡
scaleGridBottom="21");
```

If (and when) you import artwork for more than one control, you can select other styles at CSS design time using the drop-down button shown in Figure 8-12.

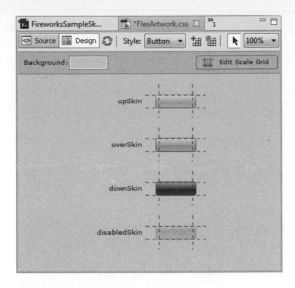

Figure 8-12. Edit Scale Grid in Flex Builder

Summary

Congratulations! You've now created your first Flex skin! Fireworks truly makes this process straightforward and easy. Now that you've stepped through the process with one control, you can do it for any control, or all controls for that matter. The process of exporting artwork from Fireworks and importing the artwork into a Flex project is really the easiest part. The most difficult and time-consuming part of skinning is the design phase. With the number of controls and states available, it can be quite a formidable task.

If you're a designer working with a team of Flex developers, you should now have an understanding of how Fireworks can help you fit into the development environment in a respectable way. You can either generate the Flex CSS yourself using Flex Builder or you can hand off images that have been named in a way Flex Builder recognizes. With the exception of customizing the nine-slice scaling, the developers can take your images and run with them. It's now up to you do define a workflow that works within your organization.

Chapter 9

CREATING ADOBE AIR PROTOTYPES

Fireworks is the starting point for many application prototypes, whether web or desktop. With Adobe's introduction of the AIR platform, it only made sense to enable rapid AIR prototypes within everyone's favorite tool for application mockups! Using Fireworks CS4 and the new Create AIR Package command, you can rapidly prototype an application within Fireworks, and then generate an actual AIR application to test the effectiveness of your design.

Creating real AIR applications directly from Fireworks lets you see your mockup in action and gain valuable insight into how well the navigation works. You can send the AIR file to colleagues or clients and get a level of feedback that is hard to obtain when passing around static images.

Before you get the wrong impression and think that Fireworks has just evolved into a development tool, let us clarify what you can and cannot achieve with the Create AIR Package command:

Things you can do:

- Create simple application mockups.
- Create applications with chromeless windows.
- Enable window dragging.
- Navigate internal pages using buttons.

Things you can't do:

- Advanced coding.
- Integrate Flash or Flex components.
- Create production-ready AIR applications.

The AIR support built into Fireworks is designed to let you take your prototype to the next level. It is not designed to be a replacement for a development environment such as Adobe Flex, Flash, or Dreamweaver.

In this chapter, we'll create a simple mockup of a portfolio viewer application as shown in Figure 9-1. We'll start by designing the layout and organizing the application using the pages feature of Fireworks. We'll then create hotspots to define buttons and link the buttons to target pages. With the basic navigation in place, we'll use some of the new AIR commands to add simple application interactivity (like window dragging). With all of the artwork in place and button events defined, we'll publish our mockup to an AIR application. So, let's get started!

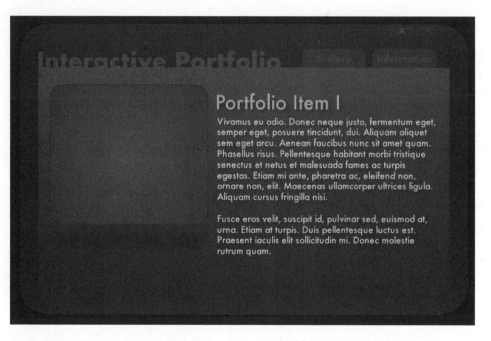

Figure 9-1. Portfolio viewer AIR application

> *If you're not familiar with AIR, which stands for Adobe Integrated Runtime, it represents a Flash-based platform for creating desktop applications. Using either the Flash or Flex authoring environments, developers can create desktop applications that run on Windows, OS X, and Linux. For more information on Adobe AIR, visit* www.adobe.com/ products/air.

This chapter assumes that you are now familiar with the core features of Fireworks CS4 discussed in previous chapters of this book. We will be skipping over the small details of each step, instead focusing on the big picture. If any of the following are unfamiliar, you might want to take a moment to review them:

- Pages
- Optimization presets
- Basic shape drawing
- Creating hotspots
- Filters and effects

Designing the master page

As we mentioned in the introduction, we're going to take advantage of the pages feature of Fireworks to create our application mockup. We'll start by defining the master page, and then add additional subpages. First, create a new Fireworks document with the following settings:

- Width: 760 px
- Height: 500 px
- Resolution: 72 px/inch
- Canvas Color: Transparent

From the Pages panel (Window ➤ Pages), right-click the only page in the list and select Set as Master Page. The artwork added to this page will now be seen on all subsequent pages that we create.

The master page can be set at any time in the process. Setting it from the very beginning just clarifies the process.

The master page for this application is going to contain the application background (a rounded gray rectangle), the application title ("Interactive Portfolio"), and two main menu buttons (Gallery and Information). You should feel free to create your own variations of this sample as you follow along, but we've included the exact dimensions of the artwork in the steps that follow should you want to replicate this layout exactly.

Defining the background

Create a rounded rectangle with the following values:

- Width: 700 px
- Height: 450 px
- X: 30 px
- Y: 25
- Corner Roundness: 38, 38, 38, 38 (TopLeft, TopRight, BottomRight, BottomLeft)
- Fill: Solid #333333

This shape will serve as the main background for our portfolio viewer.

Defining the content container

The main content of the application is wrapped with a lighter shade of gray than the solid background. Create another rounded rectangle, this time with the following settings:

- Width: 642 px
- Height: 360 px
- X: 59
- Y: 92
- Corner Roundness: 0, 0, 38, 38
- Fill: Linear Gradient, Vertical from #666666 at the top to #333333 at the bottom

You can use either the Auto Shape Properties panel (Window ➤ Auto Shape Properties) or the adorners directly on the design surface to set the corner roundness. To remove the roundness from the top-left and top-right corners of the second rounded rectangle directly on the design surface, hold down the Alt/Option key and drag the top points to the left and right respectively, as shown in Figure 9-2.

Figure 9-2. Individually adjusting the corner radius of specific corners

Adding the tabs

With the main pieces of the background in place, it's time to add the two tabs for Gallery and Information. We'll use two more rounded rectangles and position them behind the last rectangle. Use the following settings to match the tab positioning shown in Figure 9-3:

Gallery **tab:**

- Width: 100 **px**
- Height: 44 **px**
- X: 471 **px**
- Y: 63 **px**
- Corner Roundness: 11, 11, 11, 11
- Fill: Solid #484848

Information **tab.**

- Width: 100 **px**
- Height: 44 **px**
- X: 581 **px**
- Y: 63 **px**
- Corner Roundness: 11, 11, 11, 11
- Fill: Solid #484848

Figure 9-3. Final master page layout

With the tab backgrounds in place, just add the foreground text, and you're finished. We've selected Futura Medium **as the font, set the size to** 14, **and set the fill to** #666666.

Adding the application title

The final element of the master page layout is the application title. The title uses a heavier weight of Futura, and its baseline is positioned slightly below the content rectangle. We've applied the same color (#666666) to the title as the background of the content rectangle to make it look as if these two elements are joined. With this final piece in place, the master page now looks like Figure 9-3, and we're ready to move on to the additional pages of our application.

Designing the information page

The Information page of this application is like the Help ➤ About page of a traditional application. It contains some supplemental or background information about the portfolio. Start by creating a new page:

1. Open the Pages panel.
2. Click the New Page icon.
3. Double-click the page and rename it Info.
4. Switch to the Layers panel.

Your new page should look exactly like the master page you just created, and you should see a layer named Master Page Layer in your Layers panel that contains all of the elements you defined in the master page. Now, add a dummy title and description so your layout looks like that shown in Figure 9-4.

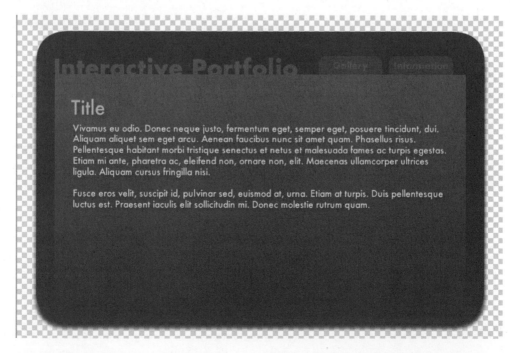

Figure 9-4. Information page

Generate filler text quickly by using the Fireworks Lorem Ipsum *command* (Commands ➤ Text ➤ Lorem Ipsum). *This command will create a new text box on the canvas that you can then size, position, and style. For more advanced control over Lorem Ipsum, check out Mayur Mundada's* Lorem Ipsum *panel on Fireworks Exchange* (www.adobe.com/cfusion/exchange/).

Designing the gallery page

The Gallery page consists of a number of thumbnails that each link to its own individual detail page. Again, start by creating a new page. We'll now create a placeholder symbol that will serve as the thumbnail icon, and then duplicate it a few times to create a total of four thumbnail icons.

Creating the thumbnail symbol

We'll start with our old friend the rounded rectangle. Create a new rounded rectangle with the following settings (or be creative and create your own look):

- Width: 246
- Height: 217
- Corner Roundness: 24 px
- Fill: Radial Gradient (#666666, #333333)

Figure 9-5 shows the gradient handle positions used to create the soft radial fill.

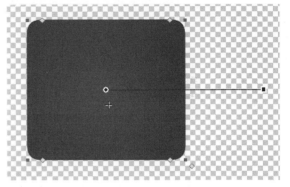

Figure 9-5. Gradient handle positions

Adding a highlight

Create a copy of this base rectangle and paste it in the foreground. We'll apply a linear, white-based gradient that adds a little more texture. Change the fill type to a Linear Gradient with the following values:

- Color Stops: White **to** White
- Opacity Stops: 100% **to** 0%

Your final gradient settings should look like those shown in Figure 9-6.

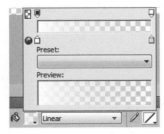

Figure 9-6. Foreground gradient stops

161

Figure 9-7. Gradient handle positions for our highlight rectangle

Figure 9-7 shows the position of the gradient handles on the design surface. By setting the last opacity stop to 0% and positioning the last handle in the middle of the rectangle, the base rectangle (with the radial gradient) is still visible beneath this new highlight.

Adding a shadow

You may have noticed a shadow in the previous figure. This shadow, which adds a little depth to the thumbnail icon, can be easily created by drawing a small ellipse beneath the rectangles. Set the ellipse's fill to black, and then apply a Gaussian Blur filter with a blur radius of approximately 14. Tweak the blur value and the underlying ellipse until your shadow looks similar to that shown in Figure 9-7.

Adding some color

We've been working with grayscale fill values up to this point. Let's add a little color to these thumbnails to help them stand out from the background. Select both of the rounded rectangles and apply a Hue/Saturation filter (Filters ➤ Adjust Colors ➤ Hue/Saturation) with the following values:

- Hue: 72
- Saturation: 25
- Lightness: 0

The resulting color is a forest green shade. Your thumbnail and layout should now look similar to that shown in Figure 9-8.

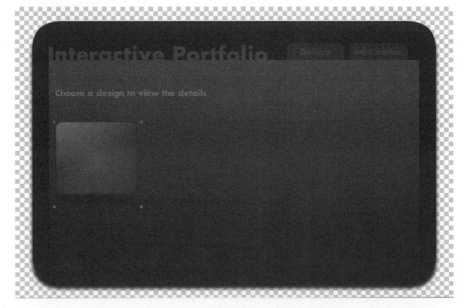

Figure 9-8. Final thumbnail design

Creating the thumbnail symbol

Now that the design of the thumbnail is complete, and knowing that we need to use it three more times, let's convert the thumbnail elements to a symbol and create multiple instances of it. Start by selecting all of the thumbnail elements: the base rectangle, the highlight rectangle, and the shadow. Then, right-click the canvas and choose Convert to Symbol. When the dialog opens, enter portfolioThumb as the name and set the type to Graphic. Finally, click OK to create the thumbnail symbol.

The three elements you just selected have now been replaced with a single symbol instance on the canvas. You can double-click the symbol instance at any time to edit the underlying artwork. Create three copies of the thumbnail and position them on the canvas so your final layout resembles that shown in Figure 9-9.

Figure 9-9. Final thumbnail layout

Building the portfolio detail pages

Each thumbnail on the gallery page will link to a specific detail page that includes a large thumbnail, a title, and a description. We'll start by creating the base layout as a new page, and then duplicate that page three times for a total of four unique detail pages.

To save a little time, we can start by duplicating the Information page created earlier. It already contains title and description elements that will make the creation of these subpages fly by. To duplicate the Information page, switch to the Pages panel, right-click the Information page, and select Duplicate Page. Adjust the position of the title and description elements, and then add an instance of the thumbnail symbol created in the last step. Size the thumbnail instance so that your final layout resembles that shown in Figure 9-10.

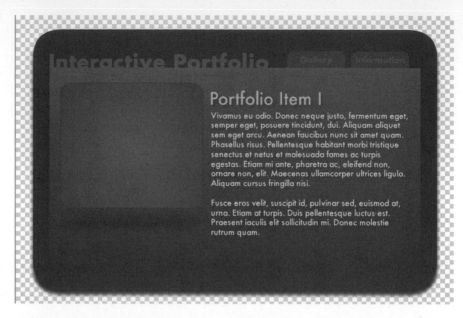

Figure 9-10. Portfolio detail page

Duplicating the pages and finalizing page names

Create three additional pages by duplicating the detail page you just created. Change the title of each page to correspond to a specific thumbnail (as in "Portfolio Item 1," "Portfolio Item 2," and so on). Also apply a Hue/Saturation filter to the large thumbnail symbol on each page to create a unique color for each page.

Now, switch back to the Pages panel one final time and update the names of your pages so that they match the page names shown in Figure 9-11.

Figure 9-11. Final page names

Adding hotspots and interaction

In the previous section, you defined all of the pages of your mock application and took the time to give each page a name that represented its content accurately. You'll now add button hotspots to each of the pages and assign actions to each hotspot that navigate between the pages when the buttons are clicked.

Global navigation

Let's start by defining the global navigation that will be shared across all pages in the application. And where would we define *global* navigation? In the master page, of course!

Creating the hotspots

Select the master page in the Pages panel, and then select the Rectangle Hotspot tool, which you will use to draw the hotspots on the navigation buttons. Draw hotspot rectangles over both of the tabs so that your document looks similar to Figure 9-12.

Figure 9-12. Tab hotspots in place

Add one more hotspot that will be used to drag the application around the screen. Select the Polygon Hotspot tool and draw a shape around the header area of the layout, making sure to exclude the tabs and leaving room for minimize, maximize, and close buttons. Your polygon should look like that shown in Figure 9-13.

Figure 9-13. Header-drag-area hotspot in place

Adding interactivity

With the hotspots in place, we can now actually make them do something. Select the Gallery tab hotspot and look at the Property inspector. The Link field displayed in the Property inspector includes a drop-down list of items that correspond to the pages defined in the document. The names in this list are based on the actual page names we defined earlier. (See, it makes sense to name pages in a meaningful way!) Select Gallery.htm as shown in Figure 9-14.

Figure 9-14. Assigning a link in the Property inspector

Continue by setting the link of the Information tab to the Info.htm page. The third hotspot's link on the master page is assigned a little differently. Instead of targeting a specific page, we want it to perform an AIR-specific action: window dragging. Fortunately, you don't have to know any code to do this. Simply select the polygon hotspot, and then select Commands ➤ AIR Mouse Event ➤ Drag from the main menu. The Link field is automatically updated with the following code:

```
events:onMouseDown='window.nativeWindow.startMove();'
```

You could have typed this code into the Link field, but using the command is much faster and eliminates the chance of error. We're sure you noticed the other commands available in the AIR Mouse Events category. In addition to Move, Fireworks includes commands for Minimize, Maximize, and Close. We're not going to add buttons for those events in this chapter, but you can follow the same steps that we've already covered to add those buttons yourself.

Defining links on the gallery page

With the master page links defined, we can move on to the Gallery page. Each thumbnail in the gallery needs to link to its corresponding detail page. Navigate to the Gallery page using the Pages panel, and then draw rectangle hotspots over each of the thumbnail symbols. Using the same technique as you did for the tab hotspots, assign the link of each thumbnail to its corresponding detail page using the drop-down. Your final layout with hotspots in place should look like Figure 9-15.

Figure 9-15. Thumbnail hotspots on the Gallery page

Creating the Adobe AIR package

And now for the part you've been waiting for—creating the AIR application! With all of the design work out of the way, our internal navigation defined, and AIR events assigned to buttons, it's time to create our application.

Launch the Create AIR Package dialog by selecting Commands ➤ Create AIR Package from the main menu. The dialog, shown in Figure 9-16, includes a number of fields that must be completed before your application can be published.

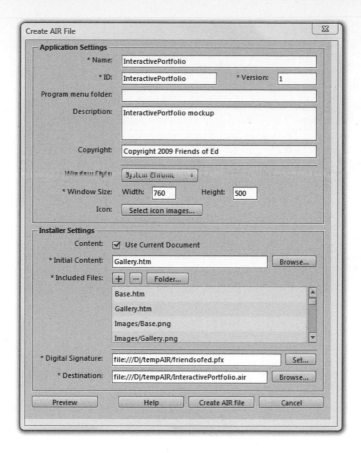

Figure 9-16. Create AIR Package dialog

The following list explains the role each field plays in the final application.

Under the Application Settings section:

- Name: The application name will be seen in installation screens and desktop shortcuts.
- ID: The unique identifier for your application. This is used internally by AIR applications and can usually be the same as the application name.
- Version: The version number of your application. This will be seen when the application is installed and is a useful reference if you create multiple interactions of your application for clients.
- Description: A custom description for your application that will be seen when the application is installed.

- Copyright: Copyright string that is also displayed in the installer.
- Window Style: Drop-down that allows you to select chrome settings for the application.
- Window Size: The default width and height settings.
- Icon: The application icon.

Under the Installer Settings section:

- Content: Option that has Fireworks automatically generate files based on all of the pages in the document. When checked, a dialog box launches so you can select a target folder for file generation.
- Initial content: The start page of the application. Click the Browse button to select the start page.
- Included Files: The list of files that will be added to the AIR file, normally generated by the Package content property.
- Digital Signature: Adobe AIR applications must have a digital signature in order to be installed. Click the Set button to browse to a digital signature file on your system. See the upcoming "Creating a digital signature" section for more details on this.
- Destination: The name and location of the generated AIR file.

For the most part, each of these fields is pretty straightforward. However, there are a couple of sections that need a little more explanation.

Packaging content

For the scenario described in this chapter, you will always check the Package content option. When you first check this box, a Folder Browser dialog will launch. Select or create a folder that will house the temporary files required for this application. Once you've selected a folder, HTML and images will be generated for all of the pages in your document and added to the folder you just specified. The generated files will then be added to the Included files list in this dialog box. Click the Browse button to select Gallery.htm from the Export folder. This will be the file first seen when the application launches.

Creating a digital signature

Adobe AIR applications require a digital signature. Click the Set button to launch the Digital Signature dialog shown in Figure 9-17.

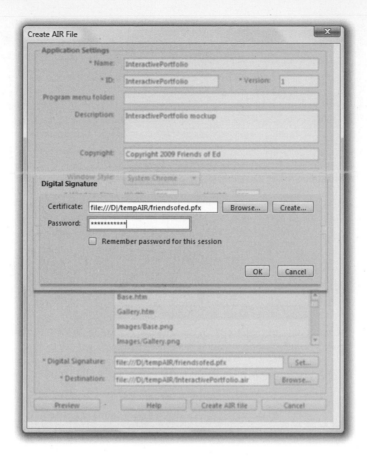

Figure 9-17. Selecting a digital signature

You can either browse for an existing signature or create one directly from this dialog. Click the Create button to launch the Create Certificate dialog shown in Figure 9-18.

In the Certificate file field, enter a name for the generated file, like MyCertificate. The certificate file will be generated in the folder you selected for the content. Complete the additional fields and enter a password for your signature file. Once all of the required fields have been completed, the Create button will be enabled. Click the Create button and this dialog box will close, returning you to the previous Digital Signature dialog shown in Figure 9-17.

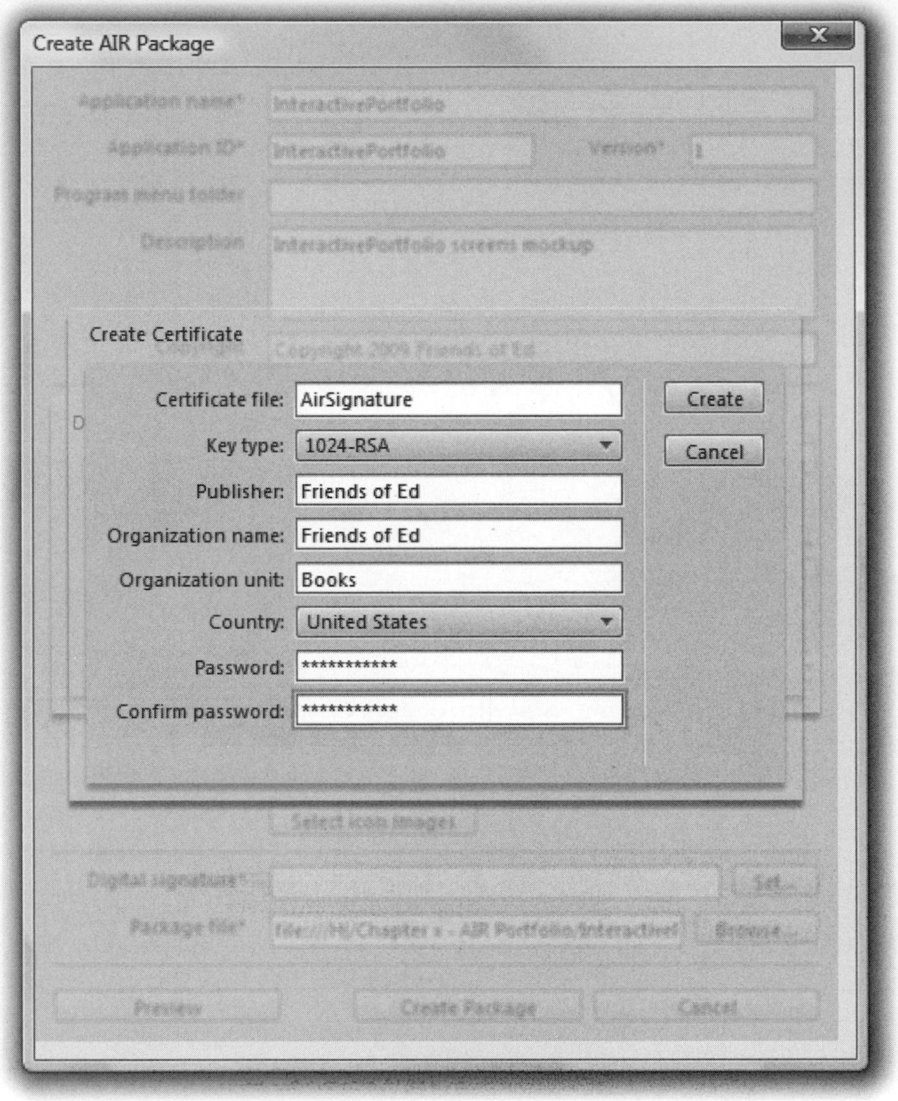

Figure 9-18. Creating a digital signature (certificate)

The certificate path should now reference the signature file you just created. Enter the password you specified and click the OK button. For subsequent AIR packages that you create, you can click the Browse button and select the signature file that you just created.

Previewing the AIR file

Before you create the AIR application, you can click the Preview button to see what your application will look like. When you choose Preview, you bypass the AIR installation process and get to a sample application immediately. This is much faster than publishing the AIR file and stepping through the installation process.

Creating and installing the AIR file

With all of the fields in the Create AIR Package dialog complete, you can now click the Create Package button. Once the dialog box closes, you can browse to the location of the AIR file you specified and double-click the file to launch the Adobe AIR Installer. Figure 9-19 shows an AIR Installer similar to the one that will be seen with your newly created file. The settings you entered in the Create AIR Package dialog should be honored in the Application Install dialog that launches.

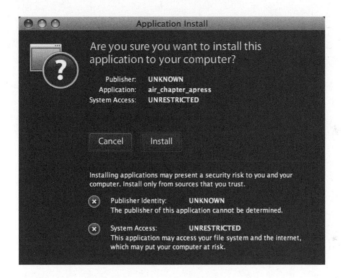

Figure 9-19. Adobe AIR Application Install dialog

With your application installed, you can now launch it from the desktop, Start menu (Windows), Applications Folder (Mac), or Dock (Mac). Figure 9-20 shows the published version of our final AIR application running on a Vista desktop. Notice the support for full alpha-channel transparency on the desktop. Nice!

Figure 9-20. Final AIR application running on the desktop

Summary

This chapter stepped you through all of the tasks required to create a true AIR application from your Fireworks mockup. You learned how to organize your document using pages, add hotspots that create interactivity between those pages, and assign AIR-specific commands to hotspots to enable window dragging, minimizing, maximizing, and closing. You can now use this knowledge to create fully self-contained AIR application mockups that you can send to clients and colleagues for immediate feedback. Use the Version field of the Create AIR Package dialog to help keep track of mockup versions as you incorporate feedback into each round of design. You should see by now that Fireworks' AIR support is not intended to replace a dedicated AIR environment, but rather takes advantage of the AIR platform to empower more sophisticated application mockups.

Chapter 10

FIREWORKS EXTENSIONS

Many of the applications in the Adobe Creative Suite include support for extensions, and Fireworks CS4 is no exception. **Extensions** are a means of enhancing the application, much like plug-ins or macros in other applications. Fireworks has a rich history of extensibility, with scores of freely (and commercially) available extensions accessible online. These extensions range in complexity from simple commands ("Distribute Frames to Pages" by John Dunning, for example) to sophisticated Flash- or Flex-based command panels (such as 3D Rotate by Aaron Beall).

Extensions add to the power of Fireworks, often automating repetitive tasks or simplifying complex operations. Here are a couple examples of the types of extensions that can be found online.

You can find command extensions that

- Generate web-safe guides and bounding boxes for various web browser sizes.
- Convert all text to lowercase, uppercase, or title case.
- Delete all of your empty layers.

- Adjust filters on all selected objects (disabling, enabling, deleting, or toggling).
- Ungroup a group and migrate all effects applied to the group to the ungrouped children.
- Migrate group effects to a group's contained children.
- And much, much more.

You can find command panel extensions that

- Show you all of the fonts used in your document.
- Rotate your object in 3D space.
- Generate slideshows.
- Resize selected objects with single-pixel precision.
- Generate *Lorem Ipsum* text.
- Import kuler palettes.
- And much, much more.

Most Fireworks extensions are developed by avid Fireworks users to solve a particular problem they've faced or automate a task that they were absolutely sick of doing over, and over, and over again. And generally, if they arrived at that need as avid Fireworks users, the odds are high that the rest of us have encountered the same need at one time or another.

In this chapter, we'll look at the default extensions available within Fireworks, touch upon a number of the Fireworks extensions that are available online, look at where extensions can be found, and show you how to manage (install, remove, enable, and disable) the extensions that you download.

Types of extensions

Practically every aspect of Fireworks can be customized or extended. If you browse to the Configuration folder of your Fireworks installation, you'll see a number of folders that support most of the features of the program that you use on a daily basis (such as autoshapes, patterns, and textures). Any of these folders may be updated and modified by third-party extensions. Let's take a quick look at the most common types of extensions. We'll then review additional types of extensions that are available.

Command and command panel extension types

The two most common types of extensions available are command and command panel extensions. Commands that are accessed via the Commands entry of the main menu are often scripts that require no user interaction (such as Commands ➤ Document ➤ Hide Other Layers). For more sophisticated commands, such as Commands ➤ Creative ➤ Twist and Fade, a custom SWF-based dialog may be presented that lets you configure the action about to be performed. Figure 10-1 shows the Twist and Fade command's dialog.

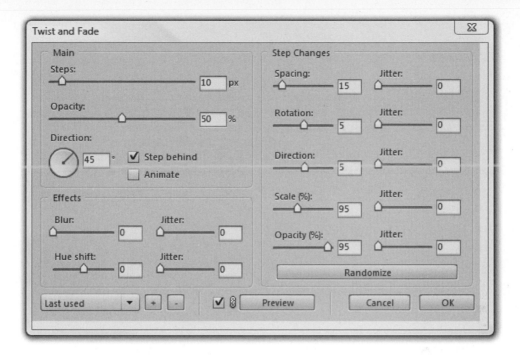

Figure 10-1. Twist and Fade command dialog

Command panels are accessed from the Window entry of the main menu. You may not realize it, but you are already familiar with command panels, which are the persistent panels that you use to modify items on the stage or adjust document settings. A couple of common command panels that you've likely already used are the Align panel (Window ➤ Align) and the Path panel (Window ➤ Others ➤ Path). When you install command panel extensions, they will be accessible from the Window menu just like the default command panels. The key difference between commands and command panels is that command panels are persistent. They can be docked, grouped, and closed with other panels just like the default panels that ship with Fireworks.

Other extension types

Extensions are not limited to commands or command panels. Here's a list of some of the additional types of extensions that are available:

- Texture libraries
- Pattern libraries
- Autoshapes
- Common Library items/additional libraries

Default Fireworks commands

You don't have to find or install any extensions to experience extensions in Fireworks. Fireworks ships with a number of powerful commands available from the Commands entry of the main menu. Figure 10-2 shows the Commands menu expanded, displaying the default commands that are available when you first install Fireworks.

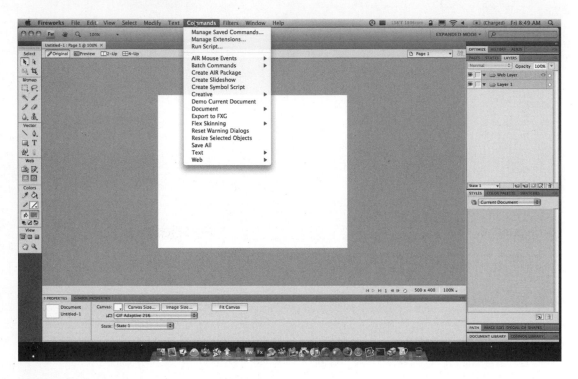

Figure 10-2. Command menu open on Mac OS X Leopard

Modifying objects

Many of the commands you'll find as extensions perform some type of operation on the selected objects on the canvas. Let's get our feet wet by using one of the default commands, Resize Selected Objects, highlighted in Figure 10-3.

Before you execute the command, you need to create a few objects on the canvas. Select the Rectangle tool and draw three rectangles, similar to what you see in Figure 10-4.

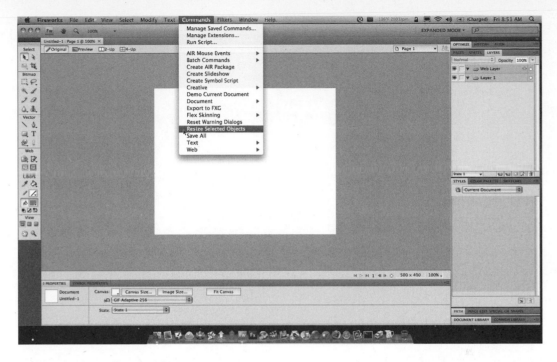

Figure 10-3. Resize Selected Objects command

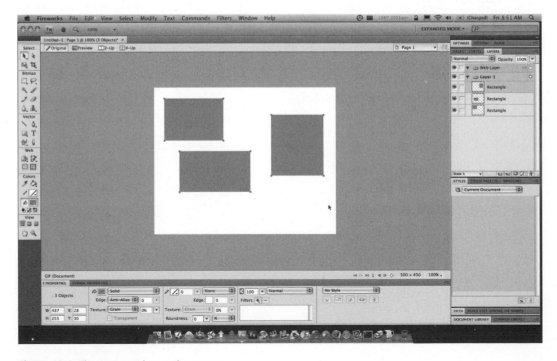

Figure 10-4. Three rectangles on the canvas

With your rectangles in place, select the Pointer tool and drag to select all three shapes (you could also press Ctrl/Cmd+A to select all shapes). With all the shapes selected, select Commands ➤ Resize Selected Objects from the main menu. You should see the Resize Selected Objects custom dialog, as shown in Figure 10-5.

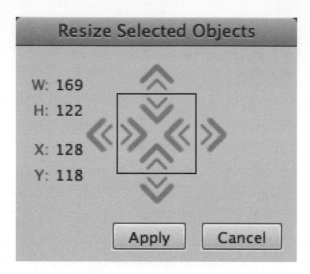

Figure 10-5. Resize Selected Objects dialog

As you click the various arrows located within this dialog, the canvas will be updated with a live preview. When you're satisfied with your changes, click Apply. All three rectangles will be resized by exactly the same amount, something that could have been achieved using the Property inspector, but you would have to resize each shape individually. With this command, you can modify the size of any number of shapes, all at once.

Modifying the document/interface

The previous command modified the selected items on the canvas. The next command we'll look at modifies interface settings, another common action performed by commands. Start by creating a new document. Create several layers and add objects (rectangles, circles, text, etc.) to each layer. Once you have three or four layers, each with objects on them, select one of the objects or layers. Now, select Commands ➤ Document ➤ Hide Other Layers from the main menu as shown in Figure 10-6.

You should now only see the one layer you selected, as shown in Figure 10-7.

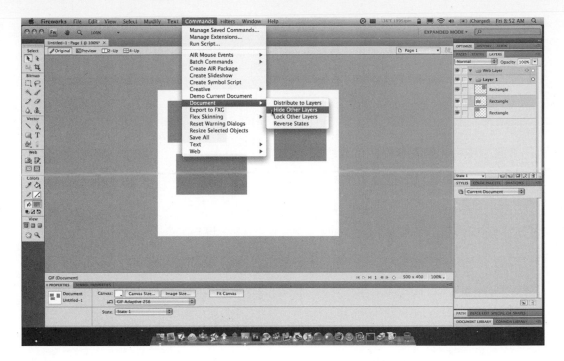

Figure 10-6. The Hide Other Layers option

Figure 10-7. Layer palette with one layer visible, displaying the one object on the canvas

Fireworks hid all of the layers except the layer that was selected (or the layer that contained your selected object). Again, you could have done this manually by clicking the eye icon for all layers except the one you're interested in, but this single command achieved all of that manual work for you. Alternatively, you could have selected Lock Other Layers from Commands ➤ Document. Instead of hiding all of the other layers, the other layers would have been locked—another common task that is often performed manually.

You've now experienced commands that present a custom dialog, commands that target selected objects on the stage, and commands that modify user interface settings. All of the command extensions that you install will fall into these categories.

Finding extensions online

A wealth of Fireworks extensions are available online, most of them for free. You just need to know how to find them. You'll find more panel, command, autoshape, and texture pack extensions than you can process. Let's start by looking at Adobe's official repository: Adobe Exchange.

Browsing Adobe Exchange: A repository of extensions

Adobe Exchange is Adobe's official, central repository for application extensions. Here you can find extensions for Fireworks, in Fireworks Exchange, and for a number of other applications in the Creative Suite. You can access Fireworks Exchange from within Fireworks directly from two locations:

- **Start page**: Click the Fireworks Exchange link.
- **Main menu**: Select Help ➤ Fireworks Exchange.

If you're not in Fireworks, you can just browse to www.adobe.com/cfusion/exchange and click the Fireworks Exchange link. From the page that appears (shown in Figure 10-8), you will be greeted with a number of featured extensions, hand-picked by the Adobe staff. Use the License type filter to find extensions that meet your licensing criteria (shareware, open source, freeware, and so forth).

Click an extension's title to visit the extension's details page and download that extension. Figure 10-9 shows the details page for the Inherit Guides extension.

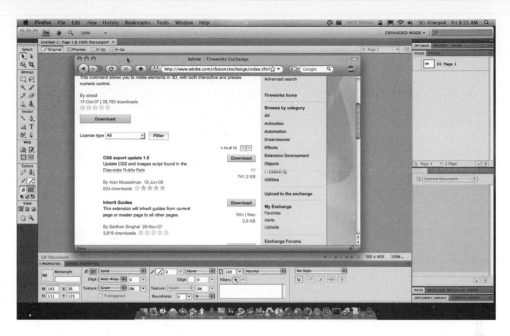

Figure 10-8. Browsing extensions at Adobe's Fireworks Exchange web site

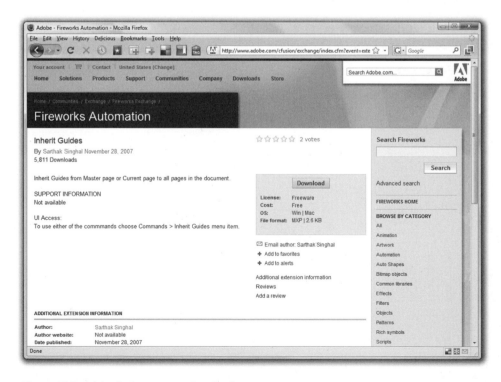

Figure 10-9. Adobe Exchange extension details page

While on the details page, you can also read reviews posted by other users and add it to or remove it from your favorites list. Once you find an extension that you would like to use, simply click the Download button. If you haven't already signed in, you will be redirected to a login screen where you can log in with your Adobe ID.

Most extensions are uploaded in the MXP file format, a package recognized by the Adobe Extension Manager. Once you've downloaded your extension, double-click the MXP file to launch the Extension Manager and install your new toy.

> *If the extension is downloaded as a ZIP file, extract the ZIP file first, and then double-click the extracted MXP file. We have encountered problems when trying to launch an MXP from a ZIP file directly.*

Additional extension resources

Adobe Exchange is a great resource for finding Fireworks extensions; however, a number of additional community and personal sites on the Web house many, many more extensions that are both free and available for purchase. The lists that follow should not be considered comprehensive, but through these sites you should be able to find your way into the web of Fireworks sites online today.

Community sites

The following are just a few of the main community sites devoted to Fireworks:

- www.communitymx.com
- http://firetuts.com
- http://fireworksGuruForum.com
- www.fireworksZone.com
- www.fwkit.com
- www.phireworx.com

Personal sites

The following are a selection of personal sites of active Fireworks community developers and enthusiasts:

- http://fireworks.abeall.com
- www.blue2x.com
- www.demontowers.com/
- www.granthinkson.com
- www.johndunning.com
- www.mattstow.com
- www.qrayg.com/

- www.senocular.com
- http://blogs.adobe.com/sarthak
- http://weblogs.macromedia.com/amusselman
- www.zaporozhye.org/dreamworld/

Using the Extension Manager

The Extension Manager, which ships with Fireworks and many other Adobe Creative Suite applications, can be launched directly from the Fireworks main menu by selecting Help ➤ Manage Extensions. This tool is used to manage (install, uninstall, enable, and disable) extensions for all of the Adobe applications that support extensions.

Following are the default locations for the Extension Manager:

- **Windows:** C:\Program Files\Adobe\Adobe Extension Manager CS4\Adobe Extension Manager CS4.exe
- **Mac OS X:** /Applications/Adobe Extension Manager CS4/Adobe Extension Manager CS4.app

Launch the Extension Manager and select Fireworks CS4 from the list of installed applications on the left. Figure 10-10 shows the Layers Commands extension has been selected in the Extension Manager.

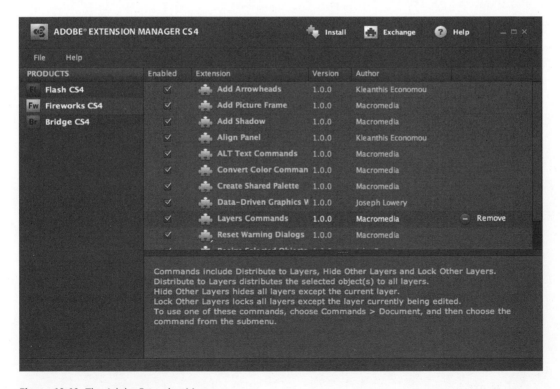

Figure 10-10. The Adobe Extension Manager

As you select a specific extension, you will see details for that extension displayed beneath the extension list. It's in this description that the extension author provides a little background information about the extension and usually lets you know where to find it once installed (such as Commands ➤ Document in the description shown in Figure 10-10).

Installing new extensions

The process of installing a new extension is very simple. Start by clicking the Install button in the top-right toolbar of the Extension Manager or by selecting File ➤ Install Extension (Cmd/Ctrl+O) from the main menu. Navigate to the directory where the MXP file was saved and select the file. Click either Select or Open (depending on your operating system) to install the extension.

> *Depending on the extension, you may be required to acknowledge that you know you're installing an extension from a third-party developer. If a dialog box appears indicating so, simply click Accept and follow through any remaining dialogs that appear.*

Once the extension is installed, you'll see it added to the list of extensions. If Fireworks is open when you install an extension, you'll have to restart it to see your changes take effect; otherwise, simply open Fireworks and enjoy the new extension. Again, the location of the newly installed extension varies based on the extension author, but most authors highlight that location in the extension's description, as shown in Figure 10-11.

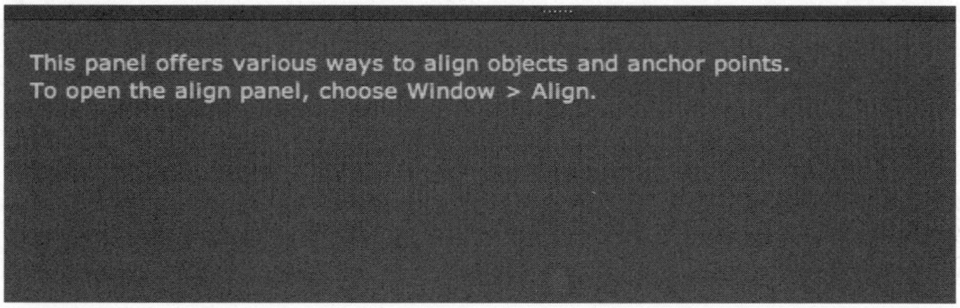

Figure 10-11. Extension description with path displayed

Disabling an extension

As you continue to install more and more extensions, you may find that you've overwhelmed your Fireworks interface with features. Fortunately, this is an easy problem to remedy. You can simply disable some extensions, and the next time you open Fireworks, those extensions will not be available. The extensions will still be listed in the Extension Manager for you to reenable at a later time. To enable or disable an extension, simply select or deselect the check mark to the left of the extension in the Extension Manager list.

> *Any time you enable/disable an extension, you must restart Fireworks in order to see the change.*

Uninstalling an extension

Unlike disabling an extension, uninstalling an extension removes the extension from the Extension Manager list completely. To use the extension again in the future, you'll have to step through the installation process once more (it's not that painful, but it is the key distinction between disabling and uninstalling). To uninstall an extension, simply select the extension in the list and click the Remove link that is displayed to the right of the name. You will be presented with a confirmation dialog, as shown in Figure 10-12. Click Yes to uninstall the extension.

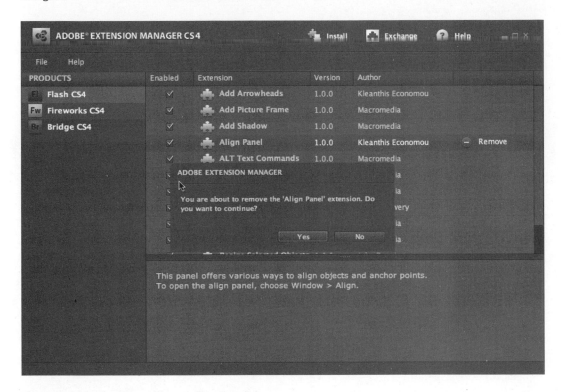

Figure 10-12. Uninstall extension confirmation dialog

Summary

You should now have an understanding of the role extensions play in the world of Fireworks. This chapter by no means covered the breadth of extension available; instead, it introduced you to the *concept* of extensions, showed you where to *find* extensions, and showed you how to *manage* extensions. It's now up to you to *explore* the world of extensions and start personalizing Fireworks.

You can find extensions to enhance your creativity, reduce your workload, and streamline your productivity, most of them for free. So, what are you waiting for—get surfing!

If this chapter has sparked new feature ideas that you think should be added to Fireworks, why not take a stab at adding them yourself? The next chapter covers all of the basics you need to get started creating the next great Fireworks extension.

Chapter 11

EXTENDING FIREWORKS: DEVELOPING AN EFFECTIVE WORKFLOW USING JAVASCRIPT AND FLASH

Adobe Fireworks includes a rich extensibility model that allows advanced users to create sophisticated custom panels (Flash panels) using a combination of JavaScript and Flash. In fact, many of the panels that ship with Fireworks, including the Align panel and the Path panel, are Flash panels. Because the Fireworks engineering team has exposed practically every aspect of Fireworks through a JavaScript extensibility model, you're really only limited by your imagination (and technical abilities, of course).

This chapter is designed to give you an understanding of the entire Flash panel development process and presents a workflow I have refined through developing a number of Fireworks panels, including the Fireworks to XAML Exporter panel and the Gradient panel. You'll see how to author Fireworks JavaScript and integrate that JavaScript in both Flash- and Flex-based custom panels for Fireworks.

This chapter is written for advanced users of both Fireworks and Flash and may be a bit overwhelming if you do you not have programming experience. If you're not a programmer, you may choose to skim through the chapter and gain a greater appreciation of what goes into creating custom panels that enhance your Fireworks experience. However, if you are a programmer and are ready to enhance to your favorite design application (Fireworks of course!), you need to be proficient with the following environments and programming languages:

189

- **JavaScript**: Intermediate to advanced
- **ActionScript 2 or 3**: Intermediate to advanced
- **Adobe Flash**: Intermediate to advanced
- **Adobe Flex**: Optional

Foundation terminology

The following terms will be used throughout the chapter and should be considered as foundational to the conversation. We'll go into more detail on these as the chapter progresses, but take a few minutes to absorb these before moving on.

- **Fireworks command**: A Fireworks command is similar to a macro in other programs. In the simplest sense, it is a recorded set of actions that can be replayed by the application. Fireworks ships with a number of predefined commands, all accessible from the main menu under Commands.
- **JSF**: JSF stands for JavaScript Fireworks. JavaScript is the programming language used to define Fireworks commands. JSF is the term used to refer to JavaScript written specifically for Fireworks. Fireworks commands are simply JavaScript files named with the .jsf extension.
- **Fireworks panel/Flash panel**: Most of the floating panels in Fireworks, such as the Align panel and the Path panel, are either Flash or Flex based. These panels are referred to as Flash panels.
- **ActionScript**: ActionScript is the programming language used by both Flash and Flex and is required when authoring Flash panels.
- **SWF**: Files compiled by Flash and Flex are saved in the SWF file format. We will use the term "SWF" throughout the chapter to refer to an exported file.
- **FLA**: Flash source files are saved in the FLA file format. We will use the term "FLA" throughout the chapter to refer to source files.
- **Fireworks API**: The Fireworks API, or application programming interface, is a set of methods and properties accessed via JSF to perform Fireworks core actions or apply changes to objects on the canvas. For example, to show the color picker in Fireworks, you call the fw. popupColorPickerOverMouse method in JSF.

Learning the basics of an advanced workflow

Before you start creating anything—JavaScript, Flash files, Flex projects, and so forth—it's important that you understand the big picture of Fireworks extensibility and get a firm grasp of the basic concepts and ideas. Consider for a moment all of the various actions you've performed while working in Fireworks: you've drawn elements on the canvas, scaled them, rotated them, applied filters to them; you've create layers and pages and named and renamed them; you've applied fill colors and strokes and edited them endlessly; and much more.

All of these actions that you have performed are core actions (or combinations of actions) that Fireworks supports. And, as we mentioned in the introduction, all of these core actions are exposed by the Fireworks API and are accessible via JavaScript. This JavaScript can be housed in a JSF text file and run via the Commands menu, or it can be compiled into a SWF and run either as a modal command window (again via the Commands menu) or as a persistent Flash panel, accessible from the Window menu like the Align panel or Path panel.

Most of the Fireworks methods exposed via the Fireworks API perform actions on the selected object (or objects). For example, the clipCopy() method assumes you have something selected on the canvas. Considering again your experience with Fireworks, this probably makes sense. You don't apply a filter to nothing; you apply it to the active selection.

Individually, the methods exposed via Fireworks are not that special. It's their combination, however, that can result in a very powerful, time-saving addition to the Fireworks toolset. Consider any operation that you perform monotonously, and then consider the subtle variations you make in executing that task each time. It's the variations that can be extracted into a custom interface, acting as variables into your repetitive task. You can then plug those variables into Fireworks API calls and reclaim some lost time.

So, with that basic overview out of the way, let's get to it!

Defining a Fireworks workflow

Since this chapter is, after all, about workflow, how about defining one? Read and reread the following workflow. The sections that follow will breathe life into these steps and give you a clear understanding of each stage in the development process.

1. Create the JSF command file.
2. Create the UI (using Flash or Flex).
3. Import the JSF command text into the UI project.
4. Execute JSF commands in Flash or Flex using MMExecute().
5. Export/Publish the SWF and test it within Fireworks.

Let's summarize that list in sentence form. Start by creating a JSF command and test that command in Fireworks. Then, create a user interface using either Flash or Flex. Once you have your interface in place, you need to have Fireworks execute your JSF command. This is achieved by calling the MMExecute() method in ActionScript and passing it the JSF you want to execute. Once you have everything in place in your UI, you publish a SWF to a special folder that Fireworks knows about.

That was the "trailer" paragraph. We hope you feel sufficiently enticed by the proposed workflow. Now for the movie!

Step 1: Creating a simple JSF command

Let's start by creating a simple JSF command. Without knowing any of the Fireworks API methods, you can quickly create a JSF file using the Fireworks History panel (select Window ➤ History from the main menu).

191

Using the History panel to create a command

Not only does the History panel show the recent actions you've performed, it lets you save a sequence of those actions as a Fireworks command file. Perform the following actions to create your first Fireworks command:

1. Create a new document.
2. Draw a rectangle on the canvas and change its fill color.
3. Select the steps you just performed in the History panel, and then click the Save icon.
4. When prompted for a command name, enter Draw Rect (see Figure 11-1).

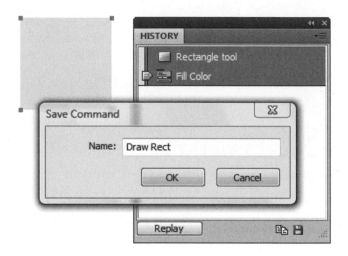

Figure 11-1. Creating a simple command using the History panel

After saving the command, you should now have a new menu item available from the main toolbar's Commands menu. Try deleting your rectangle and executing the command you just created (select Commands ➤ Draw Rect). If you saved the correct steps in your History panel, a new rectangle should appear with the same specifications as the one you previously created.

What just happened?

Fireworks created a new JSF file and saved it to a special directory on your hard drive. The file contains JavaScript code that performs the actions you selected in the History panel. Fireworks sees this new file and displays it in the list of commands in the Commands menu. When you select the command from the menu, the JavaScript within this file is interpreted and executed by the internal Fireworks JavaScript interpreter. This process is similar to a web browser executing JavaScript, and then manipulating the elements within its Document Object Model (DOM) based on the JavaScript. And, in the same way that web browsers provide a DOM that can be interacted with via JavaScript (document.getElementById(), for example), Fireworks exposes its DOM to be accessed via JavaScript.

Where is the command stored?

Fireworks commands that are saved from the History panel are stored in your user profile folder. These commands will be available only to you when logged in and not to other users. Commands can be copied to a common location so that they are available to all accounts if you are using a shared machine or if you log in with different accounts. Unlike command panels, when commands are added, Fireworks does not have to be restarted to recognize them. You can add new commands to either your user profile folder or the common folder at any time while Fireworks is running, and those commands will be available immediately via the Commands menu. The following details the location of the Commands and Command Panels folders on Windows XP, Vista, and Mac OS X.

Commands vs. command panels

Commands can either be pure JSF or SWF based. When executed, the command is run modally, meaning it has focus in the application for its entire life cycle. You cannot interact with anything else while the command is running. SWF-based commands are authored in the same way as command panels, but they cannot be persisted in Fireworks. Use commands for wizard-like operations.

Command panels use JSF to talk to Fireworks but *must* be SWF based. Command panels can be persisted in the UI and docked with other panels just like native Fireworks panels.

Note: There are some slight authoring differences between SWF-based commands and command panels not covered in this chapter.

- Commands **folder: current user**
  - **Windows XP**: C:\Documents and Settings\<User Name>\Application Data\Adobe\ Fireworks CS4\Commands
  - **Windows Vista**: C:\Users\<User Name>\AppData\Roaming\Adobe\Fireworks CS4\ Commands
  - **Mac OS X**: HD:Users:<User Name>:Library:Application Support:Adobe:Fireworks CS4:Commands

- Commands **folder: all users**
  - **Windows XP**: C:\Program Files\Adobe\Fireworks CS4\Configuration\Commands
  - **Windows Vista**: C:\Program Files\Adobe\Fireworks CS4\Configuration\Commands
  - **Mac OS X**: HD:Applications:Adobe:Fireworks CS4:Configuration:Commands

- Command Panels **folder: current user**
  - **Windows XP**: C:\Documents and Settings\<User Name>\Application Data\Adobe\ Fireworks CS4\Command Panels
  - **Windows Vista**: C:\Users\<User Name>\AppData\Roaming\Adobe\Fireworks CS4\ Command Panels
  - **Mac OS X**: HD:Users:<User>:Library:Application Support: Adobe:Fireworks CS4:Command Panels

- Command Panels **folder: all users**
    - **Windows XP**: C:\Program Files\Adobe\Fireworks CS4\Configuration\Command Panels
    - **Windows Vista**: C:\Program Files\Adobe\Fireworks CS4\Configuration\Command Panels
    - **Mac OS X**: HD:Applications:Adobe Fireworks CS4:Configuration:Command Panels

Editing and understanding the JSF

Now that you know where commands are stored, browse to the file that you just created, Draw Rect.jsf, and open it using your text editor of choice. At this stage in the process, the lightweight Notepad++ is a great choice that provides syntax highlighting. (Just select Language ➤ JavaScript so that Notepad++ interprets the JSF file as JavaScript.) If you followed our example earlier and saved the same history steps we did, you should see code similar to the following:

```
line 1: fw.getDocumentDOM().addNewRectanglePrimitive ➡
({left:36, top:39, right:101, bottom:104}, 0);
line 2: fw.getDocumentDOM().setFillColor("#99cc33");
```

Let's break this down so you understand what's happening. The two history steps you saved have been translated into two lines of JavaScript, each representing a specific history item. Notice that both of these lines begin with fw.getDocumentDOM(). This method call gets a reference to the DOM of the active Fireworks document. All of the methods that we call to operate on objects on the canvas are housed on the document's DOM.

> You can also access specific documents directly using the fw.documents object: fw.documents[documentIndex] returns the DOM for the specified document.

So, following the requisite call to access the current document's DOM is the actual method call. On line 1, the addNewRectanglePrimitive method is called. This method accepts two arguments: a boundingRectangle argument (of type Rectangle) and a roundness argument (of type double, where 0 equals no roundness and 1 equals 100% roundness). The Rectangle type includes four properties: left, top, right, and bottom, each of type float. The syntax used as the first argument for addNewRectanglePrimitive({left: 35, top: 39, right: 101, bottom: 104}) is a common way to define an object in JavaScript (and other languages).

> If you're wondering how we know what parameters these methods are expecting, we'll cover this later in the section "Navigating the Extending Fireworks documentation."

We could also have explicitly declared an object, and then set left, top, right, and bottom properties:

```
var myRect = new Object();
myRect.left = 36;
myRect.top = 39;
myRect.right = 101;
myRect.bottom = 104;
```

```
var cornerRadius = 0;
fw.getDocumentDOM().addNewRectanglePrimitive(myRect, cornerRadius);
```

That pretty much covers the details of line 1. A rectangle will be created with the specified bounding box and corner radius. The second line sets the color of the newly created rectangle by calling the setFillColor method. setFillColor accepts a hexadecimal color string of the format #RRGGBB or #RRGGBBAA, where AA represents opacity (alpha).

Remember how we said earlier that most methods operate on selected objects? You may be wondering how we selected the rectangle that was just added. The answer is that we didn't need to. Consider any time that you've drawn a rectangle on the canvas—after drawing the rectangle, it's automatically selected, right? The same is true when you add an object via code; it becomes the active selection.

Experiment with the values passed to addNewRectanglePrimitive and setFillColor, save Draw Rect. jsf, and rerun the command within Fireworks. You can get immediate feedback on changes to your code via the Commands menu. You have now performed actions that you will perform countless times if you proceed with Fireworks extension development (change code, save, test in Fireworks).

Step 2: Creating a Flash UI

The first phase of this workflow focuses on creating a working JSF file and testing that file in Fireworks. The sample we looked at was extremely simple and didn't require much testing. Really complex panels, however, can often be difficult to debug. It's sometimes hard to determine whether the bug is in your JSF or in your panel's ActionScript. By working with and testing pure JSF via the Commands menu before moving into a panel, you can be confident that the underlying JSF is working correctly.

Creating a document and adding a button

Now that you have a working, tested JSF file, it's time to create a command panel that gives the underlying command a face. We'll keep things simple at first and show you how to create a panel in Flash that executes the JSF code defined in Draw Rect.jsf.

1. Start by creating a new Flash document (select an ActionScript 2 project for now).

2. Set the document width to 250 pixels (px) and the height to 300 px. The size that you define on your document becomes the minimum size of the panel in Fireworks. The panel can be sized larger than this in Fireworks but never smaller.

3. Now, add a Button component to the stage (note that Flash uses the term "stage" instead of "canvas"), and give it an instance name of executeJSF_btn.

4. Set the component's Label property to Execute JSF, as shown in Figure 11-2.

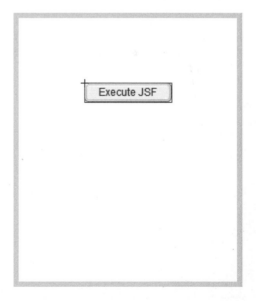

Figure 11-2. Adding a Button to the stage in Flash

195

Steps 3 and 4: Importing and executing the JSF

Flash panels pass JSF to Fireworks via the MMExecute() method in ActionScript. When an exported SWF is run inside Fireworks as a Flash panel, MMExecute() passes the JavaScript directly to Fireworks. Fireworks then executes the JavaScript and returns the resulting value to Flash (if any):

```
var result = MMExecute(jsfCode);
```

The JavaScript is passed to MMExecute() as a string, which means you must escape quotation marks and potentially double-escape text that has already been escaped in JavaScript strings. That sounds more confusing than it actually is. The following example executes the setFillColor() line of code in Flash using MMExecute():

```
MMExecute("fw.getDocumentDOM().setFillColor(\"#99cc33\");");
```

Notice that the entire string is wrapped with quotation marks, and the inner quotes surrounding #99cc33 have been escaped: \"#99cc33\". For single lines of JavaScript, this method of execution works well. As your JavaScript grows in complexity, however, escaping large sequences of code becomes laborious and introduces the potential for error.

One way around this for simple commands is to paste the JSF into a Flash TextField. Let's use this approach for our Draw Rect example:

1. Create a new TextField on the stage.
2. Change its text type to Dynamic Text and give it an instance name of jsfCode_txt (see Figure 11-3).
3. Move this TextField off the stage so that it is not visible at runtime.
4. Paste the contents of the Draw Rect command directly into this TextField.

The Fireworks JavaScript is now available to you directly within the Flash document, accessible via jsfCode_txt.text, and you didn't have to make any modifications to the code at all.

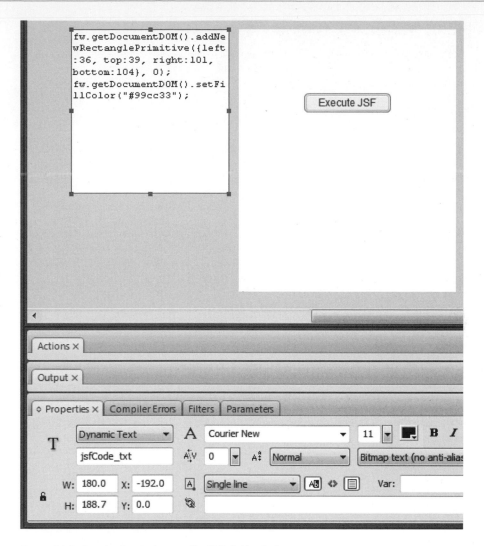

Figure 11-3. Copying JavaScript to a TextField in Flash

Adding the Mouse.onRelease event handler

With all of the pieces in place on the Flash stage, it's now time to add an event handler to the button's onRelease event and execute the JSF:

1. Create a new layer in the timeline.
2. Change the layer name to Actions.
3. Lock the layer.
4. Open the Actions panel and add the following code to Frame 1 of the Actions layer:

```
executeJSF_btn.onRelease = function() {
    MMExecute(jsfCode_txt.text);
}
```

When the button is clicked, MMExecute() will be called with the value of the TextBlock passed as the argument.

Step 5: Publishing and testing the SWF

You're now ready to publish your new command panel as a SWF and test it in Fireworks. This is the exciting part! Refer to the "Commands vs. command paths" section earlier in this chapter to locate the correct Command Panels folder for your operating system. Once you have the correct path, export your current file as Draw Rect.swf to that location.

> *Because this is the first time you are exporting the file, you will have to restart Fireworks in order to see the new command panel in the* Window *menu of Fireworks. For subsequent exports, you can just close the panel in Fireworks and reopen it to see your latest version.*

Once you've restarted Fireworks, open the new panel from the main menu by selecting Window ➤ Draw Rect. You should now see your Execute JSF button in a new panel. Let's test this thing! Create a new document, and then click the Execute JSF button. If you've followed along correctly, a new rectangle should appear on the stage, just as it does when you select Draw Rect from the Commands menu.

Congratulations! You've now created your first custom Flash panel for Fireworks!

> *Change the publish path in Flash via* File ➤ Publish Settings *to the Command Panels folder you just exported to. Publish by selecting* File ➤ Publish *(press Alt+F+B to navigate the main menu quickly) or by pressing Shift/Cmd+F12, all from the comfort of your keyboard.*

This simple example illustrates an effective workflow for developing Flash panels. You started by creating a JSF command and testing that command within Fireworks. When you knew it was performing as expected, you copied the JSF into a Flash TextField. You then added code to execute the JSF when a button was clicked within Flash.

Building a functional UI in Flash

The Draw Rect sample covered just the basics. You saw how to execute JSF from a command panel, but the panel didn't provide any enhanced functionality at all. It performed the exact same action as the Draw Rect.jsf run from the Commands menu. Let's build on the Draw Rect sample and create a functional UI.

The scenario: Update the Draw Rect UI to include left, top, height, width, and cornerRadius TextBlocks and a ColorPicker component. To support this behavior, we need to update the JSF, converting the inline code into a function that can be called.

In the following JSF code, we've created a function named CreateRectangle that accepts all of these values as parameters:

```
// Test the CreateRectangle Function
CreateRectangle(10,10,100,50, 10, "#FFCC00");

function CreateRectangle(left, top, width, height, cornerRadius, color)
{
   var rect = new Object();
   rect.left = left;
   rect.top = top;
   rect.right = left + width;
   rect.bottom = top + height;

   fw.getDocumentDOM().addNewRectanglePrimitive(rect, cornerRadius);
   fw.getDocumentDOM().setFillColor(color);
}
```

Draw Rect.jsf updated with the CreateRectangle function

The CreateRectangle function accepts width and height instead of right and bottom parameters. Thinking in terms of a bounding box is unnatural for most people, so we do the translation from width and height to right and bottom in the CreateRectangle function. Notice that we have a sample function call in the preceding listing. Remember, we do as much testing in the JSF via the Commands menu as possible to ensure that the JSF is working correctly.

After a couple of run-throughs and corrections (the first time we tested we forgot the .getDocumentDOM() before setFillColor), we are confident in the function. We will now copy the function to the TextBlock inside Flash. Figure 11-4 shows the updated TextBlock.

```
function
CreateRectangle(left,
top, width, height,
cornerRadius, color)
{
var rect = new Object();
rect.left = left;
rect.top = top;
rect.right = left +
width;
rect.bottom = top +
height;

fw.getDocumentDOM().addNe
wRectanglePrimitive(rect,
cornerRadius);
fw.getDocumentDOM().setFi
llColor(color);
}
```

Execute JSF

Figure 11-4. Flash TextBlock housing JSF code

It's now time to update the UI to support the added flexibility provided by the new JSF.

Start by creating four instances of the NumericStepper component (available from the Components panel as shown in Figure 11-5) and name them nsX, nsY, nsWidth, nsHeight, and nsCornerRadius.

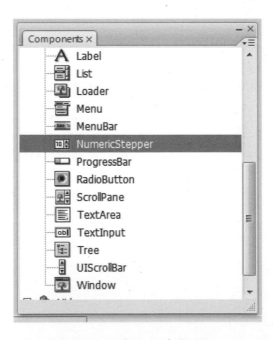

Figure 11-5. Selecting the NumericStepper component

Figure 11-6 shows the new layout with all of the NumericSteppers in place. We've also added labels to make it clear what each control represents and some moderate styling to give this panel a little personality.

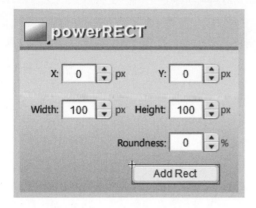

Figure 11-6. Updated panel layout in Flash

Using a NumericStepper instead of a TextInput component will let us enforce certain value ranges—you don't want someone entering "thirty" for the width, for example. For all of the controls besides nsCornerRadius, set the minimum property to 0 and the maximum property to 10,000. For nsCornerRadius, set the minimum to 0 and maximum to 100. Even though the CreateRectangle function expects a cornerRadius in the 0–1 range, we think users will expect a value in the 0–100 range. A simple division by 100 will take care of the discrepancy. Figure 11-7 shows the Component inspector in Flash with the nsCornerRadius NumericStepper control selected.

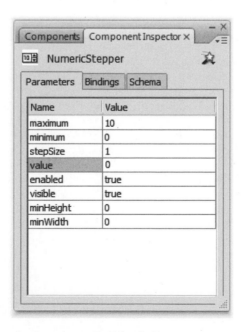

Figure 11-7. Setting NumericStepper values via the Component inspector

With all of the controls in place, with the exception of the ColorPicker, it's now time to update the ActionScript event handler for the Add Rectangle button. The ColorPicker will be a little more involved, so we'll add it in a minute. Return to the executeJSF_btn.onRelease event handler on the actions timeline and update the ActionScript with the following:

```
executeJSF_btn.onRelease = function() {
    // Execute the JSF, creating the CreateRectangle function
    MMExecute(jsfCode_txt.text);

    // Calculate the CornerRadius value
    var cornerRadius:Number = nsCornerRadius.value / 100;

    // Call CreateRectangle
    MMExecute("CreateRectangle(" + nsX.value + "," + nsY.value + ➥
"," + nsWidth.value + "," + nsHeight.value + "," + ➥
cornerRadius.toString() + ", '#FF0000');");
}
```

The first thing we do is execute the JSF contained in the TextBlock. Instead of the original JSF that created a rectangle when executed, this just registers the function definition. Now the function CreateRectangle will be available as long as Fireworks is running. After executing the JSF, the value of the nsCornerRadius NumericStepper is divided by 100. This gives us a value in the 0–1 range—the value expected by the Fireworks createRectanglePrimitive method. With those two housekeeping steps out of the way, it's now time to actually call the CreateRectangle function, passing it values from Flash UI elements. Again, use MMExecute(), this time dynamically building the parameter string, directly injecting the NumericStepper values. For now, we'll use a hard-coded color value (#FF0000). Later this value will be replaced with a value from the ColorPicker.

Working with returned values: Adding a ColorPicker

It's great that we can now define the size and location of a rectangle from within our panel, but we're still missing the crucial color component. We could just add a TextBlock and accept a straight hexadecimal string, or we could take advantage of Fireworks' built-in ColorPicker. Remember, just about everything that the Fireworks core is capable of has been exposed via the API, and the ColorPicker is no exception. We can launch the ColorPicker by calling the fw.popupColorPickerOverMouse() method. Notice that this method is defined directly on the Fireworks (fw) object and not the DOM object. This is because the ColorPicker itself isn't performing an action on a specific document but is instead providing general-purpose functionality. When called, the native Fireworks color picker will be launched. Once a color is selected, the value will be returned in the #RRGGBBAA format. Figure 11-8 shows the command panel updated with a new MovieClip named ColorPicker_mc. This MovieClip has a custom method named SetColor that, when called, paints the ColorPicker with the specified color. (Open the sample files for this chapter to see how this is achieved.)

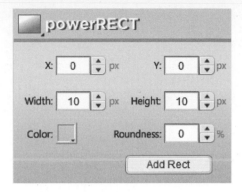

Figure 11-8. ColorPicker MovieClip added
to the stage

With the MovieClip in place on the stage, add an event handler for its onRelease event and call
fw.popupColorPickerOverMouse() via MMExecute(). MMExecute() will return a color value in the
#RRGGBBAA format that can then be passed to the SetColor method defined on ColorPicker_mc.
Following is the ActionScript event handler for ColorPicker_mc.onRelease:

```
var currentColor:String = "#FF0000";
colorPicker_mc.onRelease = function()
{
    currentColor = MMExecute("fw.popupColorPickerOverMouse('" + ➥
currentColor + "',false,false);");
    colorPicker_mc.SetColor(currentColor);
}
```

The popupColorPickerOverMouse method accepts three parameters: initialColor, allowTransparent,
and forceWeb216. The resulting value is stored in the variable currentColor and passed directly to the
SetColor method of ColorPicker_mc. The following code demonstrates how the SetColor method
works with the Fireworks-returned color value. Like many values returned from Fireworks (or Flash
values going to Fireworks), the value has to be massaged into a format that makes sense to Flash.

```
function SetColor(color:String)
{
    rectTarget_mc.clear();
    rectTarget_mc.moveTo(0,0);
    rectTarget_mc.beginFill(parseInt("0x" + color.substr(1, 6)), 100);
    rectTarget_mc.lineTo(22,0);
    rectTarget_mc.lineTo(22,22);
    rectTarget_mc.lineTo(0,22);
    rectTarget_mc.lineTo(0,0);
    rectTarget_mc.endFill();
}
```

In this method, the Flash Drawing API is used to draw a rectangle directly into an empty MovieClip named rectTarget_mc. rectTarget_mc is prepositioned on the stage and serves as the selected color swatch. The third line of ActionScript

```
(rectTarget_mc.beginFill(parseInt("0x" + color.substr(1, 6)), 100);)
```

demonstrates how to convert the color string returned from Fireworks into a hexadecimal value that Flash can use in its beginFill method. This solid color conversion example is an easy one. The Gradient panel that I wrote has to convert back and forth between the Fireworks gradient format and the Flash gradient format constantly throughout its life cycle. After publishing the SWF (press Alt+F+B or Shift/Cmd+F12) and testing Draw Rect.swf, the ColorPicker now works as expected, launching the native Fireworks color picker and drawing the selected color in the Flash panel. However, there's still one piece missing: the Add Rect button's event handler needs to be updated to take advantage of the selected color. Back to the code:

```
executeJSF_btn.onRelease = function() {
    // Execute the JSF, creating the CreateRectangle function
    MMExecute(jsfCode_txt.text);

    // Calculate the CornerRadius value
    var cornerRadius:Number = nsCornerRadius.value / 100;

    // Call CreateRectangle
    MMExecute("CreateRectangle(" + nsX.value + "," + nsY.value ➡
+ "," + nsWidth.value + "," + nsHeight.value + "," ➡
+ cornerRadius.toString() + ", '" + currentColor + "');");
}
```

Notice that the hard-coded #FF0000 color string has been replaced with the currentColor variable in the second MMExecute() call. After publishing again, you can select a color, click Add Rect, and the selected color is applied as expected!

This is just one example of many cases where Fireworks and Flash values vary to a certain extent. You have to know the differences between ActionScript requirements and the Fireworks object model and convert these values into something that can be used.

Streamlining your workflow with the Fireworks developer toolbox

So far we've shown you how to execute JSF inline via MMExecute() and by including the JSF in a TextBlock on the design surface. You'll never get away from the first method completely, but you should not have to rely on it exclusively. The TextBlock method gives you a way to import your JSF without having to escape all of your JSF. This is great for small chunks of JSF but introduces another manual step that can result in errors. Having to copy and paste all of your JSF code from a text editor to the design surface in Flash becomes laborious, and it's one of those steps that can drive you crazy.

Fortunately, there's another approach that can streamline your workflow even further, and it doesn't change the workflow proposed at the beginning of this chapter. It actually continues to enable it for complex projects that include large amounts of JSF. Instead of copying the JSF to a TextBlock, you can export the JSF as a single ActionScript variable defined in an AS file, and then use ActionScript's #include to import the variable into your project. You then use MMExecute() just as you did with the TextBlock, only this time passing it the variable name defined in the external AS file. This actually requires that you escape the entire JSF file again, something that we were trying to get you away from earlier. Fortunately, this is not something you have to do manually. While creating the FW to XAML Exporter panel, I created the Fireworks Developer Toolbox (FDT), a utility that does the escaping and conversion to ActionScript for you automatically, which you'll see how to use momentarily. First, let's review where we've come from and see how this latest solution is really just another evolution of the process. In the first MMExecute() examples, we defined the JSF string inline as the method parameter:MMExecute(fw.popupColorPickerOverMouse(),"),.

We then moved the JSF directly to a TextBlock and accessed the TextBlock's text property to execute JSF:MMExecute(jsfCode_txt.text);.

What we haven't demonstrated is how to define a variable that houses the JSF code, and then pass that variable to Fireworks via MMExecute(). In this approach, we have to escape the string values again:

```
var jsfCode:String = "fw.getDocumentDOM().setFillColor(\""#FF0000\");";
MMExecute(jsfCode);
```

Taking this one step further, instead of defining the variable jsfCode inline in the Flash file, we can create an external AS file that defines the variable:

```
// Contents of jsfCode.as
var jsfCode:String = "fw.popupColorPickerOverMouse();";
```

We can now use #include to include the contents of the external AS file. The variable jsfCode can be accessed exactly as if it had been defined inline:

```
// ActionScript within Flash File
#include "jsfCode.as"
colorPicker_mc.onRelease = function()
{
    // Execute JSF defined in jsfCode variable,
    // housed in external jsfCode.as file
    MMExecute(jsfCode);
}
```

This may seem like a step in the wrong direction, having to convert the JSF code to a string variable. Fortunately, the FDT will do this automatically.

Converting JSF to AS using the FDT

Converting the JSF file to an ActionScript file is easy using the FDT. Launch the FDT (which is available with the files for this chapter or at www.granthinkson.com/tools/fireworks), and then select the ActionScript Conversion tab as shown in Figure 11-9. On this tab, you select your source JSF file and the destination AS file, and define the ActionScript variable name that the JSF will be assigned to. Once you've targeted your files and defined the variable name, just click the convert button, and the AS file will either be created or overwritten. You can also check the Auto Convert when Source File Changed option on this tab. When enabled, the FDT will watch for file changes and automatically perform the conversion in the background. When you step back to Flash, you don't have to remember to click convert in the FDT.

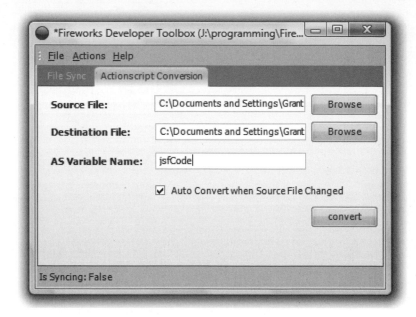

Figure 11-9. FDT ActionScript conversion

Following is the original `CreateRectangle` function introduced earlier in the chapter, housed in `Draw Rect.jsf`:

```
function CreateRectangle(left, top, width, height, cornerRadius, color)
{
    var rect = new Object();
    rect.left = left;
    rect.top = top;
    rect.right = left + width;
    rect.bottom = top + height;

    fw.getDocumentDOM().addNewRectanglePrimitive(rect, cornerRadius);
    fw.getDocumentDOM().setFillColor(color);
}
```

The following code listing shows the contents of `Draw Rect.as` after being converted to an ActionScript variable using FDT:`var jsfCode:String = "":`

```
+ "function CreateRectangle(left, top, width, height, ➥
cornerRadius, color)\n"
+ "{\n"
+ "    var rect = new Object();\n"
```

```
+ "    rect.left = left;\n"
+ "    rect.top = top;\n"
+ "    rect.right = left + width;\n"
+ "    rect.bottom = top + height;\n"
+ "    \n"
+ "    fw.getDocumentDOM().addNewRectanglePrimitive(rect, ➥
cornerRadius);\n"
+ "    fw.getDocumentDOM().setFillColor(color);\n"
+ "}\n"
+ "";
```

The entire contents of the JSF source file specified in the FDT have been converted to a string, escaped correctly, and assigned to the variable name specified, in this case jsfCode. You can now use the #include method introduced earlier and reference this AS file. With the AutoConvert option enabled, you'll be able to edit, save, and test your JSF, and then switch to Flash and recompile, without having to manually import/update the JSF code in your Flash project.

Updating the Draw Rect panel

Now that you have an external AS file housing your JSF, you can remove the code-housing TextBlock that you added earlier in the chapter. The only other thing you need to do is update the ActionScript on your Actions layer to reference the external file and execute the JSF variable:

```
#include "jsfCode.as"
executeJSF_btn.onRelease = function() {
    // Execute the JSF, creating the CreateRectangle function
    MMExecute(jsfCode);

    // Calculate the CornerRadius value
    var cornerRadius:Number = nsCornerRadius.value / 100;

    // Call CreateRectangle
    MMExecute("CreateRectangle(" + nsX.value + "," + nsY.value ➥
+ "," + nsWidth.value + "," + nsHeight.value + "," ➥
+ cornerRadius.toString() + ", '" + currentColor + "');");
}
```

With the exception of adding the #include statement, the only other change required in the ActionScript is the MMExecute() statement—jsfCode_txt.text was replaced with jsfCode, the variable name defined in the FDT. This now concludes the workflow section of the chapter. We've worked our way from the ground up, starting with a simple JSF command and ultimately creating a fully functional Flash panel.

Defining Flash panel resize behavior

When creating Fireworks panels, you must be aware that the user can resize the panel, just like any other panel you encounter in Fireworks. When authoring panels in Flash (and not Flex), we have to manually define the resize behavior. Flex provides layout panels that automatically react to stage resizing, so this section can pretty much be ignored if you're planning to exclusively author your panels in Flex.

By default, Flash SWFs scale when resized—not the behavior expected by users. Go ahead and try resizing the Draw Rect panel you just created. All of the elements should scale in size, as if you had zoomed in on the stage in Flash. Scaling can easily be prevented by adding the following ActionScript to Frame 1 of the Actions layer in the movie's main timeline:

```
Stage.scaleMode = "noScale";
Stage.align = "TL";
```

The first property tells Flash not to scale/stretch its content when resized; the second property tells Flash to anchor its content to the top-left (TL) corner of the Flash Player window. Go ahead and update your Draw Rect panel with these changes, republish, and then test the panel. Figure 11-10 shows these settings in action.

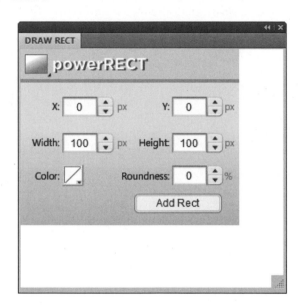

Figure 11-10. Basic scaleMode and align properties set

The panel is no longer scaling, but none of the elements on the stage actually react to the resizing, they just *don't* scale. Cosmetically, this is definitely an improvement, but it still doesn't get us all the way there. Take the Add Rect button, for example. It is common practice to have the main dialog command button anchored to the lower-right corner of the dialog window. This can be achieved by handling the stage object's onResize event in ActionScript:

```
Stage.onResize = function()
{
    // Define a common margin
    var MARGIN:Number = 10;

    // Manually update the position of executeJSF_btn
    executeJSF_btn._left = Stage.width - executeJSF_btn.width - MARGIN;
    executeJSF_btn._top = Stage.height - executeJSF_btn.height - MARGIN;
```

```
        // TODO: Manually update positions of all other elements on stage
}
```

Updating the position of the single button was not that bad—it just took a couple of lines of ActionScript. However, that's just for the single button on the stage. We really want the header and background artwork to stretch as the panel is resized. For panels with more UI elements, our resize desires will grow in complexity. Enter the AlignmentManager extension for Flash. I wrote this Flash panel a few years ago to save time when creating resizable Flash layouts. (Note: This panel was written in ActionScript 2 and will not work with ActionScript 3 projects. I don't currently have plans to update this as I see the Flex layout controls as a replacement for this panel.)

The AlignmentManager is included as an MXP in the Utilities folder of the resource files for this chapter. After installing it via the Flash Extension Manager, you should see AlignmentManager listed in the Components panel under the Infragistics section, as shown in Figure 11-11.

Drag an instance of the component onto the stage, and then open the Component inspector in Flash (Window ➤ Component Inspector). Figure 11-12 shows the custom Property inspector for the AlignmentManager component. The managed MovieClips listed are elements on the Draw Rect stage.

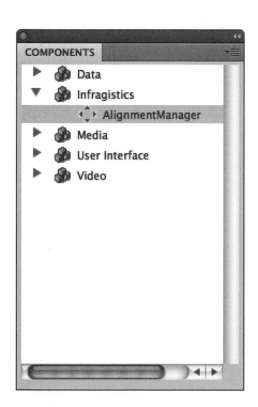

Figure 11-11. AlignmentManager Flash component

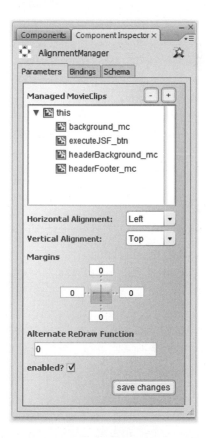

Figure 11-12. Managing MovieClips with the AlignmentManager

209

The AlignmentManager can manage only objects that are MovieClips, so the header artwork has been converted to a MovieClip and given an instance name of headerBackground_mc. With the headerBackground_mc item selected in the MovieClip tree, you can specify values for HorizontalAlignment, VerticalAlignment, and Margins. After making changes, you have to click the save changes button (an admitted quirk of the panel).

We've included an alternative version of the Draw Rect sample file that uses the AlignmentManager to completely define the resize behavior of the panel. (See the version of Draw Rect.fla located in the source projects folder as "Draw Rect/4. Using the Alignment Manager/Draw Rect.fla".) The final version behaves nicely as it is resized in Fireworks. Republish Draw Rect.fla to see the final layout behavior in Fireworks as the panel is resized:

- The background artwork stretches to fill the panel.
- The header background stretches horizontally.
- The logo remains anchored to the top-left corner.
- Configuration fields remain anchored to the top-left corner.
- The Add Rect button anchors to the lower-right corner.

Coding this resize behavior by hand would have taken a long time and be very frustrating to maintain. Using this panel empowers you to deliver expected layout results in a fraction of the time you would spend hand-coding the same behavior.

Responding to Fireworks events

Up to this point, we've been pretty much oblivious to what's been going on around us in Fireworks. We haven't cared about selection changes or tool changes or documents opening or closing. We've just focused our attention on one thing: creating rectangles. For content creation panels, this is fine, but for panels that need to respond to selection changes (such as the Gradient panel), we need a way to react to such changes. Fireworks provides a number of events that we can listen for and handle directly via ActionScript. We'll show you how to handle these in ActionScript 2 (since we've been using ActionScript 2 exclusively so far) and save the ActionScript 3 demonstration for the section "Building panels with ActionScript 3" later in the chapter.

Detecting change of selection

Let's start by handling the onFwActiveSelectionChange event. This event is raised any time you select a different object on the Fireworks design surface. With the Gradient panel, we handle this event and redraw the brush preview based on the fill of the selected object. Fireworks event handling is a little different from traditional event handling. In Fireworks, you simply define an ActionScript function with the name of the event you wish you handle. When Fireworks checks for event handlers, it will find your matching function name and register it. Any time the event is raised, your function will be called.

The following ActionScript defines a function named onFwActiveSelectionChange. When the selection changes in Fireworks, an alert box is displayed.

```
function onFwActiveSelectionChange()
{
    MMExecute("alert('Selection Changed!');");

    // Do something with the selected object, like retrieve its color
    // var currentColor:String;
    // currentColor = MMExecute("fw.selection[0].pathAttributes➡
    .fillColor");
}
```

> *This function needs to be defined at the _global level, meaning you should define these event handlers either on the* Actions *layer or in an #include ActionScript file. Defining event handlers on nested MovieClips will render them useless.*

Detecting tool changes

When the active tool changes in Fireworks (from the Pointer to the Text tool, for example), the onFwActiveToolChange event is raised. Because no arguments are passed with this event, you have to define a variable named fwActiveToolForSWFs in order to access the name of the active tool. Once this variable is defined, Fireworks will update its value with the name of the currently active tool. The following ActionScript defines the fwActiveToolForSWFs variable and handles the onFwActiveToolChange event. When the event is raised, the name of the active tool is displayed in an alert box.

```
// Define variable to hold name of Active Tool
var fwActiveToolForSWFs:String;

// Active Selection Change Event Handler
function onFwActiveToolChange()
{
    MMExecute("alert('Tool Changed: " + fwActiveToolForSWFs + "');");
}
```

These are two of the most common events that you'll need to handle in your custom panels, though there are a number of other events raised by Fireworks, such as onFwStartMovie and onFwStopMovie, raised when your panel starts and stops, respectively. The list of Fireworks events can be found in the *Extending Fireworks* documentation at Cross-Product Extensions ➤ Flash panels ➤ Events ➤ Creating event handlers.

Building panels with ActionScript 3

We've spent most of the chapter looking at how to create Flash panels using ActionScript 2. ActionScript 2 is more accessible for most hobbyist programmers than ActionScript 3, and you'll find most examples of Flash panels available online today have been authored with ActionScript 2 (either because they were authored prior to ActionScript 3, or because ActionScript 2 *is* more accessible). However, many of the panels that ship with Fireworks CS4 have been reauthored using Flex and ActionScript 3.

In this section, we'll first show you how to use ActionScript 3 in Flash to author custom panels, and then introduce you to Flex panel authoring.

Creating ActionScript 3 panels in Flash

The concepts we've covered so far are all still valid when creating ActionScript 3–based panels. There are just a few things that we have to do differently to ensure communication between the SWF and Fireworks. When authoring ActionScript 3 panels, start by specifying a document class for the FLA. Figure 11-13 shows the class DrawRect specified as our document class in Flash.

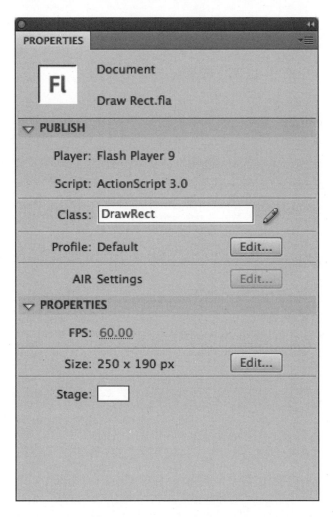

Figure 11-13. Specifying a document class using the Flash Property inspector

Now create a Draw Rect.as file and save it in the same folder as Draw Rect.fla. We've re-created the original Draw Rect layout in a new ActionScript 3 file and added the actions layer as we did earlier.

ActionScript 3 still supports the concept of "including" external files, only you don't need to include the # symbol. So, the first thing we do is update the include statement:

```
// Import External JSF
include "jsf/jsfCode.as"
```

The rest of the code will be moved to the new Draw Rect.as file and will need to be modified slightly. Start by defining the package and DrawRect class:

```
package {
    import flash.display.*;
    import flash.events.*;
    import flash.text.*;
    import flash.external.ExternalInterface;
    import adobe.utils.*;

    public class DrawRect extends MovieClip
    {

    }
}
```

Note that the flash.external.ExternalInterface and adobe.utils.* packages have been imported. These are required in order to communicate with Fireworks. Now assign event handlers to the buttons, this time using the addEventListener method:

```
public class DrawRect extends MovieClip
{
    // Add Button Event Handlers
    executeJSF_btn.addEventListener(MouseEvent.CLICK,
                                    executeJSF_onRelease);
    colorPicker_mc.addEventListener(MouseEvent.CLICK,
                                    colorPicker_onRelease);
}

// Event Handlers
function executeJSF_onRelease(e:Event):void
{
    // Execute the JSF, creating the CreateRectangle function
    MMExecute(jsfCode);

    // Calculate the CornerRadius value
    var cornerRadius:Number = nsCornerRadius.value / 100;

    // Call CreateRectangle
    MMExecute("CreateRectangle(" + nsX.value + "," + nsY.value + "," +
            nsWidth.value + "," + nsHeight.value + "," +
            cornerRadius.toString() + ", '" + currentColor + "');");
}
```

The changes here are minor and no different than any ActionScript 2 to ActionScript 3 migration. With the event handlers in place and assigned, this FLA can be published and executed in Fireworks. The functionality should be equivalent between the two. Note that MMExecute(jsfCode) has remained the same. Since ActionScript 3 supports the include statement, our workflow has remained relatively unchanged.

Responding to Fireworks events in ActionScript 3

Responding to Fireworks events in ActionScript 3 is a bit more structured than in ActionScript 2. Whereas in ActionScript 2 you simply define a function with the name of the event, in ActionScript 3 you must register an event handler for the events you want to listen to (just like we registered event handlers for our buttons using addEventListener). The following code shows how to register Fireworks events using the ExternalInterface object:

```
// Constructor
public function DrawRect()
{
  // Register all Fireworks Event Handlers
  ExternalInterface.addCallback("IsFwCallbackInstalled", ➡
IsFwCallbackInstalled);
  ExternalInterface.addCallback("onFwActiveToolChange", ➡
onFwActiveToolChange);
  ExternalInterface.addCallback("setfwActiveToolForSWFs", ➡
setfwActiveToolForSWFs);
  ExternalInterface.addCallback("onFwActiveSelectionChange", ➡
onFwActiveSelectionChange);
}

// Fireworks calls IsFwCallbackInstalled whenever an event is generated
// Return true when you wish to handle the event.
function IsFwCallbackInstalled(funcName:String):Boolean
{
  switch( funcName )
  {
    case "onFwActiveToolChange":
      return true;

    case "setfwActiveToolForSWFs":
      return true;

    case "onFwActiveSelectionChange" :
      return true;

    default :
      return false;
  }
}
```

```
// onFwActiveSelectionChange Event Handler
// Get the color of the currently selected object
// (only works for solid fills)
function onFwActiveSelectionChange()
{
  currentColor = MMExecute("fw.selection[0].pathAttributes.fillColor");
  colorPicker_mc.SetColor(currentColor);
}
```

The first event that we are handling is IsFwCallbackInstalled. Before sending an event like onFwActiveSelectionChange to the panel, Fireworks first raises the IsFwCallbackInstalled event as a sort of polling mechanism. The event passes a single string argument representing the name of the event Fireworks is about to raise. If you want to handle the event, your function should return true; otherwise, it should return false. This is commonly achieved by using a switch statement, as demonstrated in the previous code sample.

When you return true, the actual event is raised on your panel, and your event handler code is executed. So, handling Fireworks events in ActionScript 3 is really a two-step process. You first handle the IsFwCallbackInstalled event and respond with the true value to events that you want to handle, and then you actually handle the event you're interested in.

The updated sample in the AS3 Flash Panel folder includes a fully working ActionScript 3 version of the Draw Rect example. In the ActionScript 3 version, the onFwActiveSelectionChange event is handled, and the value of the ColorPicker is updated based on the fill value of the selected object.

Creating ActionScript 3 panels in Flex

This section assumes you are familiar with the Flex environment and the Flex programming model. Aside from the differences between Flex and Flash, enabling your Flex project to work with the workflow presented in this chapter is a natural evolution of what you've seen thus far. The following code shows the <mx:Application> tag of DrawRect.mxml, the Flex version of the Draw Rect example we've been using:

```
<mx:Application
    xmlns:mx="http://www.adobe.com/2006/mxml"
    layout="absolute"
    minWidth="250" minHeight="190"
    initialize="init()"
    creationComplete="UpdateLayout()"
    width="250" height="200">

    <mx:Script>
      <![CDATA[
      include "jsf/jsfCode.as";

      import mx.containers.HBox;
      import adobe.utils.*;
        ...
```

Notice that we are handling both the initialize event and the creationComplete event. The init() method specified as the event handler for initialize registers all of the Fireworks event handlers that were previously handled in the DrawRect constructor of the Flash ActionScript 3 project. We can still use the include statement to read in JSF code. We've done this on the first line in the <mx:Script> section: include "jsf/jsfCode.as". The jsfCode variable defined in the external file is accessible as a member of this application, which means we can continue to load the external JSF variable using MMExecute(jsfCode).

Note also that adobe.utils.* is now imported and flash.external.ExternalInterface is not. Following is the init method, defined in the CDATA section of <mx:Script />:

```
private function init():void
{
    // Register all Fireworks Event Handlers
    ExternalInterface.addCallback("IsFwCallbackInstalled", ➡
IsFwCallbackInstalled);
    ExternalInterface.addCallback("onFwDocumentOpen",onFwDocumentOpen);
    ExternalInterface.addCallback("onFwDocumentClose", ➡
onFwDocumentClose);
    ExternalInterface.addCallback("onFwActiveToolChange", ➡
onFwActiveToolChange);
    ExternalInterface.addCallback("setfwActiveToolForSWFs", ➡
setfwActiveToolForSWFs);
    ExternalInterface.addCallback("onFwActiveSelectionChange", ➡
onFwActiveSelectionChange);

    // Handle Resize Event of Panel
    this.parent.addEventListener(Event.RESIZE, UpdateLayout);
}

private function UpdateLayout(e:*=null):void
{
    this.width  = this.parent.width;
    this.height = this.parent.height;
}
```

As in Flash ActionScript 3 projects, ExternalInterface.addCallback is used in Flex to register event handlers for Fireworks events, like onFwActiveSelectionChange or onFwDocumentOpen. We have also added an event handler to the Event.RESIZE event of the movie. When this event is fired, the UpdateLayout method is called, which updates the size of this application to match the size of the parent window. Without this event handler in place, the Flex layout will not resize in Fireworks as expected. Figure 11-14 shows the DrawRect Flex project open in Adobe Flex Builder. We have used the native Flex components to re-create the original Flash panel in Flex. Instead of using a component like AlignmentManager to handle layout, we now rely on the Flex panels and their support for dynamic repositioning and scaling at runtime.

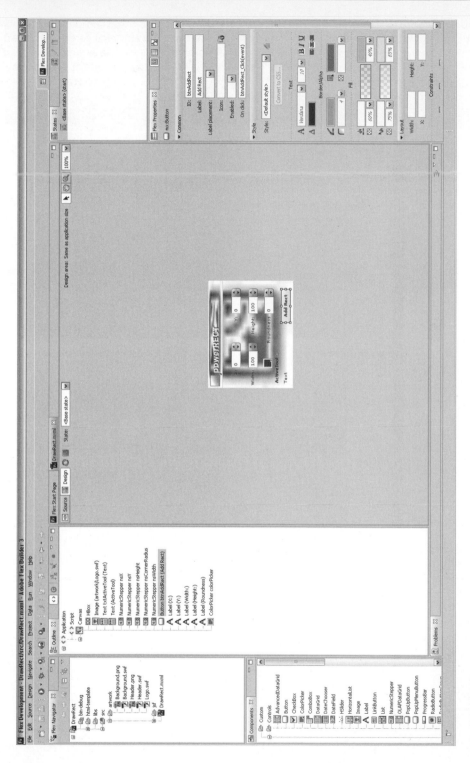

Figure 11-14. Authoring DrawRect in Flex Builder

And, just like setting the publish path in Flash, we always set the Flex build path of the active project to the Fireworks Command Panels folder for fast testing. You can change the Flex build path by right-clicking the project in the Flex Navigator panel in Flex Builder and selecting Properties. From the resulting dialog, shown in Figure 11-15, select the Flex Build Path category on the left, and then change the Output folder field on the right to match the path of your Command Panels folder.

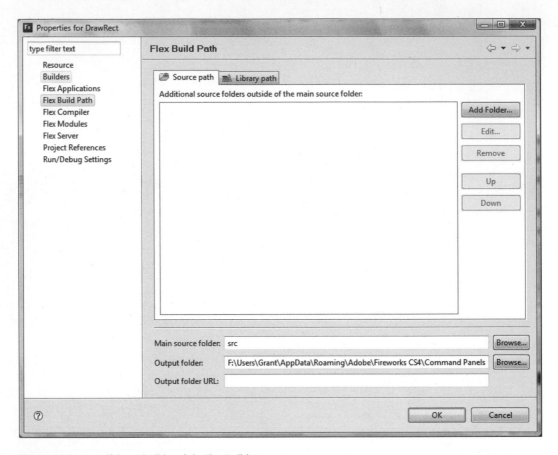

Figure 11-15. Specifying a build path in Flex Builder

With that setting changed, you can now select Project ➤ Build Project from the main menu in Flex Builder, immediately switch to Fireworks, and test your updated panel.

Packaging and deploying your panel

Throughout this chapter, we've been working with exported SWF files. To add a custom panel to Fireworks, we just copied the SWF to the correct folder, restarted Fireworks, and then accessed the panel from the Window menu. This is fine for development, but when you're finished with your panel and want to share it with the world, you need to package your panel into an MXP file that can be double-clicked and automatically installed using the Adobe Extension Manager.

Creating an MXP is a relatively simple task. You start by authoring an XML-based file saved with the .mxi extension. We've included a starter MXI file in the files that accompany this chapter (StarterMXI.mxi, also available at C:\Program Files\Adobe\Adobe Extension Manager CS4\Samples\Fireworks). Following is a snippet from this file:

```
<macromedia-extension
    name="Draw Rect Panel"
    version="1.0"
    type="Command Panel">

    <!-- List the required/compatible products -->
    <products>
    <product name="Fireworks" version="10" primary="true" />
    </products>

    <!-- Describe the author -->
    <author name="Grant Hinkson, www.granthinkson.com" />

        <files>
            <file name="Draw Rect.swf"
                destination="$fireworks/Configuration/Command Panels/" />
        </files>
```

Most of the sections of this file are used for display purposes in the Extension Manager, such as the name attribute and the <author /> section. The <files> section, however, is where you reference the SWF (or SWFs) that you want installed with this particular MXP. The name attribute of the <file /> tag is a relative reference to the file you want packaged. Since there is no folder name specified, the Draw Rect.swf file is expected to be located in the same folder as the MXI. Open the sample MXI to see the handful of remaining sections that you can customize. Once you've edited the MXI and are satisfied with the results, it's time to create a compiled MXP file that you can share with other Fireworks users. You can simply double-click the MXI file to launch the Adobe Extension Manager. It will automatically create an MXP for you, prompting you first to specify a name and location for the new file, as shown in Figure 11-16.

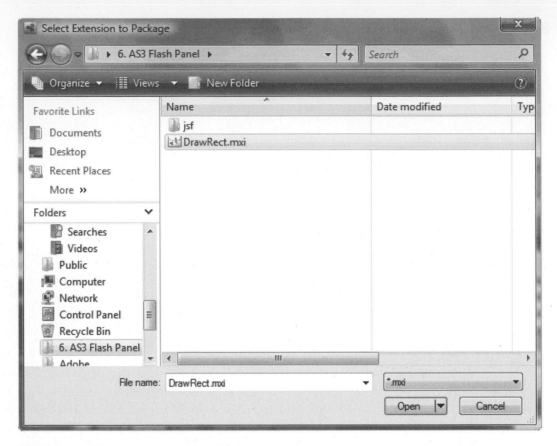

Figure 11-16. Saving an extension in the Adobe Extension Manager

Now that you have an MXP file, you can either double-click the file to launch the Extension Manager or select File ➤ Install Extension from the Extension Manager main menu. Once installed, your panel will appear in the list of installed extensions as shown in Figure 11-17.

Figure 11-17. Installed extension displayed in the Extension Manager

Learning the Fireworks object model

This chapter has primarily concerned itself with defining an effective workflow for developing Fireworks panels. We've shown you how to do this in both ActionScript 2 and 3, using both Flash and Flex. Along the way, we've used certain Fireworks methods and handled Fireworks events that you probably didn't even know existed. You may have wondered how we knew that calling `fw.popupColorPickerOverMouse()` in JSF would launch the color picker or how calling `fw.selection[0]` would give us a handle to the first selected object. We learned our way around the Fireworks object model using the following resources and methods:

- The *Extending Fireworks* documentation
- The History panel method—demonstrated at the beginning of this chapter
- The FWAPI_Inspector panel
- Online samples, tutorials, and articles

The Extending Fireworks documentation

The *Extending Fireworks* documentation is available online and can be found by selecting Help ➤ Fireworks Help from the main menu (or directly via `http://help.adobe.com/en_US/Fireworks/10.0_Using/`). Select Extending Adobe Fireworks CS4 from the main menu on the left. This documentation covers all of the methods, events, objects, and properties available to you as a Fireworks panel author.

The History panel method

The History panel method introduced at the beginning of this chapter is a fast way to come up to speed with the methods that Fireworks is calling as you use the tool. You simply perform steps within Fireworks that you want to know how to achieve via JSF, and then select the steps you just performed in the History panel (Window ➤ History). With the steps of interest selected, click the Copy button to copy the JSF directly to your clipboard. You can then paste the JSF into your authoring tool and review the code. Learn more about the methods used by looking them up in the *Extending Fireworks* documentation.

The FWAPI_Inspector panel

Learning to navigate the Fireworks object model is a fundamental step in Fireworks panel development. Often, navigating the *Extending Fireworks* documentation can be confusing. Fortunately, Aaron Beall has written a panel that displays the property tree of the currently selected element on the stage (see Figure 11-18). You can see the values for each property and even edit the properties that aren't read-only. Using this panel, you can learn the hierarchy of Fireworks objects and properties and predictably code against selected objects.

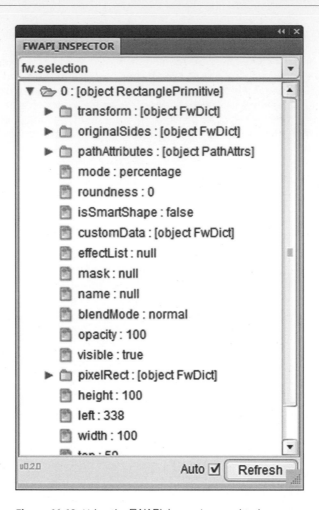

Figure 11-18. Using the FWAPI_Inspector panel to browse the Fireworks DOM

You can download the panel and its source file at Aaron's Fireworks web site: http://fireworks. abeall.com/extensions/panels.

Aaron has a number of great Fireworks commands and command panels available for download and just happens to be the author of the Path panel that ships with Fireworks.

Summary

We've covered a lot in just one chapter! You should now have a solid understanding of what it takes to create and deploy Fireworks panels. We've tried to give you a big-picture understanding of all the moving pieces in this exciting world of extension development. It's now up to you to dig into the documentation and really learn the Fireworks API.

You now have a number of additional tools at your disposal (like the FWAPI_Inspector panel), and you have a number of source files to start from (included with the resources for this chapter). In addition to the files included with this chapter, you'll find a number of great articles available online at the Fireworks Developer Center (www.adobe.com/devnet/fireworks/). We also recommend visiting www.fireworksguruforum.com, where you can learn from an active community of Fireworks enthusiasts.

Part 3

FIREWORKS IN ACTION

You should now be well on your way to becoming a Fireworks pro. You probably have a sea of ideas swirling in your head after reading the previous part. Maybe you're dreaming of new effects that you can create or thinking about the next set of Flex skins you're going to design. Maybe you're thinking of a new command panel that will save you tons of time. Or maybe you're combining all of your ideas into a new command panel that will automate that fancy new effect you're thinking of! Regardless of where your head is, we think you'll agree that Fireworks enables a world of possibilities.

In this last part, we'll ground those possibilities with three end-to-end case studies. You'll see how various features of Fireworks come together to support the varying workflow requirements demanded by each project. Watch for similarities and differences in approach, and think about how your real-world projects can map to each of these chapters.

Chapter 12

WEB SITE CASE STUDY #1: BLOG

Fireworks is a powerful end-to-end web design tool. It is as useful for rapid prototyping and wireframing as it is for creation of vector art, logos, and pixel-perfect design detail and nuance. This example is going to walk through designing a blog site, a relatively simple and standard format on the modern Web. Over the last several years, blogs have developed some fairly solid formatting conventions, much like books, and thus make a good, simple design case. We will be designing a fictitious blog about pop culture, film, music, and industry gossip called PopDiary.com.

In our careers as web developers, in the freelancing, secondary education, and corporate sectors, we have encountered a wide variety of clients. We are going to outline a process alongside the design process that we have found helpful in minimizing the frustration and heartache that can go into designing a masterpiece, only to have that design rejected outright, seemingly arbitrarily, by a stakeholder. Discreet design phases with incremental progress, clear communication, and frequent signoff on design direction help to make the best use of everyone's time and to ultimately arrive at a superior product.

Phase 1: Project planning and preparation

A good proposal and contract can be the most important phase of the entire project. Specify as much detail as possible. This is for the protection of you and your client. It protects your relationship and will determine the success or failure of the project.

A good proposal is based on a requirements document that outlines what type of content will be in the site, core functionality of the site, promotional elements, and advertising requirements. In Fireworks, these requirements will translate into pages, layers, design elements, and states.

Once you have determined requirements for the project, you'll want to gather as much actual content as possible. In the world of blog design, this might mean making (or collecting) some actual posts that will go live on the site, any "about the blog" text, author info, and so forth. The more real content you have to work with, the more accurately you can design and build your project, and the easier it will be to pitch the design to the client or other stakeholders.

This is also the time to discuss the site's **brand**—its voice, tone, and mood—as well as general ideas for the site's look and feel. These will guide you in the later phases of the site's design.

Project details example

We have been given a requirements document asking for a very simple blog with the following types of pages:

- A home page listing the 5 most recent posts
- A permalink page with a comments listing and comment form
- A category archive listing page with 10 posts from that category
- A tag archive listing page with 10 posts from that tag
- A search results page with 25 search results (headings and a short excerpt)
- An "about" page (generic design for other static pages)

In addition, each page should have the following elements:

- Two advertisements: a Google ads leaderboard (728×90 px) and a medium rectangle ad (300×250 px)
- Most recent comments listing displaying the last 5 commented posts
- "About the author" excerpt with a link to the full "about" page
- A blogroll (with about 20 blogs linked)
- A "featured stories" spot displaying 5 featured posts
- A search bar

Phase 2: Exploring layouts with wireframes

After requirements are decided upon and a good contract is signed and in hand, it is time to crack open Fireworks and start rolling. In the first phase we perform wireframing, which involves making decisions about what goes where, and how much emphasis and space to give everything. Every client and stakeholder wants to have everything "above the fold" and vastly emphasized. The trick is finding the right balance.

Each page type outlined in the requirements document will become a page in Fireworks. Most blogs (and sites in general) have at least some consistent elements, such as navigation controls. Elements that are going to be standard across all pages of the site can be part of the **master page**, which is set using the Pages panel menu. Having a master page allows you to quickly change these common elements in every page of your document. Subsequent pages can be used for the different types of pages in the design, as well as different iterations of those page types. Having a good naming convention is helpful here so that the pages are easily scannable and you won't have to try to guess which page was, say, your search results wireframe.

In a wireframe, it is wise to stay very barebones and rough. Don't get caught up in detail. Make it ugly on purpose. This will help all stakeholders to stay focused on the task at hand in this phase, determining positioning of elements, and not get caught up in font sizes, colors, margins, and so forth.

Create a single PDF file of all your page wireframes (select File ➤ Export and choose Adobe PDF from the Export select box) that you can e-mail to the decision makers. They can then use Adobe Acrobat to make annotations and send the PDF back to you for changes. Repeat this cycle until you have agreement on element placement. A successful wireframing phase will allow you to much more quickly come to these decisions than spending a lot of time on design detail, only to have to throw away detail work in subsequent iterations.

Wireframe example

First we will block out the common elements of the site. Create a header, the sidebar, and navigation area containing all the elements that should be common to each page. Use your best guess for the sizes of these elements, but don't worry about being too precise. You want to get a feel for relative element placement, not exact pixels. Figure 12-1 shows approximately what a basic wireframe would look like for this example.

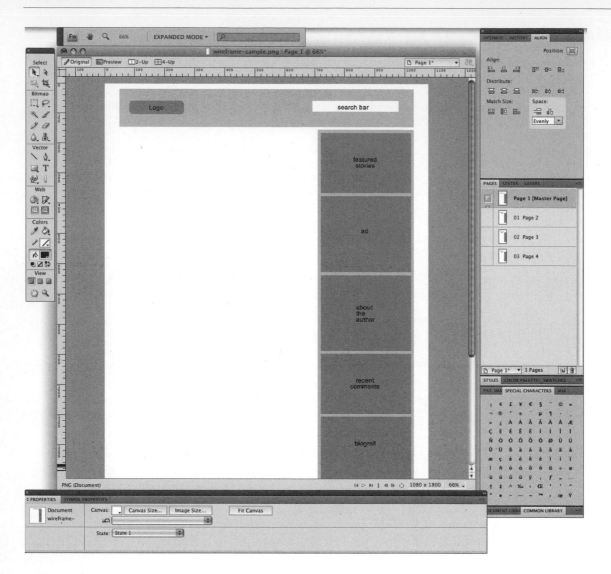

Figure 12-1. A basic wireframe shows approximate size and placement of each element.

Once you have blocked in these pieces, go to the Pages panel, select Page 1, go to the Pages panel menu, and select Set as Master Page. You now have a set of common elements that will be applied to each new page you create in this document.

Next, we will create the wireframe for the home page. Create a new page by selecting New Page from the Pages panel menu, by clicking the Add/Duplicate Page button, or by right-clicking a page in the Pages panel and selecting New Page from the contextual menu as illustrated in Figure 12-2.

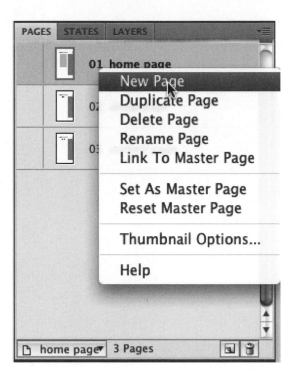

Figure 12-2. Right-clicking a page brings up this contextual menu.

Notice that the elements from the master page appear here. Now we will rough out the placement for the five most recent articles. We usually use simple gray boxes to represent these posts. This is a quick exercise, and again the idea is to sketch out a very high-level view of the site's structure. Figure 12-3 illustrates this.

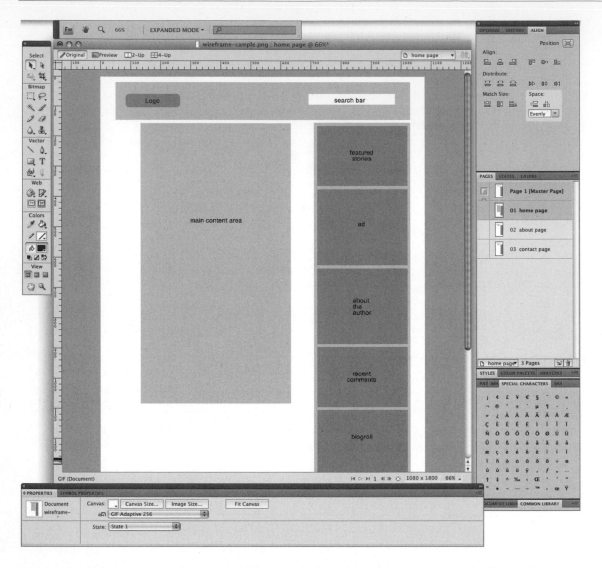

Figure 12-3. Wireframes are a very basic but helpful exercise in determining placement and size of each page element.

Create a new page and continue the preceding process for every other type of page in the require-ments document. If you have several good ideas, create several versions of each and be prepared to discuss the benefits and drawbacks of each layout.

Phase 3: Turning wireframes into gray frames

Once you have signoff on your wireframes, it is time to get to some detail. Here we usually create a new file and start with a fresh slate. A gray frame is a chance to establish your grid, play with typography, and start to explore the visual hierarchy of your design, without yet getting into the color and fine-grained detail of added textures and effects.

Gray framing is an optional stage, but we have found it to be a very useful one. When working with a large team, it helps to keep the focus of the discussion narrow, and therefore can save time. Keep a broader eye open for which parts of the page need to "pop out" of the design, try to determine how much visual weight to give different elements, and explore typography, without getting distracted with textures, colors, and effects.

As in wireframing, different types of pages will be individual pages in your Fireworks document. In this phase, you might want to have different design iterations be separate documents.

As in Phase 2, export your gray frame pages as a single PDF file to e-mail to the decision makers.

Gray frame example

Starting with a new file, we will follow the same basic process that we did in Phase 2, but this time with attention to detail. The foundation of any good graphic design is a grid. Fireworks has its own grid functionality that can be useful in aligning elements by site, but we prefer to create our own grids using rectangle shapes and lines. There are several good resources available to use as guides in creating a grid system. We highly recommend Nathan Smith's 960.gs templates (http://960.gs), or you can create your own. The grid provides a structure ordering the graphical elements of text and images in your design.

Your grid can be determined by known constraints such as predetermined element sizes. For example, in our design, we know that we will need to fix a 300✕250 px ad graphic placement area in our design. This can nicely define the width of the sidebar.

In this example, we are going to choose a 960-px-wide, 16-column grid (40-px-wide columns with 10 px margins to create 20 px "gutters") into which we'll start to lay our elements. We will create guides for the columns and their margins (illustrated in Figure 12-4) to get a feel for how we should arrange things. Nathan has kindly offered these templates to us as part of his downloadable 960.gs templates. When using these templates, you can making the pink (transparent red) grid columns invisible, leaving a great set of guides for you to align your elements with. Click the visibility toggle (the eye icon) next to the layer containing the grid columns to make them invisible.

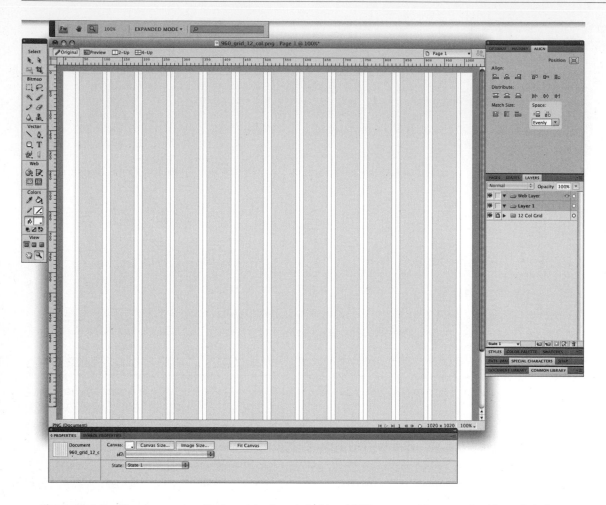

Figure 12-4. A grid system, such as the templates found at http://960.gs, provides a set of guides to help lay out content columns and other graphic elements in an orderly fashion.

As in Phase 2, we will create a master page with the persistent site elements, this time with an eye to detail, dimension, alignment to the grid, and visual hierarchy. Create space for your header with a logo, navigation, search bar (we like to put ours in the header or top of the sidebar), and the leaderboard ad. Set in the sidebar content at 300-px wide to include the following: featured stories, medium rectangle ad, "about the author" area, most recent comments, and the blogroll.

In our gray frames, we use darker and lighter shades of gray to approximate the visual weight we are going to give to each element via color, graphical decoration, font size and weight, and so forth. Figure 12-5 shows the beginnings of this gray frame.

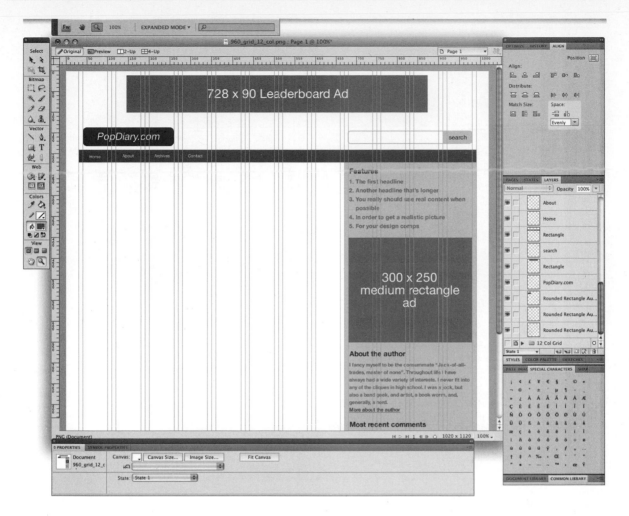

Figure 12-5. In gray framing, you add more detail to your design to start exploring visual "weight" and establishing a visual hierarchy for your design elements.

Having created the master page, go on and create the rest of the pages with the same eye to detail. As in Phase 2, create a new page for the home page (and subsequent pages). For the home page, include one or two sample posts with their headlines, possibly a photo, and accompanying metalinks: comments links, permalinks, and other functionality you'd like for each post. This step is illustrated in Figure 12-6.

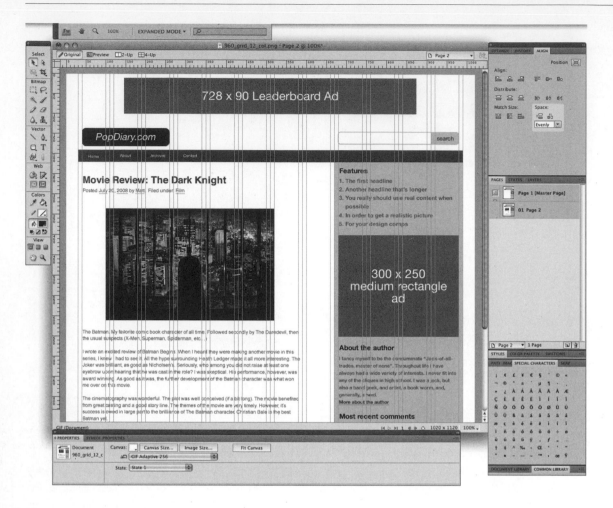

Figure 12-6. Adding real content to your gray frames helps you to realistically explore font size and weight.

A good finished product will be a Fireworks document with several pages, possibly several states in each page for hover effects of navigation elements, with attention paid to typography, grid alignment, and visual hierarchy, that will provide the foundation for you to adorn with color, texture, and other visual effects.

Phase 4: Creating a logo for the design

This phase can be accomplished at any point once you have a requirements document and a discussion about the site's voice and tone. We like to base logo design off of choices made and agreed upon for font and color.

Logo example

We want to add a very simple graphic element to it to help communicate its nature as a blog: a speech bubble. Cliché? Perhaps. Overused? Definitely. But it serves us perfectly here (see Figure 12-7).

Figure 12-7. Logos are easy to create in Fireworks. This is a simple example for our sample web site.

In order to create this logo, we will create a new document; 500×500 px is sufficient for our purposes. Use the words "Pop Diary," change the font to Killed DJ (or any other distressed, retro font) and font size to 60 px (size doesn't matter much here), and then create the bubble. To do this, first select the Rounded Rectangle tool and create a rectangle that is 350 px wide and 100 px tall. Grab one of the yellow diamonds in the corner and drag it toward the center of the graphic as far as it will go to create a "pill" shape.

To create the arrow portion of the speech bubble, select the Smart Polygon tool and drag out an 80×80 px polygon. Grab the bottom-left yellow diamond and drag down to reduce the number of sides until you have a triangle. Position the triangle into place on the bubble, and place its layer under the bubble layer with the Send to Back command (Ctrl/Cmd+Shift+Down arrow).

We chose yellow (#D68019) for our text and a deep brown (#18080B) for our bubble. That's all there is to this site's simple logo.

Phase 5: Putting all the pieces together: The design composition

Once element placement, a grid system, visual hierarchies, color palettes, and typography have been settled upon, it's time to pull out the stops and decorate your gray frames! Time to break conventions (except useful ones), hide your grid, erase your outlines, wow your neighbors, and create the next masterpiece that will be featured on CSS Beauty (www.cssbeauty.com/)! Now you'll combine all the expertise you have and all the techniques we've discussed thus far in the book and put together a final design composition based on decisions made in the previous phases.

Design example

To start with, we typically save a duplicate copy of our gray frame document and use that as a base to start the composition. The first obvious step for us is usually to insert the logo we created in the last phase into the placeholder in our gray frame. Do this in the master page of the document (see Figure 12-8).

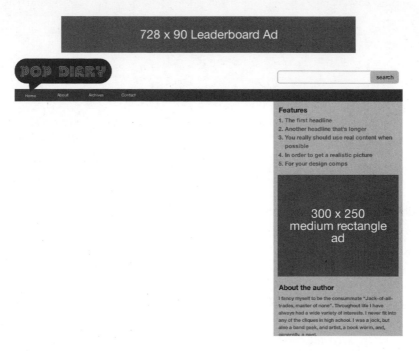

Figure 12-8. Add your logo to the master page of your file; this will cause it to appear on all subpages.

Next, we like to experiment with background patterns as a sort of a foundation to build on top of. Here we have selected vector art we purchased as a stock graphic and are using pieces of it, remixed a bit, to form the background. At this point we also have widened our document's canvas from 1020 px to 1220 px to let the background show through more, and to allow us to consider how to repeat or fade the background graphic out. Figure 12-9 shows the results.

Next we start to "paint" our gray frame using the colors red (#AB0019), yellow-orange (#D68019), brown (#18080B), and a complementary blue for links (#0A80A0). We typically do this by selecting the rectangles and other shapes created in the gray frame phase and adding color (with color fills), adding textures (with effects, painting with brushes, etc.), replacing blocks with graphics (photos or vector art), or deleting them to let the background show through. See a simple example of this in Figure 12-10. Do not feel constrained by your gray boxes. Remove them altogether if you like. We find the constraint helps to keep our designs focused and sharp, as we are not particularly talented graphic artists.

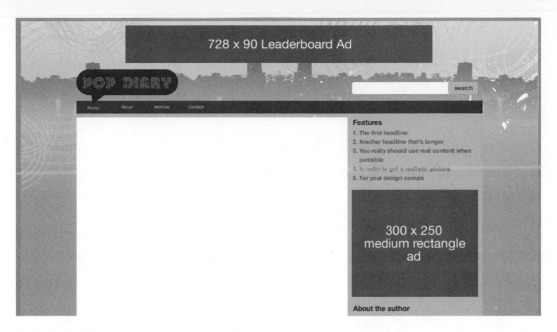

Figure 12-9. Widen your document and play with background patterns and graphics.

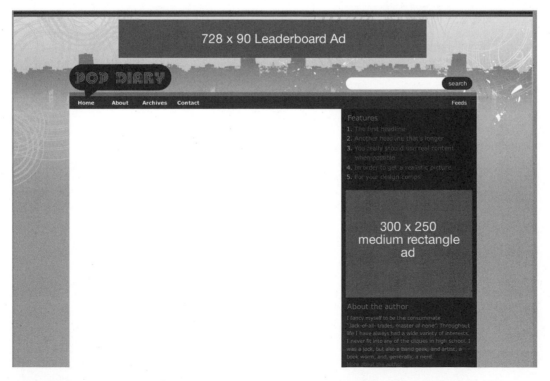

Figure 12-10. Add color and texture to the blocks you created in your gray frame, replace them with other graphics, or remove them to let background art show through.

Next we can switch to our separate pages for some minor typographic adjustments to fit the theme created by the logo and background graphics. Now we're zeroing in on a very simple, yet effective, design! See the results in Figure 12-11.

Figure 12-11. A final design comp can then be sliced up for export to HTML.

At this point, it's possible to add hotspots over your various navigation elements to link your different pages together in order to export them to HTML; doing so lets you show off a working prototype so that stakeholders can click through the site and observe basic functionality. Most professional web designers will skip to something like Phase 6 at this point, but we'll walk through this process briefly so you understand the functionality.

First, in the master page, create a rectangular hotspot over the navigation elements you want to link to (see Figure 12-12).

Figure 12-12. Hotspots can be added over navigation elements to export them to a prototype HTML document.

Next, select the first hotspot. In the Property inspector, set the Link property to the page you want to associate with that link, as shown in Figure 12-13. In this example, our home page is Page 2 in the Pages panel (the "about" page is Page 3, archives is Page 4, and contact info is Page 5).

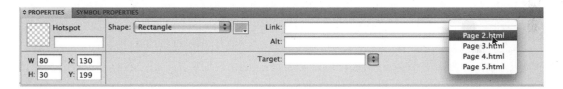

Figure 12-13. In the Property inspector, you can associate a hotspot with a page in your document or an external link.

Repeat this process for each hotspot you create. Select one of the HTML-based export options (see Chapter 5), and these pages will be linked together.

Phase 6: Build-out: From graphics to code

And finally, we arrive at our favorite part of the design phase: the build-out. This is where we get to slice our graphics up and breathe life into our design with HTML and CSS. When we are done with this phase, we will have a working prototype of a blog with clickable links and copy-able text. There is something satisfying about seeing a fresh design in this state.

It is possible to use Fireworks' native capability to export to CSS and images for a very rapid build of your design. This can be useful for a very quick demonstration of the functionality of your design; however, it is not the way a professional web developer will work. In order to produce the most efficient code, you will want to build the HTML and CSS by hand, which is the subject of another book or three. We highly recommend *CSS Mastery: Advanced Web Standards Solutions* by Andy Budd, Cameron Moll, and Simon Collison (friends of ED, 2006), as well as *HTML Mastery: Semantics, Standards, and Styling* by Paul Haine (friends of ED, 2006).

But to be complete, the basic process goes something like this:

1. Slice and export graphics (see Chapter 5).
2. Place content in a plain text file.
3. Add semantic markup to the content.
4. Add "pseudo-semantic" markup to define content divisions (.e.g., header, footer, sidebar).
5. Build the page layout with CSS.
6. Apply your look and feel with CSS, applying classes sparingly and adding nonsemantic markup sparingly as necessary.

Phase 7: Integrating into a CMS

The only thing that remains in order to start publishing your content and watching the traffic numbers soar is to integrate your beautiful design into a content management system (CMS) of some sort. There are some obvious choices among the big players: WordPress, ExpressionEngine, Movable Type, Textpattern, and others. All offer basically the same functionality with some benefits and drawbacks to each.

Those who are less inclined to run their own hosting setup may want to consider one of the hosted solutions that exist. Some smaller companies are doing amazing things and can offer the added benefit of personal support. Two we have worked with in the past that provide excellent functionality and excellent service are Markup Factory (http://markupfactory.com/) and MonkCMS (www.monkcms.com/). Give them a look.

Summary

Breaking a project down into discrete phases and communicating with stakeholders at each phase can make an otherwise frustrating project very efficient and manageable. Fireworks makes this process simple by allowing for efficient file management, rapid execution of each phase, easy exportation for reviewing documents and prototype markup, and final export of production-quality graphics.

In this chapter, we walked through a simple project of creating a basic blog. From wireframe creation to more detailed gray frames and logo design, to putting it all together as a final composition ready for export to production, Fireworks is the right tool for every phase of web graphic design.

Chapter 13

WEB SITE CASE STUDY #2: CSS SPRITES

Exporting a completed Fireworks document for web use makes for some interesting situations. For instance, how can you export graphical images that need hover, active, or click states while still maintaining an optimized user experience? You could use Fireworks' built-in button exporting features to export each of the image states to separate files, but a more efficient way would be to export all of the image states to a single file or **sprite sheet**, as it's often called (see Figure 13-1).

Figure 13-1. Example of a sprite sheet

In this chapter we'll show you a site design that requires some graphical navigation with hover and selected states. We'll use the pages feature in Fireworks and create the navigation as a single exportable bitmap sprite sheet. Then, we'll show you how to use CSS to create a viewport over that image and slide the sprite sheet around underneath it to display the appropriate image states.

Creating site navigation with sprites

Figure 13-2 shows a completed site design built in Fireworks. Notice that the navigation, located at the top center of Figure 13-2, is mocked up to show a hover state as well as active, focus, or selected state scenarios. To allow this type of functionality in a working web site, we'll need to re-create the navigation on its own page and export it out as a single bitmap separate from the rest of the export slices.

Figure 13-2. Example site design

Preparing a new page

Open the Pages panel (press F5) and click the Add/Duplicate Page icon in the lower-right corner. The new page will take the same canvas size as the existing document, but we want this navigation page to be as small as possible for optimization reasons. So, we will need to figure out the width and height of our navigation page. In this example, each one of the four navigation buttons is 100 px (pixels) wide by 28 px tall. We also know that we want to have three navigation states: normal, hover, and active. Through some simple math we come up with 4 × 100 = 400 px and 28 × 3 = 84 px. As a result, our navigation page will be 400 px wide by 84 px tall. Go to Modify ➤ Canvas ➤ Canvas size and enter the appropriate dimensions.

Next, we can copy over our navigation states from our main site page. We'll make the top row the normal state, the middle row the hover state, and the bottom row the active state. Figure 13-3 shows exactly what we're talking about.

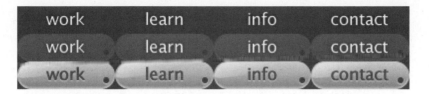

Figure 13-3. Navigation image (nav.png)

Now all we need to do is export this image as a single flattened bitmap. Using the Optimize panel, we've set the export format to PNG 24 and then used the Export command (File ➤ Export). Figure 13-4 shows the export settings for this particular page.

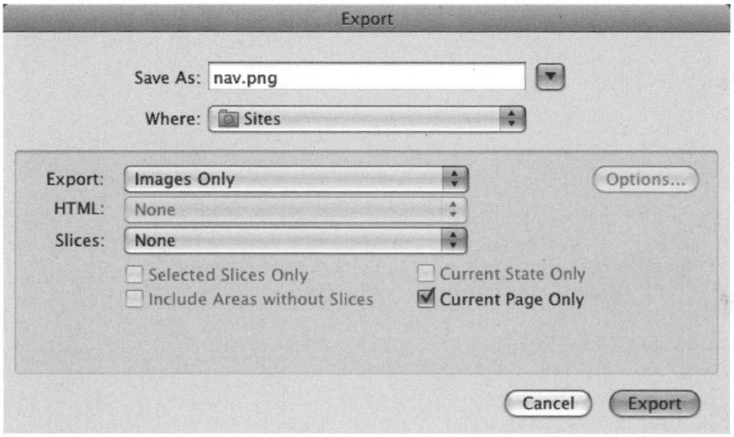

Figure 13-4. Export window for the navigation page

Now that we have our new page, the next step is to add the navigation system to it.

Writing the HTML

For this example, we're going to use a standard unordered list to represent our navigation. We prefer using lists to define our navigation, as we feel it allows for a great deal of control when styling. By greater control, we mean that an unordered list of links contains three sets of nested tags that can be hooked into via CSS. This is by no means the only way to write out web site navigation, but for this example we feel it will work best.

```
<ul id="nav">
<li id="nav-work"><a href="#" class="selected">Work</a></li>
<li id="nav-learn"><a href="#">Learn</a></li>
<li id="nav-info"><a href="#">Info</a></li>
<li id="nav-contact"><a href="#">Contact</a></li>
</ul>
```

As you can see in the code block, we've done some things that might raise some eyebrows. We've added id attributes to each of the list item tags so that we can use them as hooks when applying the CSS. We've also added an optional class attribute with a value of selected, which can be used to display the third row of the nav.png image. You can move the class attribute to any of the other anchor tags or remove it entirely if you wish.

Figure 13-5 shows the resulting HTML when viewed in a web browser. The unordered list looks plain and boring right now but will soon be given life through the wonders of CSS.

Figure 13-5. A plain unordered HTML list that's about to become styled with CSS

Writing the CSS

There are many, many ways to create the CSS for our page, but we've decided to go with an image replacement technique that will hide the HTML text and replace it with selected portions of our exported nav.png bitmap. This technique involves displacing the text with a negative text-indent value that will force the text off of the web page without causing horizontal scrollbars. With the text safely hidden from sight, we can replace the blank anchor tag with a background image. Here's what the CSS looks like:

```
<style type="text/css">
#nav,#nav li {
margin: 0;
padding: 0;
list-style: none;
}
```

```
#nav li {
text-indent: -9999px;
}

#nav a {
margin: 0 20px 0 0;
background: url(nav.png);
width: 100px;
height: 28px;
display: block;
float: left;
}

#nav #nav-work a {
background-position: 0 0;
}

#nav #nav-work a:active,
#nav #nav-work a:focus,
#nav #nav-work a.selected {
background-position: 0 -56px;
}

#nav #nav-work a:hover {
background-position: 0 -28px;
}

#nav #nav-learn a {
background-position: -100px 0;
}

#nav #nav-learn a:active,
#nav #nav-learn a:focus,
#nav #nav-learn a.selected {
background-position: -100px -56px;
}

#nav #nav-learn a:hover {
background-position: -100px -28px;
}

#nav #nav-info a {
background-position: -200px 0;
}

#nav #nav-info a:active,
#nav #nav-info a:focus,
#nav #nav-info a.selected {
background-position: -200px -56px;
}
```

```
#nav #nav-info a:hover {
background-position: -200px -28px;
}

#nav #nav-contact a {
background-position: -300px 0;
}

#nav #nav-contact a:active,
#nav #nav-contact a:focus,
#nav #nav-contact a.selected {
background-position: -300px -56px;
}

#nav #nav-contact a:hover {
background-position: -300px -28px;
}
</style>
```

At first glance it seems like there's a lot going on with this CSS, but if you look closely you can see that a large portion of the code repeats for all four navigation buttons and their individual display state scenarios. We'll go over the code blocks to explain exactly what's happening.

List reset

Plain and simple, the following code is just a reset of the margin, padding, and list style so that the unordered list doesn't have any indentations or bullet symbols.

```
#nav,#nav li {
margin: 0;
padding: 0;
list-style: none;
}
```

Figure 13-6 shows what the reset unordered list looks like in a browser.

Figure 13-6. The unordered list reset with no bullets or indentation.

Extreme negative text indent

In the next code block, we set the text indent to an extreme negative value on all list items inside the unordered list so that there's virtually no chance that the HTML text will display over the top of the background image.

```
#nav li {
text-indent: -9999px;
}
```

Figure 13-7 shows what the navigation would look like if we didn't set the text indent to a negative value.

Figure 13-7. Text indent set to its default value

Defining the dimensions

The next code block is where we call nav.png and set it as the background image for all of the anchor tags within the unordered list.

```
#nav a {
margin: 0 20px 0 0;
background: url(nav.png);
width: 100px;
height: 28px;
display: block;
float: left;
}
```

We also define the width and height, which will act as our viewport to the background bitmap. We've set the display element to block so that the entire dimensions of the 100 × 28 px navigation item is clickable in all browsers. The float element is set to left so that the navigation items flow horizontally across the page, and we've added a 20-px margin to the right, which will make the navigation feel less cramped. Figure 13-8 shows the progress so far. Now all we need to do is position nav.png for the appropriate navigation items and display scenarios.

Figure 13-8. The navigation items all set to the same value

Sliding the background into position

In the next code block, we start by showing the CSS for the third navigation item so we can better illustrate exactly how we tell the CSS to slide the background image.

```
#nav #nav-info a {
background-position: -200px 0;
}
```

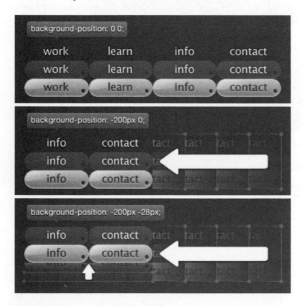

The values for the background-position property are telling the browser to move the background image 200 px to the left and 0 px down. A positive number in the first position slides the image right, while a negative number slides the image left. Likewise, a positive number in the second position slides the image down, while a negative number slides it up. Figure 13-9 is a visual representation of the background image moving from its starting position in the upper left or 0 0 position to the -200px 0 position, and then to hover position at -200px -28px.

The following bit of code takes care of the active, focus, and selected states by sliding the nav.png image 200 px to the left and 56 px up:

Figure 13-9. Background-position coordinates

```
#nav #nav-info a:active,
#nav #nav-info a:focus,
#nav #nav-info a.selected {
background-position: -200px -56px;
}
```

We then place the hover section after the active, focus, and selected sections because we want the hover to retain its effect even when a nav item may be in the active position. In other words, we'd like visual feedback for the hover scenario regardless of the original state of the item.

```
#nav #nav-info a:hover {
background-position: -200px -28px;
}
```

It's amazing what a little CSS can do. Figure 13-10 shows the exact same unordered list as in Figure 13-5, only this time CSS is being applied to replace the anchor tags with background images. When the user moves his or her mouse over the items, or uses the Tab key in some browsers, the CSS instantly slides the nav.png image to the appropriate viewing state. There are no delays or HTTP requests back to the server to load a new image, as everything is loaded into cache from the nav.png image.

Figure 13-10. Our plain unordered list is now all grown up and handsome.

Summary

Fireworks CS4's pages feature works incredibly well for setting up sprite images within your existing design files. By using CSS sprites for the multiple navigation display states in our example, the final working web site will send fewer image requests to the server. This will in turn make all of the pages load and interact with mouse movements as fast as possible for all users, no matter what type of Internet connection they may have. So, a user viewing this page via a dial-up modem will have the exact same experience as another user across the globe viewing it through a corporate OC3.

Chapter 14

WEB SITE CASE STUDY #3: E-COMMERCE

Earlier in this book, you learned that Fireworks is unique because of its strengths as a prototyping tool. In this case study, we're going to showcase that strength as we create a prototype for a fictitious T-shirt store and related checkout pages common on most e-commerce sites. Along the way, you'll also get an in-depth view of Fireworks' abilities as a graphic design workhorse as you learn how to create a wide range of custom graphics for this faux store.

Checking out with shared layers and pages

This glimpse into the world of designing for e-commerce is made possible by the fictional T-shirt company Boxtees. Boxtees approaches you, the designer, to create a new logo, a fresh visual design, and some new pages for their online store that will better market their shirts and get customers through the checkout process easier.

With this as the backdrop, we'll show you step by step how to create a simple, yet attractive logo with vector shapes and text. We'll also demonstrate how to draw a stylized T-shirt graphic with the Pen tool that is modular, making for easy and efficient mass production. And what is an e-commerce site without buttons? We'll reveal a quick-and-easy way to create a custom-made button to match the site's visual design instead of depending on those ugly default browser buttons.

Most importantly, we'll do all this within one Fireworks file using a combination of shared layers and a feature called pages to create each screen of the checkout process for buying a Boxtees T-shirt.

Setting up the workspace

Before we get started, we need to make some decisions about our project. We need to think about several aspects of our design, including page size (width), color scheme, navigation, and page layout. For the purposes of this exercise, let's just say we've already made those decisions, we've sketched out some preliminary layouts, and we're ready to start prototyping with Fireworks.

Designing the site's background

We've decided that we want a canvas size of 1,000 pixels (px) wide to accommodate a fixed-width layout that works well in most modern screen resolutions. In order to have room for all of our content, we'll give our canvas a height of 1,100 px. To establish this in Fireworks, select Modify ➤ Canvas ➤ Canvas size.

Using the Rectangle tool, we're going to draw each section that makes up our page—a basic one-column layout for the store section of this site.

Let's start off with the background of our page, drawing a rectangle that fills the height and width of our canvas, as previously stated—1,000 px wide and 1,100 px tall. The background rectangle will have a linear gradient that spans between medium tan (hex #BFBFB5) and light tan (#EFEFE0).

Creating a header

Next, we'll draw a solid brown (#493929) rectangle that spans the width of our canvas (1,000 px) and is 70 px tall. We'll add some style to the header by creating a decorative border at the bottom of the header rectangle. The decorative border is a series of smaller, overlapping rectangles with varying opacity to create the multiple-color pattern.

Defining the page body

Now we'll draw the body of the page by placing a white rectangle, 800 px wide, centered horizontally in the middle of the canvas. At the bottom of the body rectangle, we'll add a footer, which is a tan (#DDDDD0) rectangle, 800 px wide and 26 px tall.

Establishing the site's navigation

Lastly, a simple site navigation scheme is necessary as well; we'll add one inside the header. This base layout is illustrated in Figure 14-1.

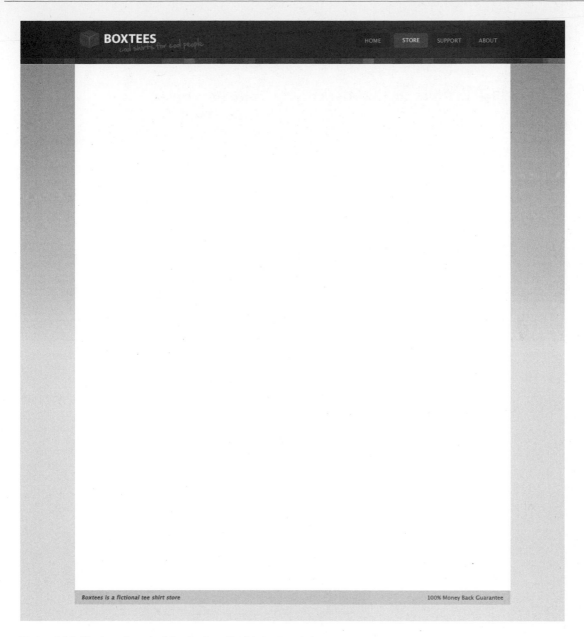

Figure 14-1. The base layout of the Boxtees T-shirt store prototype

Organizing the document's objects and layers

At this point, we've got the foundation of our page finalized. These are the elements that are static—they stay the same from page to page. We need to start organizing our layers, so let's open the Layers panel. To do this, you select Window ➤ Layers in the menu, or you can select Layers from the Tools panel to the right of your document. All objects we've created are contained in layers. Everything we've done to this point is most likely contained in a layer called Layer 1. We'll rename that to Base. Next, we need to make sure this layer stays "on the bottom" so that anything we do going forward appears on top of this base layer. Additionally, locking this layer is helpful, as it prevents us from inadvertently selecting elements in this layer and messing up our base layout.

Organizing the site design into pages

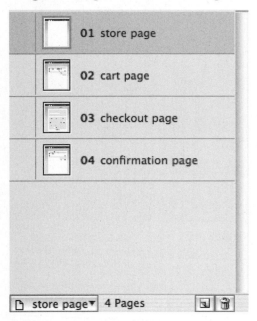

Figure 14-2. The Pages panel with our four added pages

Now that we have our base layer set, we can start creating all the necessary pages for our project. We'll do this through a feature called pages, a concept we discussed back in Chapter 1. Adobe introduced this feature in Fireworks CS3. Pages allows you to be super efficient in creating prototypes by holding all the pages of your design in one file, rather than creating a separate Fireworks file for each page of a prototype. By sharing layers between pages, we have an efficient method for keeping all the pages of our prototype consistent and flexible. Our base layer effectively becomes our master page; all other pages are overlaid on top of this master page. Any object you need to be present on all pages needs to be placed on the master page.

Select Window ➤ Pages from the menu or select the Pages panel in the Tools panel to the right of your document. By default, you'll see one page already exists, Page 1. Let's create three more new pages using the New Page button at the bottom of the panel. Renaming the pages will help us keep things organized going forward. At this point, we should have a page for each screen or step in our prototype: Store, Cart, Checkout, and Confirmation (see Figure 14-2).

Now, we need to make sure our base layer shows up on each of our freshly created pages. Making sure we're back on Page 1 (now named Store), let's select the layer named Base and unlock it. Next, right-click on that layer and select Share Layer to All Pages. Remember to relock that Base layer. Now you can navigate from page to page and see that the Base layer is carried over to each one.

Fireworks provides more than one way to bounce between pages in the document. One way is on the Pages panel itself. Merely clicking a page will change what appears on the canvas. Another way is by using the handy drop-down menu at the top-right corner of the Fireworks document. The Page Up/Pg Up and Page Down/Pg Dn keys on the keyboard allow you to scroll between pages.

Because the Base layer is a shared layer, any changes made to the Base layer within any page get propagated across each page, making changes and modifications fast and efficient.

Now we have a nearly finished Base layer and all the necessary pages for our e-commerce prototype. We're ready to start creating the graphical elements that make up each page.

Building all the graphics in Fireworks

Before we get into building individual pages for our make-believe online T-shirt store, we need to take some time to create some graphics to give the site some distinctiveness and character. We'll walk through how to create a logo, a T-shirt image, and a button. This is a good opportunity to showcase the power of Fireworks as a graphics creation tool.

Every site needs a good logo to portray the online identity of the company. For Boxtees, we just want something simple, yet memorable. We'll create a three dimensional-looking box with some strong typeface elements to achieve our goal.

Creating the logo

Let's open a new document to save our logo file so we can interact with it apart from our prototype document.

Defining the logo's basic shape and color

First, use the Smart Polygon tool to draw a hexagon. To use the Smart Polygon tool, select the Rectangle tool button in the Tools panel and hold down with the mouse. This will expose buttons for several other vector drawing tools. From there, select Smart Polygon. After you draw a polygon with the Smart Polygon tool, you'll notice several yellow diamond-shaped markers around the polygon. Each marker can be clicked/dragged to affect the characteristics (size, rotation, number of sides, number of sections) of the polygon. Use the yellow diamond-shaped marker located near the bottom-left corner of the object to select the number of sides for your polygon. In this case, just select six sides. Also, give it a fill color of medium brown (#7D5733) to coordinate nicely with the color of our site's header.

Next, ungroup the object so we can modify the path of the polygon. To ungroup an object, select the object and then select Modify ➤ Ungroup. Using the Subselection tool, select the top point of the polygon and use the down arrow key to move the point down 20 px. Holding the Shift key down while using arrow keys will result in a 10-pixel adjustment. Hence, to move the top point down 20 px, just hold the Shift key down while pressing the down arrow key twice.

We'll want to similarly move the bottom point of the polygon, but in this case, move the point up 10 px. Adjusting the top and bottom points of the object like this subtly changes the perspective of our polygon, giving it a more realistic look, which will become more obvious as we progress (see Figure 14-3).

Figure 14-3. The base polygon shape (enlarged) with top and bottom points adjusted

Adding some detail and dimension

The next task is slightly more difficult, but it will give our simple polygon the effect it needs to look like a three-dimensional cube rather than a flat polygon.

1. Use the Pen tool to draw a straight-lined vector shape, which will effectively add a corner to our polygon and give it some slight highlighting. Starting at the top-left corner of the polygon, click with the Pen tool to start a path.

2. Click in the exact middle of the polygon to establish the next point in the path, and then click again on the top-right corner of the polygon.

3. Go back to the middle of the polygon and make another point a few pixels below the middle point.

4. Continue the path by clicking the bottommost corner of the polygon and then back to the middle point, again a few pixels from the center point.

5. This last step will take us back to where we started by continuing our path back to the first point we made. Clicking the first point will close the shape, resulting in a Y-shaped object on top of our polygon, as shown in Figure 14-4.

Figure 14-4. The Y-shaped object on top of the base polygon (enlarged)

Polishing it up

To polish off the logo and make sure the effect is realistic, you may need to use the Subselection tool to line up the points and ensure the shape is symmetrical. Also, change the fill color of the Y-shaped object to white and set the opacity to 25%. This will create the subtle effect that we're looking for to turn our flat polygon into a cube. Add the word "Boxtees" set in the Myriad Pro typeface (or similar) and a fun tagline set in the Hand of Sean typeface (or other script-like font), and the logo is finished. Figure 14-5 shows our finished version of the logo.

Figure 14-5. The finished Boxtees logo

Drawing a T-shirt graphic

As with most e-commerce sites, good-quality product shots are important. People want to know what they're buying and be confident that what they see online is representative of what they'll actually get. Many sites use photographs to establish the nature of their products. For Boxtees, we could have used actual photographs of T-shirts, but because our product is so simple and everyone knows what a T-shirt looks like, we can use a custom designed T-shirt graphic instead, which gives the site a more casual, fun look and also provides flexibility in showcasing T-shirts in the future.

Recall that the logo we created consisted of only two objects, which worked to great effect to change a "flat" object into an image with depth and dimension. We'll achieve a similar effect with the T-shirt graphic, but this time we'll need a few more complex objects.

The first step is to draw the outline shape of a T-shirt with the Pen tool. Starting at the top right, create the shoulder outline and working your way clockwise around with points until you get back up to the top of the shirt's collar piece. Connecting the points to the first point you started with will close the shape and fill it with the document's current fill color, as shown in Figure 14-6. Right now it doesn't really matter what the fill color is because we will be changing it later.

Figure 14-6. Flat T-shirt-shaped object

The next step is to create the shapes that will serve as "shadows" to mimic what it would be like if the shirt had a few slight wrinkles or gathering in certain areas. Again, use the Pen tool to create several abstract-looking shapes on the shoulder, the collar, and around the armpit area of the T-shirt. Also add a few wrinkles to the sleeves and to the bottom of the shirt (see Figure 14-7).

Next, we need to group all the shadow shapes together so we can interact with them as one object going forward. Now we basically have two layers—the T-shirt object and the shadow object. We need to ensure that the shadow object is on top. Then we change the fill color to black and the opacity of the layer to 45% to create the subtle shadow effect, which works nicely to give our "flat" shirt some added dimension. Figure 14-8 shows the finished product.

Figure 14-7. Drawing the shadow shapes   **Figure 14-8.** The final T-shirt graphic

Making a button

The final custom graphic that we need to create is a button. Buttons are critical to all e-commerce sites because they are the primary method through which the user interacts with the page to progress through the shopping and checkout processes. Sure, we could just use a default browser button, and even the Fireworks Common Library is full of browser interface elements. However, default browser buttons do nothing to support the visual identity of a site. Additionally, each browser displays buttons differently, which may or may not be a good thing for Boxtees. To circumvent all these issues, we'll just create our own buttons.

The button is the easiest of the graphics we need to create. As with most graphics, we'll start off with the bottommost layer and work our way up from there, building each element, layer by layer, on top of the base element.

For this button, the base element is a simple rectangle with a width of 134 px and a height of 30 px. Next, give the rectangle a linear gradient fill of light blue (#EAF1FE) at the top to a medium blue (#CCE0FF) at the bottom. Next, give it a "shadow" by duplicating the shape and changing the fill color to a solid medium blue (#C2CFE5), slightly darker than the medium blue in the gradient. Then, ensure the shadow rectangle is behind the gradient-filled rectangle. You should have something that looks like Figure 14-9.

Figure 14-9. Base rectangle of the button with shadow (enlarged)

Next, we'll create an area within the rectangle to hold the text of the button. We'll use some basic techniques to give this area a "chiseled-out" look, which will add a dimension of depth to our button. To do this, create another rectangle, slightly smaller than the base rectangle. Set the width to 100 px and the height to 25 px. We'll fill this smaller rectangle with a linear gradient, but reverse the colors that we used in the base rectangle. Align the smaller rectangle so it fits uniformly inside the larger rectangle and offset to the right, leaving an open area on the left. We'll need that space later. For the chiseled look, we just need to add some highlighting and shadowing effects to the smaller rectangle, which we can achieve by adding two simple, 1-pixel paths—a darker path that borders the left and top of the rectangle and a lighter path that borders the right and bottom. To achieve the right color of these paths, the darker path has a line color of black, and the lighter path has a line color of white. Adjust the opacity of both path objects—in this case, black 10%, white 50%. Figure 14-10 illustrates our progress.

Figure 14-10. The inset rectangle on top of the base rectangle (enlarged)

Now all we need to do is add some text (here, we've used the Lucida Grande typeface, but any sans-serif font would work well) inside our "inset" rectangle and a stock icon of a plus sign to the empty space on the left, and we're all set. For this project, we've used a royalty-free stock image; alternatively, you could create your own plus sign graphic. You can imagine how easy it would be to simply change the wording of the text and the icon to create a completely different button, which we will need to do in our prototype. Figure 14-11 shows the finished product.

Figure 14-11. The completed custom button graphic

Assembling the pages

Now that we have set up our prototype document and created some custom graphics, its time to start building some pages and putting everything together. As stated before, the Boxtees prototype will consist of four pages, or screens—Store, Cart, Checkout, Confirmation. Each page will have a title bar at the top with the page title and a short page description. Since this is going to be different on each page, we did not make it part of the master page. Before we build the details of our pages, let's go through each page (using the page drop-down in the top-right corner of the document to navigate from page to page) and insert a page title and page description, with a light blue background behind our text. Figure 14-12 illustrates this. Now we're ready to start filling in the details of each page, starting with the Store page first.

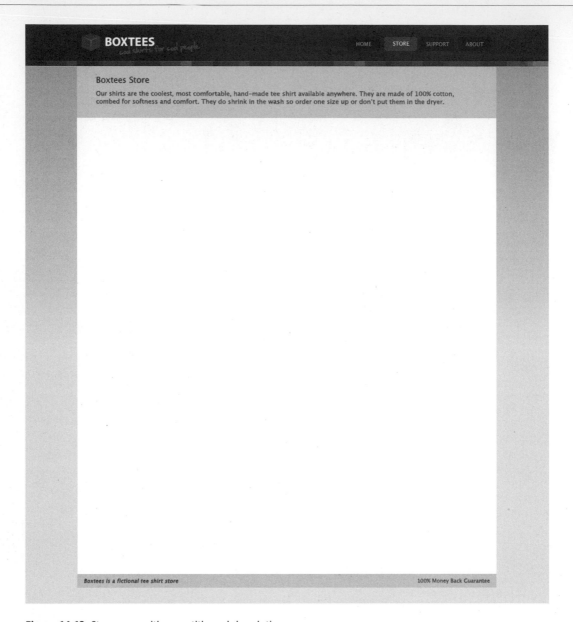

Figure 14-12. Store page with page title and description

Building the Store page

The Store page needs to have a simple layout in order to adequately display the T-shirts as well as information about them. For the purposes of this case study, we'll set up a gallery type layout. Our layout will constitute a grid of three rows and two columns. This will give us plenty of room to show a nice-sized T-shirt graphic and the accompanying information and actions for each product. To ensure our grid is of consistent size and that all of our elements align properly, let's add a few guide lines to our document. (Note that guide lines are page-specific, and therefore will not be shared across pages.) To establish some guide lines, first make sure canvas rulers are visible (View ➤ Rulers). This will show rulers at the top and left of our canvas. From there, click anywhere on a ruler and just drag a guide line onto the canvas. Figure 14-13 shows the guide lines we'll use.

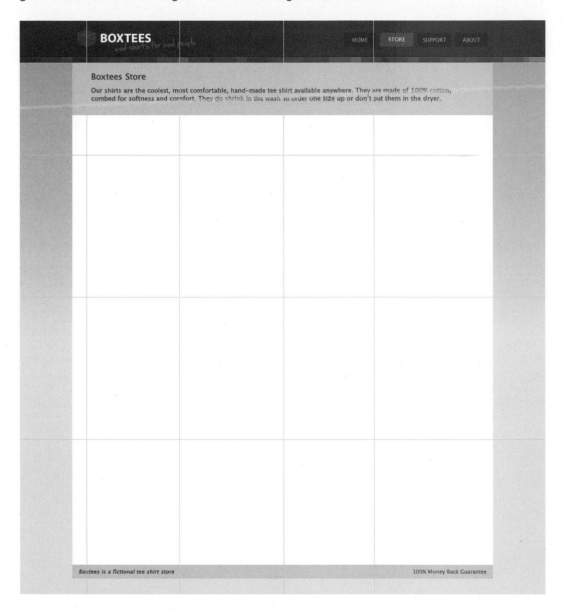

Figure 14-13. The Store page showing only guide lines

Now we're ready to populate the product listings. Boxtees sells one basic T-shirt, but it comes in six different colors. We'll list each color T-shirt out as a separate "product," named for the color of the shirt. The shirt is the showcase piece here, but we also need to leave room for price, available sizes, a size selection drop-down menu, a quantity field, and a button.

Using symbols for efficient workflow

All the product information is the same for each T-shirt. Once we get the first set of product information placed exactly where we want it, we can convert that group of objects into a symbol. In Fireworks, you can use symbols much the same way a developer uses "includes." Developers embrace a common methodology called D.R.Y.—Don't Repeat Yourself. If you have to repeat yourself, you are not working efficiently.

Symbols are a perfect way to prevent repetitive actions. Symbols should be used when you have an element (or group of elements) that is repeated multiple times on a page or across a network of pages. To convert an object to a symbol, select the object/group and then select Modify ➤ Symbol ➤ Convert to Symbol. The symbol can then be named and an instance is placed in a document library or in the Common Library for use in other projects, if desired. A document library is a storage area within a Fireworks file that can contain objects or groups of objects. The Common Library, as you may recall, is a library of graphics that can be used within any Fireworks file.

Instead of duplicating that group of static elements, we can place multiple instances of that symbol on the page. Now if we want to change the price from $16 to $20, we can make the change in the symbol, and every instance on the page and throughout the document will be automatically updated. This is much easier and faster than changing the price of the T-shirt in six (or more) different locations.

To edit a symbol that you've already created, just double-click the element, and the element will appear on its own subcanvas. In the top-left corner of the canvas, you'll see what looks like a file path from the page to the symbol you're currently editing. When you're finished editing, just click the page name, and the symbol subcanvas will close, returning you to the main page canvas. Double-clicking the subcanvas will also allow you to exit editing mode.

In this prototype, there are potentially several items that could be converted to use as a symbol, but we've used this efficiency technique on three elements—the product information listing and the text/ logo design on each T-shirt. As mentioned before, any element that will be used in multiple places is a candidate for converting into a symbol.

Now that we have created symbols for some of our page elements, we're ready to propagate the Store page by placing an instance of the product information symbol next to each T-shirt, making sure to use our guide lines to align everything neatly. Lastly, each T-shirt graphic should be changed to the correct color. All we have to do is select the T-shirt shape with the Subselection tool and change the fill color to the desired hue. The semitransparent shadow layer should be intact, creating a nice effect on each T-shirt graphic. Figure 14-14 shows the Store page with T-shirt images, product names, product information, and cart actions.

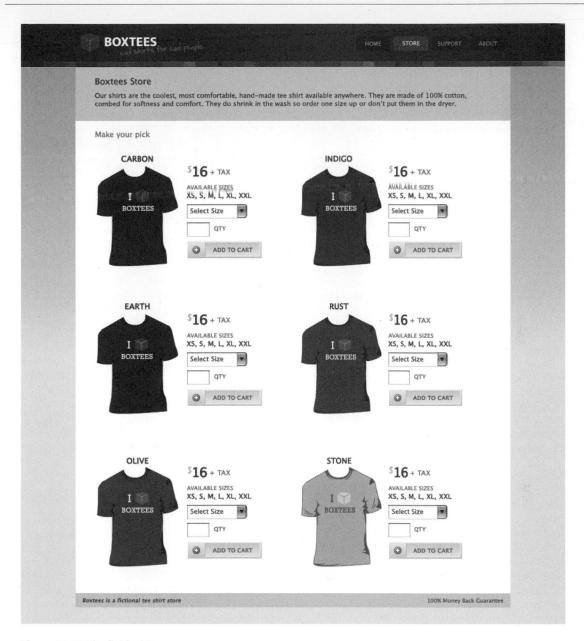

Figure 14-14. The finished Store page

Creating the Cart page

Let's say someone shopping on the fictitious Boxtees site clicked the Add to Cart button on the Store page. That would take him or her directly to the Cart page.

The Cart page is a simple page that displays the items in the customer's shopping cart. In addition to the product the customer selected, we'd like to show him or her a short product description and a small product image. We'll also carry over the size selection drop-down menu, the quantity field, and the price from the Store page. We'll lay out the Cart page in more of a tabular view so the prices align on the right-hand side; that way the customer can visualize how the math works out as we display the price of his or her items and the cart total.

The distinct feature of the Cart page is the Checkout button. We want to make it easy for people to buy these T-shirts, so placing a clear, simple button with the word "checkout" on it is one way to make it clear what the next step should be. Since we built our button in such a modular method, it is easy to duplicate the Add to Cart button and modify it slightly. To differentiate the Checkout button from the Add to Cart button, we'll just swap out the "plus sign" stock icon with a "check mark" stock icon (and change the text to "checkout").

Figure 14-15 depicts the finished Cart page with the product information organized into a tabular format.

Making the Checkout page

We've mentioned that Fireworks is a powerful prototyping tool. One of the things that makes Fireworks so useful for creating prototypes and wireframes is the built-in HTML elements available in the Common Library. It is much easier to drop in premade elements rather than building your own text fields, radio buttons, and drop-down menus. The Checkout page contains several text fields and other HTML elements, so it is the perfect page to demonstrate how we can use these elements from the Common Library.

Because this is a fictitious site, we have the luxury of not worrying about every edge case in terms of shipping, payment options, country of origin, and so forth. So we're not going to worry about all that, which allows us to condense all the checkout information onto one page.

We'll start off with usual fields requesting a mailing/shipping address. Each field set is bounded by a shaded rectangle to distinguish the types of information we're asking for. Within each field set, we've used the built-in HTML elements from the Common Library for our text fields, radio buttons, check boxes, and drop-down menus. Again, we'll use guide lines to ensure our text fields and other HTML elements have some semblance of alignment as you scan down the page.

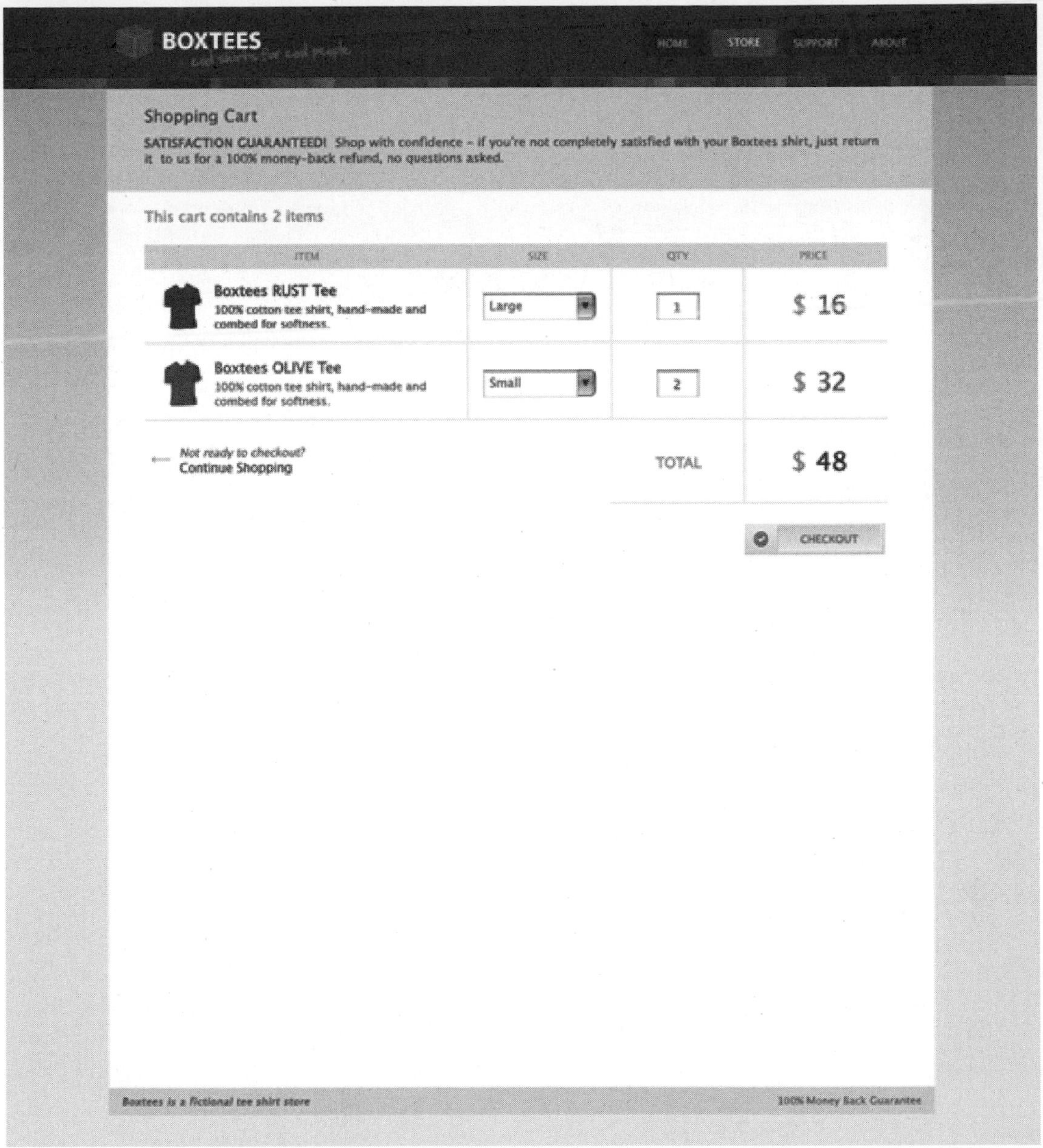

Figure 14-15. The finished Cart page

At the bottom, we need to use another custom button the customer can click to confirm his or her order and make the purchase, as shown in Figure 14-16. On the finished Checkout page, we've used the same button from previous pages, but this time we've changed the color to a green gradient rather than blue. The green color stands out at the bottom of the page and draws attention to itself, which is what we want so that we can sell more T-shirts. Additionally, the green color gives the customer confidence that it's OK to proceed.

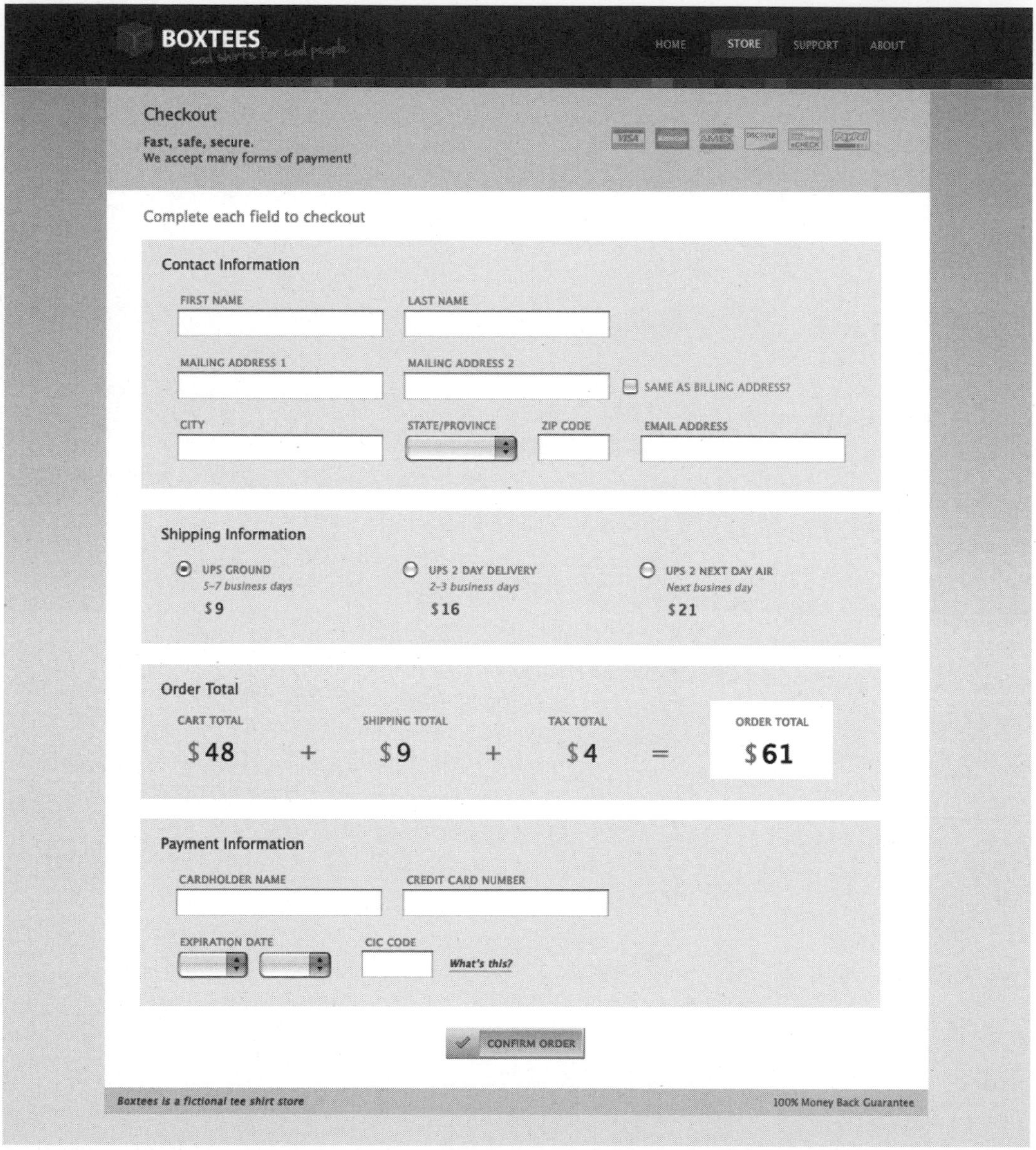

Figure 14-16. Completed Checkout page

Building the Confirmation page

The Confirmation page is essentially a repeat of the Cart page. The difference is the Confirmation page is not editable, containing no text fields requiring input from the customer; it only shows the result of the customer's order. Also included in the table are shipping and tax line items. Add in a confirmation number and customer-support phone number, and this Confirmation page doesn't look all that different from most—not much to it. Figure 14-17 illustrates the completed Confirmation page.

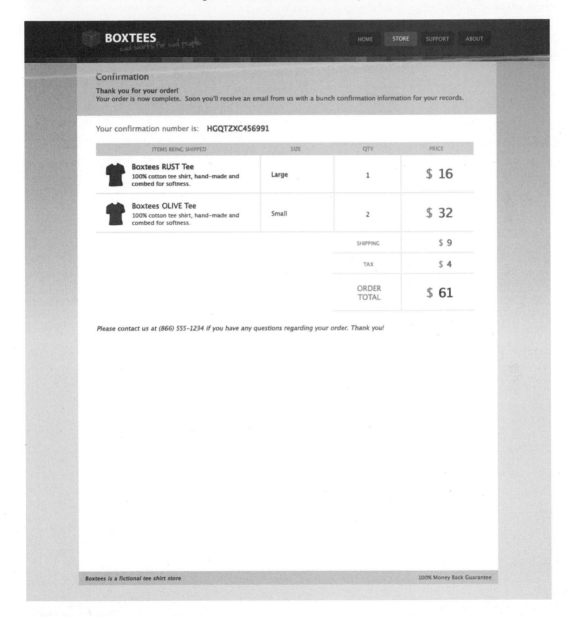

Figure 14-17. The finished Confirmation page

Summary

In this chapter, we've built a prototype for Boxtees, an online T-shirt store. The finished product is one Fireworks file that has been created with efficiency in mind. Thanks to shared layers, pages, and symbols, if any changes need to be added to this mockup or even if a new page needs to be added, it can be done quickly and easily. The file is ready to be sliced up and integrated into real-live HTML/CSS to work in a browser.

The examples we used to create the Boxtees store illustrated how Fireworks can be employed as a powerful prototyping tool. We also demonstrated how Fireworks can be a graphic design workhorse, perfect for creating web-ready images that are scalable, flexible, and easy to modify.

INDEX

S

scaleModel and align properties, basics in action, 208

Scale Points command, in Edit Points section, 69

Scale setting, in Vector File Options dialog, 27

Select All Points command, in Select Points section, 67

Select Contour command, in Select Points section, 67

Selected Slices Only option, images-only Export dialog, 89

Select First Point command, in Select Points section, 67

Select Inverse Points command, in Select Points section, 67

selections, converting to paths and vice versa, 37–38

selection tools, 33–37

selective compression, optimizing JPEG images with, 82

Select No Points command, in Select Points section, 67

Select Points section, commands in, 67

Select/Deselect Next/Previous Points command, in Select Points section, 67

Select Top/Right/Bottom/Lefts Points command, in Select Points section, 67

SetColor method, how it works with Fireworks-returned color value, 203

setFillColor method, 195

shared layers and pages, 255–256

Share Layer to All Pages option on Base layer, 258

Sharpen JPEG edges, selecting in Optimize panel, 83

Sharpen Points command, in Edit Points section, 70

Sharpen tool, 41–42

Shift key, as selection technique, 34

Show Preview option, in Photoshop File Import Options dialog, 20

sight design, example of, 246

Simplify Paths command, in Alter Paths section, 62

site navigation, creating with sprites, 246

skin
  importing in Flex, 148
  naming, 145

skin images, importing, 149–152

slices, tips to consider when creating, 76

Slices select box, deciding how you want slices treated in, 89

Slice tool, 4
  in Fireworks, 76
  vs. Hotspot tool, 76

Smart Polygon tool, using, 259

Smith, Nathan, 960.gs templates by, 233

Smoothing setting, for JPEG images, 83

Smooth Points command, in Edit Points section, 68

Smudge tool, 44

Specific components radio button, for skinning a specific component, 145

Split Paths command, in Paths panel, 58

sprites, creating site navigation with, 246

sprite sheet, example of, 245

state delay, between states when animation is playing, 130

states, duplicating and reversing, 138–139

States panel, 129–132
  with options menu open, 129

Store page
  building, 264–266
  propagating, 266

Straighten Points command, in Edit Points section, 68

styles
  in Fireworks CS4, 109–110
  reviewing applied in Property inspector, 110

Styles panel, launching, 147

Styles panel, selecting style library in, 109

Subdivide Points command, in Edit Points section, 71

Subselection tool, 6
  using in vector graphics, 51

SWF files, 190
  keyboard shortcut for publishing, 204
  updating Add Rect button event handler, 204

Symbol Properties panel, setting properties on selected control with, 9

symbols
  editing, 266
  indicating properties of color in slice's color palette, 81
  using for efficient workflow, 266

T

terminology, for developing effective workflow, 190

TextBox method, for importing your JSF, 204–205

text elements, adding to web headers, 119–120

text indent, extreme negative, 251

Text option, in Import Fireworks Document dialog, 29

Text Properties panel, 54

Text tool, in Vector tools section of Tools palette, 54–55

texture fills, 105

The Essential Guide to Flash CS4 with ActionScript, by Paul Milbourne, et al., 29

thumbnail symbol
  adding a shadow or color to, 162
  adding highlights to, 161
  converting thumbnail elements to, 163
  creating for AIR application, 161–163
  gradient handle positions for, 161

TIFF (Tagged Image File Format)
  available for use in Fireworks, 78
  preview window, 95

Tolerance property, added to Magic Wand tool, 36

Tools palette, Vector tools section of, 50

Tools panel, bitmap tools housed in, 32–33

Transparency property, in image optimization, 81

Trim Paths command, in Paths panel, 61

T-shirt graphic, drawing, 261

Twist and Fade command dialog, 176

U

Uniform color palette, available in palette index, 80

Uninstall extension confirmation dialog, 187

Union Paths command, in Paths panel, 59

unordered list reset, with no bullets or indentation, 250

V

Vector File Options dialog, 12
  settings in, 26–28

vector graphics, working with, 49–73

Vector Path tool
  in Vector tools section of Tools palette, 52
  random line drawn with, 52

Vector tools, using, 50–56

Version field, in Create AIR Package dialog, 167

visual effects, creating, 101

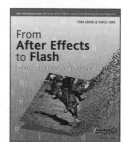